Collective Bargaining in Public Employment

Michael H. Moskow
Temple University

J. Joseph Loewenberg
Temple University

Edward Clifford Koziara
Drexel Institute of Technology

Consulting Editor: **Albert Blum,** *Michigan State University*

collective bargaining in public employment

 Random House · New York

preface

In recent years the central stage of employee relations has featured a new cast and plot: collective bargaining for public employees. Unions have dramatically increased their membership among public employees. Bargaining for employees of federal, state, and local governments has also increased rapidly. Every indication points to further increases in membership and bargaining activity in the future. The growth and nature of bargaining activities in public employment, including the proliferation of strikes, have captured the attention of the public and have challenged those engaged in labor relations.

This book describes and analyzes the developments in public-employee bargaining. The emphasis throughout is on bargaining and labor relations rather than on administration of public personnel. After the environment of government and public employment is introduced in Chapter I, Chapters II–V are devoted to a description of the bargaining. Chapter II discusses the employee organizations and collective-bargaining activities for federal employees; Chapter III, those for employees of states, counties, and municipalities; Chapter IV, those for teachers; and Chapter V, those for police and fire fighters. Interrelationships exist in labor relations among the above groups of employees, but a separate chapter is included for teachers and for police and fire fighters because of the special developments in these sectors. The remaining chapters (VI, VII, and VIII) analyze the participants (or actors, in industrial relations terminology), as well as the process of public employee bargaining. Comparisons are made among different levels of government as well as with bargaining in the private sector of the economy. The final chapter presents the authors' conclusions and predictions.

The authors have attempted to survey an enormous field consisting of 11.5 million employees (or almost 15 percent of the total labor force) and tens of thousands of different employers, including federal and state agencies and installations, municipalities, school districts, counties, and special districts. Two additional factors complicate the analysis: the widely varying legal situations and the very recent introduction of formal labor relations, which causes rapid change in practices and procedures. The book is not intended to be a comprehensive study. Rather, its purpose is to give the reader an insight into the uniqueness and similarities of the large, complex, and evolving field of public employee bargaining.

This book will be of interest to laymen as well as to labor relations students and practitioners. Only a handful of persons are experienced in more than one sector of public employment labor relations; in fact, most practitioners still have not had experience in public employee bargaining. The book can be used as a basic text, supplemented by outside readings, in a course in public employee bargaining and as outside reading in traditional courses in labor relations, labor economics, and collective bargaining.

A brief word about terminology is in order. The authors use the term "collective bargaining" throughout the book to describe the bilateral determination of conditions of employment in both the public and the private sectors. Other terms, the most common of which is "collective negotiations," have been used instead of "collective bargaining" in references to public employees. The Taylor Committee of New York State used the term "collective negotiations."[1] to emphasize the important differences between public and private employment. The National Education Association, an organization of over 1 million public school teachers,

[1] State of New York, Governor's Committee on Public Relations, *Final Report,* March 31, 1966.

uses "professional negotiations" and objects strenuously to "collective bargaining." One of the authors of this book has previously used "collective negotiations"[2] to describe bargaining for public school teachers to avoid argument over terminology, even though little difference was apparent between "professional negotiations" and collective bargaining. For this book, the authors believe the term "collective bargaining" is appropriate. They do not think that the difference between bargaining in the public sector and that in the private sector necessitates a new term. Furthermore, the special problem of terminology among teachers is no longer pressing. .

The authors are indebted to many persons too numerous to mention. Over 150 union officials, management representatives, mediators, arbitrators, and students of public employee bargaining were interviewed. Research directors of employee organizations and government agencies provided invaluable information. The authors are particularly grateful to Seymour L. Wolfbein, Dean of the School of Business Administration of Temple University, for granting two of them released time, travel funds, and encouragement to conduct a large part of the research for this book. The Temple University Manpower Research Institutional Grant from the U.S. Department of Labor provided partial support for the research of this book.

Philadelphia
May 1969

M. H. M.
J. J. L.
E. C. K.

[2] Myron Lieberman and Michael H. Moskow, *Collective Negotiations for Teachers* (Chicago: Rand McNally, 1966).

contents

ix

Collective Bargaining in Public Employment

government and public employment

Collective bargaining practices vary widely among industries partly because of different economic factors, participants, and organizational structures. A first step in analyzing collective bargaining in any industry is to observe the environment and the characteristics that will affect collective bargaining. This chapter describes government, the public sector of our economy, as an industry that renders services for the public. The first part of the chapter discusses the main government services and some of the social, economic, and political trends that have prompted expansion of the public sector. This discussion is followed by an examination of government finances and by an analysis of government's growing labor force. The final section presents the unique aspects of government as an employer.

Government Services

Government has undertaken the responsibility for certain services considered essential to the public that the private economy has been unable to provide. In many cases, government has ventured into areas where the private profit margin is equal to or less than zero, but where the benefits to society are presumably worthwhile. Hence, much government activity does not yield a profit.

Government has a monopoly on many of its functions. This monopoly position is not due to the government's superior efficiency, larger size, or greater innovativeness, but rather to the absence of sufficient profits to motivate competition from private enterprise, in most cases.

Federal, state, and local governments provide highly diverse goods and services. Society as a whole benefits from some services, such as national defense, and society pays for such services through general taxation. Other services assist the individual directly, and are paid for as they are used; examples are the post office and toll roads. Still other services are considered advantageous for all of society, in addition to helping individuals. Education enhances an individual's earning potential, but society, too, gains from a literate, educated citizenry. Public transport serves the passenger and may also result in fewer vehicles on the road, reducing congestion of roadways and air pollution. Welfare services aid individuals and also satisfy the public concept of social and economic equity.

Government Finances

TRENDS IN GOVERNMENT EXPENDITURE

In 1900, output for all three levels of government accounted for 6 percent of the gross national product (GNP), the value of all goods and services produced in that year. By 1968, government accounted for over 23 percent of GNP.

Since 1900, the federal government has accounted for an increasing proportion of total government expenditures. In 1902, local governments were responsible for 58 percent of all government expenditure; today the federal government is responsible for 58 percent. Nearly one-half of all federal expenditures is applied to national defense. Without defense expenditures the federal government would be responsible for 23 percent, state governments for 27 percent, and local governments for 50 percent, of all government civilian expenditures. The federal government increased its share of total government civilian expenditures from 17 to 23 percent between 1902 and 1964.

The most costly civil functions performed by government are education, highway construction and maintenance, public welfare services, and public health. Table I–1 lists the combined govern-

Table I–1
Percentage Distribution of Government Expenditures on Major Civil Functions

	1902	1927	1938	1948	1963	1966–67
Education	20.7%	26.0%	19.2%	29.2%	28.1%	29.5%
Highways	14.1	21.1	15.6	11.6	12.6	10.2
Public welfare	3.3	1.9	8.9	8.1	6.4	7.0
Health and hospital	5.1	5.0	4.9	7.3	7.6	6.9
Other	56.8	46.0	51.4	43.8	45.1	46.4
All civil functions	100.0	100.0	100.0	100.0	99.8*	100.0

* Percentages do not total 100 because of rounding.

SOURCE: U.S. Bureau of the Census, *Historical Statistics of the United States: Colonial Times to 1957* (Washington, D.C.: 1960), U.S. Bureau of the Census, *Government Finances in 1963* (Washington, D.C.: 1964), and U.S. Bureau of the Census, *Governmental Finances in 1966–67*, series GF67, No. 3 (Washington, D.C.: 1968), 22.

ment expenditures in these four areas. Education has consistently led all major civil expenditures.

What are the reasons for the increase in governmental civilian expenditures?[1] One explanation is that for the first time our society can afford the luxury of systematically providing for health, welfare, and security. In other words, the success of private enterprise, the private sector, allows resources to be channeled into meeting public needs.

A changing social and economic order, a changing theory of the proper role of government, and a changing concept of democracy have further stimulated the growth of the public sector. For example, technological advancement often changes the economic and social order. The development of automobiles, airplanes, radio, and television all resulted in demands on the public sector, because rules and regulations are needed for channeling transportation and communication flows. The public sector must provide expressways, bridges, highways, airports, beacons, radio beams, and so on. Similarly, the growth of industry brings with it abuses to the public welfare, which have to be corrected by the government. The population increase, the growth of cities, and industrial expansion cause complex problems of health, welfare, housing, sanitation, and air pollution. The government becomes involved in many of these areas because the private sector does not allocate sufficient resources to them. Finally, a revised concept of democracy has led to a changing view of the role of government. Public policy now emphasizes increased economic security as well as political equality. Unemployment compensation, old-age and survivors insurance, minimum wage laws, medicare, and price supports reflect this trend. All these factors have expanded the sphere of government activity, expenditure, and employment.

Federal, state, and local government revenues have increased rapidly. Federal revenue soared from less than $5 billion in 1939 to $111 billion in 1967. State and local revenues rose from $10 billion in 1939 to $70 billion in 1967.

The bulk of federal revenues comes from individual income taxes ($56 billion in 1967) and corporate income taxes ($34 billion in 1967). Excise taxes, estate and gift taxes, customs charges, and other sources round out federal income. Although there is a trend toward higher state and local income taxation, in 1967 property and sales taxes still accounted for over one-half the revenues of state and local governments. Significantly, federal grants now amount to 15 percent of state and local incomes.

Local governments encounter difficulties because sales and property taxes, the main form of state and local revenue, do not adequately respond to increases in gross national product (GNP). The federal government does not face this problem because the income tax is quite responsive to changes in GNP. In fact, increases in GNP yield a more than proportionate increase in federal revenues.[2]

Responsibilities for the execution of government functions have never been clearly divided among the federal, state, and local levels. Time has blurred rather than clarified the role of each level. The present system of "cooperative federalism" calls for cooperation among various levels of government to provide for public wants. Unless state and local tax structures change drastically, however, it seems likely that the federal government will have to play a larger role in the collection of taxes and in the disbursement of revenues to state and local governments. Some combination of these alternatives probably will be used as projected increases in tax revenues lag behind expenditures.

Important limitations are placed on the powers of state legislatures to tax. The federal Constitution prohibits state taxes on imports and exports. Because interstate commerce is controlled by the federal government, such commerce may not be taxed by the states. The states may tax property used in interstate commerce, but they may not tax an act of interstate commerce. The states are not allowed to tax the federal government or any of its instrumentalities.

State tax laws must satisfy the Fourteenth Amendment of the Constitution that no state shall "deprive any person of life, liberty, or property, without due process of law." As judically interpreted, this statement means (1) that the state may tax property and rights only within its jurisdiction; (2) that taxes may be levied only in the public interest; and (3) that all persons or all things within the same classification must be taxed alike.

Municipalities, counties, school districts, and other local governments have no inherent power to tax. The power to tax is given to local governments by the states through charter, statute, and constitutional provisions. Legislatures dictate to local governments what is to be taxed and the maximum rates that can be set. Only cities that have received home rule charters from the state legislature have the power to levy taxes.[3]

Governments borrow money to finance appropriations that cannot be paid out of current revenues. Congress imposes limits on the federal debt. State governments are limited both by the U.S. Constitution, which prevents states from borrowing by issuing bills of credit (paper money), and by state constitutions, many of which set limits on the amount states may borrow. Local governments are constrained by state constitutions and by state laws in the amount they may borrow. This constraint is often phrased in terms of assessed valuation of taxable property in jurisdiction of the local government.

THE BUDGET

Prior to World War I, financial management at state and local levels was quite different from what it is today. At that time, state and local government agencies pressured their legislatures or councils for needed appropriations. The agencies would then spend money subject to an auditor's check on the legality of expenditures.[4]

Since World War I, governments have concentrated on the need for overall sound planning in the formation of a budget. Budget formation forces government officials to decide on the cost of government for a fixed time period and on the sources of the necessary financing. To develop formal budgets, government officials must decide which programs should be implemented.

A budget is usually prepared by the office of the chief executive. In some jurisdictions a commission composed of representatives from the executive and legislative branches prepares the budget. Agencies generally make requests to the executive or the commission for quarterly or yearly allotments. Requests are subject to negotiation, and agency heads may be asked to support their requests before the legislature or the council. Requests are usually classified by the agencies under the separate headings of personnel costs, material costs, and capital outlays. In most jurisdictions, funds may be transferred from one classification to another if the executive officer gives his approval. Interagency transfers are not usually permitted. For example, a pay increase for road construction employees may come from funds set aside for the purchase of new earth-moving equipment but not from funds appropriated for the construction of a new university building or for the purchase of new police patrol cars.

Methods of Government Employment

Two types of employment exist in government service: patronage and the merit system. Patronage is a system of employment whereby supporters of the winning candidates are appointed to government jobs. Supporters of the losing candidate are removed from office or are not reappointed. The employment decision is based primarily on party loyalty. Under a merit system, on the other hand, theoretically the most capable workers are employed and promoted. A system such as civil service is established to place the most qualified individual in a given job. Promotions are determined by a combination of criteria, including efficiency ratings, examinations, seniority, and administrative judgment. Discipline is exerted through loss of seniority, demerits, suspension, and demotion. The merit system is most pervasive at the federal level, although many federal jobs are still appointive. Over one-half the states have comprehensive merit programs for state employees. Most of the larger cities, but only 10 percent of the counties, have some form of merit system. The quality of the systems is uneven, ranging from scrupulous implementation of the merit principle to patronage in disguise. In some situations where a formal merit system has been adopted, the merit principle does not operate. Politicians may use pressure on civil service commissioners to see that their constituents are rewarded with jobs or promotions. The decision to punish and the nature of the punishment may also be influenced by political considerations.

The first permanent merit system for federal employees was passed by Congress in 1883. Twenty years later Illinois and Wisconsin became the first states to pass such legislation. A 1939 amendment to the Federal Social Security Act requires all states to have the merit system for employees administering federal funds for public assistance and employment security. Limited merit systems covering certain departments or services exist in some states and in other jurisdictions. In other states—for example, Arkansas (1939) and New Mexico (1941)—civil service legislation has actually been repealed. Some states have sought to make civil service a constitutional provision in order to guarantee a permanent system. One example is Michigan's 1937 civil service law, but some aspects of the law that were favored by good-government groups were repealed in 1939. Although the civil service programs and the merit system have worked imperfectly, advocates argue that they have raised the quality of public employees over that of employees hired under the patronage system.

Composition of the Public Sector's Labor Force

The composition of the public sector's labor force and the historical trends that have influenced its present composition have implications for the public labor force in the future. In turn, the composition of the labor force will affect the development of employee organizations.

TOTAL EMPLOYMENT

Government employment has been rising in absolute terms and as a percentage of the total civilian labor force. Between 1940 and 1967 the number of government employees has more than tripled. Table I–2 shows that by 1968 government employed over 15 percent of the nation's labor force.

Table I–2
Government Employment and the Labor Force

YEAR	NUMBER OF GOVERNMENT EMPLOYEES	PERCENTAGE INCREASE IN GOVERNMENT EMPLOYMENT	TOTAL LABOR FORCE	GOVERNMENT EMPLOYMENT AS PERCENTAGE OF TOTAL LABOR FORCE
1940	3,592,952	—	55,640,000	6.5%
1950	5,553,997	55%	62,208,000	8.9
1960	7,849,997	41	69,628,000	11.3
1968	12,342,000	64	78,804,000	15.6

SOURCE: *Economic Report of the President,* January 1964 (Washington, D.C.: 1964), Table C-19, p. 230, and U.S. Department of Labor, *Employment and Earnings Statistics for the U.S.,* Bulletin 1312–5, October, 1967. U.S. Bureau of the Census, *Public Employment in 1968,* series GE68, No. 1 (Washington, D.C.: 1969), 7. U.S. Bureau of Labor Statistics, *Monthly Labor Review,* Vol. 91, No. 12 (Washington, D.C.: December 1968), 78.

Table I–3 indicates the distribution of government workers and of salary payments in the various public services at the federal level and the state and local levels. As of October 1968, almost one-half of all federal personnel worked in national defense and international relations, and over one-half the state and local workers were employed in education.

The need for professional and white-collar government workers will increase in the future. In 1962 the federal government employed almost 250,000 professional workers, about 20 percent of whom were women.[5] Nonprofessional white-collar jobs—for example, those requiring secretarial or clerking skills—also provide

Table I-3
Public Employment and Payrolls, by Level of Government and by Function, October 1968

Function	Employment, Full time and Part time (thousands)			Payroll (millions of dollars)		
	ALL GOVERN-MENTS (CIVILIAN)	FEDERAL GOVERN-MENTS (CIVILIAN)†	STATE AND LOCAL GOVERN-MENTS*	ALL GOVERN-MENTS (CIVILIAN)	FEDERAL GOVERN-MENTS (CIVILIAN)†	STATE AND LOCAL GOVERN-MENTS*
Total	12,342	2,984	9,358	$6,889.2	$2,137.3	$4,751.9
National defense and international relations	1,353	1,353	—	943.4	943.4	—
Postal service	714	714	—	455.4	455.4	—
Space research and technology	33	33	—	36.0	36.0	—
Education	4,847	18	4,829	2,557.9	13.1	2,544.8
Highways	604	6	598	301.9	6.0	295.9
Health and hospitals	1,130	193	937	544.4	126.3	418.1
Police protection	489	26	463	294.6	24.5	270.1
Natural resources	394	216	178	256.5	169.1	87.4
Financial administration	321	88	233	183.1	75.6	107.5
General control	379	40	339	163.2	34.3	128.9
All other	2,080	298	1,782	1,152.1	253.6	898.5

NOTE: Statistics for local governments for 1968 are subject to sampling variation. Because of rounding, detail may not add to totals.

* —Represents zero.

† Comprises all federal civilian employees, including those outside the United States. Data include civilian employees of the National Guard paid directly from the federal treasury (in October 1968, 39,000 persons, with $28 million of payroll for the month). On a full-time equivalent basis federal employees totaled 2,901,000.

SOURCE: U.S. Bureau of the Census, *Public Employment in 1968,* series GE68, No. 1 (Washington, D.C.: 1969), 7.

significant employment opportunities. In 1962 there were over 1.3 million nonprofessional white-collar employees in the federal service; over one-third of these were women.[6]

The call for more professional and nonprofessional workers in traditionally female occupations will raise the proportion of women in all levels of government. In 1960, all levels of government employed three out of every twenty working women. Because participation of women in the labor force has increased, particularly in the rapidly expanding areas of education and public health, over three times as many women were employed by government in 1967 as in 1940. Two-thirds of all female government employees work for local governments.

NEGRO EMPLOYMENT

The number of Negroes in civilian federal jobs has risen steadily over the last thirty years. In 1940 Negroes filled 5.6 percent of all federal positions; by 1956 Negroes held one out of ten federal jobs.[7] By 1967 Negroes held 14.9 percent of such positions, whereas Negroes constituted 11 percent of the total U.S. population.[8]

The increased number of Negroes in federal jobs has been accompanied by significant increase in the number of Negroes employed in higher pay classifications. From 1962 to 1967 the percentage of Negroes rose 13.3 percent in relatively low-paying jobs, 50.7 percent in the lower-middle, 65.4 percent in the higher-middle, and 125 percent in the highest-paying classifications[9] (see Table I–4).

Negro employment at the state and local levels has been increasing more rapidly than at the federal level. In 1940, one-half of all nonwhites in government jobs were concentrated in the federal service. By 1962, with the growth of state and local employment continuing to outstrip federal employment, the proportion of nonwhites filling state and local government jobs equaled the number in federal positions.[10]

Although no comprehensive study has been made of Negro employment in local government, a number of individual studies have been conducted. A 1963 study in Pennsylvania found Negro state employees concentrated in clerical, sales, and service positions. The number of Negroes in state employment was roughly pro-

Table I–4

Percentage Distribution of Negro Employment in Federal
Government by Wage-Level Classification*

WAGE-LEVEL CLASSIFICATION	1962	1967
GS–1 through GS–4	18.1%	20.5%
GS–5 through GS–8	7.7	11.6
GS–9 through GS–11	2.6	4.3
GS–12 through GS–18	0.8	1.8

* Federal employees are classified for pay purposes under various schedules. The largest schedule, the General Schedule for the Classification Act of 1949, as amended includes almost one-half of all federal employees and is composed of 18 pay-grade classifications. A fuller explanation of this system will be found in Chapter II.

SOURCE: U.S. Civil Service Commission, *Study of Minority Group Employment in the Federal Government* (Washington, D.C.: 1967), p. 7.

portional to the state's Negro population, but Negroes constituted less than 1 percent of the skilled workers. At the same time, Negroes were employed in less than 2 percent of the unskilled jobs.[11]

AGE

Between 1950 and 1960 the total civilian labor force grew 12.9 percent. Yet the proportion of workers between the ages of twenty-five and thirty-four actually declined because of the low birth rates during the Depression. On the other hand, the proportion of older workers (forty-five years old and above) in the labor force increased by 24 percent. The number of workers younger than twenty-five years of age also increased disproportionately.

World War II and the postwar baby boom will also affect the future age distribution of the total U.S. labor force. Between 1960 and 1970 there will be a 48.2 percent increase of workers under age twenty-four and a 1.8 percent decrease of workers over thirty-five. Projections for 1980 indicate that 49 percent of the labor force will be thirty-five or younger.[12]

IMPLICATIONS FOR EMPLOYEE ORGANIZATIONS

The changing composition of the labor force implies a more difficult job for union organization of the public sector. Historically, women have been harder to organize than men, and Negroes have proved distrustful of unionization. White-collar workers have been poorer union potential than blue-collar workers; professionals have tended to join associations rather than unions. If unionization in the public sector is to increase, the traditional difficulties in organizing groups of workers, who constitute an ever-growing proportion of public employees, will have to be overcome.

The projected younger labor force and the growth of government suggest a decrease in the average age of government employees. The influx of younger workers into the labor force may be a positive factor in organizing public employees. Certainly the 1960s did not produce an apathetic or a silent generation. Civil rights demonstrations, peace marches, draft card burning, and demands for student participation in university policy drew on a verbal, committed, and involved youth. If these traits are carried into the work place, the prospects for union growth in the public sector would be bolstered and some of the previous difficulties offset.

Unique Aspects of the Public Employer

By definition, an employer hires persons to work for wages or salary. He sets the overall goals and individual tasks of workers, supervising their efforts directly or though delegated authority. These functions are shared by all employers.

The decision-making environment in which the functions are carried out differs for public employers and private employers. The major differences discussed in this section include finances, separation of powers, and the sovereign nature of the state. The extent to which these differences affect collective bargaining in the public sector will be presented in Chapters II–V and will be analyzed in Chapters VI–VIII.

FINANCES

The principal differences in financing between government and private industry are economic constraints and independence of action in financial matters. In the private sector the market economy acts as a constraint on demands of workers for higher wages and more favorable terms of employment. Increasing labor costs are offset by higher worker productivity, lower employer profits, or higher prices to consumers. The employer's ability to pass increased labor costs on to consumers depends on consumer willingness to purchase the product at a higher price. This willingness is conditioned by competition for the consumer's disposable income.

Government is a growth industry that receives little competition from other industries; in fact, it is usually the sole dispenser of the goods and services it offers the public. Therefore, government is not faced with the market competition that characterizes the private sector of the economy. Consumers have no choice in the purchase of most government products. Usually they are required by law to pay for government services through taxes, regardless of whether they use the services. Price increases are passed along in the form of higher taxes, without fear of losing customers.

Although market competition is lacking, government is not entirely free in its economic actions. In a democratic society, the government must obtain consent for tax increases from the citizens or their representatives. Thus, political constraints limit the government's ability to tax or to find other sources of revenue.

In terms of financing, public corporations such as turnpike commissions are intermediate between public and private employers. These corporations raise funds through the sale of bonds to the public. In such cases, financing is limited only by revenues produced by sale of services.

Some local political subdivisions may not take independent fiscal action. All states set millage limits for local subdivisions. Many subdivisions have already reached the limit of these millage allowances and can increase revenues only through action of the state authority. In other cases, the budgets of local subdivisions must be approved by local taxing authorities.

Individual public employers must operate within the limits of their budgets. In many states and political subdivisions, expenditures cannot exceed revenues in each budget period; the law may also restrict flexibility within the total budget. The transfer of funds between projects or departments of the public employer is generally much more difficult in the public sector than in the private.

Unlike the employer in private industry, the public employer has neither property rights nor a profit incentive to motivate him and direct his decisions. The absence of market constraints does not excuse the public employer from considering economic opportunities and spending constraints. His performance may be judged on his ability to balance budgets or his skill in finding new sources of revenue. Such evaluation, however, is expressed in political rather than in economic terms.

SEPARATION OF POWERS

The public sector is marked by a diffusion of authority within levels of government. This contrasts with the private sector, where the chief executive officer is the focus of all authority in the organization. In the public sector, wages and working conditions may lie within the jurisdiction of the legislative branch or the civil service commission. Matters affecting budgets may be beyond the control of the nominal public employer. The civil service commission of a state often establishes its own procedures to hear grievances of employees of other state agencies. In fact, the "employer" in the public sector appears to be multiple persons or agencies rather than a single authority on all matters.

A complicating factor in analyzing authority of employers in the public sector is the distribution of powers *among* levels of government as well as *within* a single level of government. For instance, pension plans for municipal employees may come under the jurisdiction of the state legislature. The federal government may regulate working conditions of state employees in federally supported programs.

SOVEREIGN NATURE OF THE STATE

Sovereignty may be defined as the supreme, absolute, and uncontrollable power by which any independent state is governed.[13] The sovereign is the person, body, or state in which supreme authority is vested. In the United States, sovereignty rests with the people. Sovereign power, however, is exercised for the people by the federal and the state governments. These governments delegate some of their power to counties, municipalities, and special districts.

The orthodox position on sovereignty maintains that government has sole authority which cannot be given to, taken by, or shared with anyone. Sovereign immunity can be limited, however. Along with the increase in government functions has come a tendency to restrict the absolute power of the sovereign in democratic governments. Such a course is necessary if the government's authority is not to become oppressive.

In many instances sovereignty has been limited by the legislation that has waived sovereign immunity. In the nineteenth century American citizens were allowed to petition a court of claims if they believed their property had been taken by the federal government without proper compensation. Under the Federal Tort Claims Act of 1946, tort claims may be filed against the federal government. The Tucker Act of 1948 allows contract claims to be brought against the federal government. Similarly, states have waived their sovereign immunity in certain instances. Court decisions have also limited the sovereignty of federal, state, and local governments.

With regard to employer-employee relations in the public sector, the orthodox position on sovereignty would permit only the government to establish terms and conditions of employment. Collective bargaining under which employee organizations jointly determine terms and conditions of employment is obviously incompatible with this position. The orthodox position on sovereignty has been used repeatedly in arguments against collective bargaining in the public sector. In the early 1960s this position was one of the major arguments against recognizing representative organizations of public employees. By 1968 the argument was used less frequently as some government agencies agreed voluntarily to bargain with employee organizations and as others were required to do so by state laws and executive orders. Nevertheless, some persons still use the argument; sovereignty was the basic reason advanced in the 1968 Nevada Attorney General Opinion to forbid public employees in the state to join organizations whose goal was collective bargaining.[14]

Aside from its intrinsic logic, the sovereignty concept has long been used by those who fear the impact of collective bargaining on government. Government officials often have wished to continue unilateral determination of conditions of employment. They feared that collective bargaining would infringe on management prerogatives, weaken authority, and affect adversely the efficiency of government operations. In addition, many feared that collective bargaining in government would inevitably lead to strikes against the government.

The proponents of collective bargaining in public employment argue that, in addition to its express powers, government also has implied powers necessary to carry out express powers. For example, government has the long-recognized right to enter into contracts for the personal services of doctors, teachers, and other employees. The argument that government can contract for employment individually but not collectively seems difficult to defend. In fact, a number of courts have ruled that, in the absence of legislative prohibitions, government authorities may voluntarily enter into collective bargaining agreements with their employees.

The position of the federal government and of many state governments today is that they can *agree* to bargain collectively but can *be compelled* to do so only by law. There is no unwritten "law of sovereignty" which prohibits the state from participating in bargaining. In fact, it may be said that in so doing the state is exercising its sovereign power. The following chapters will indicate the extent of this position and its effect on collective bargaining in the public sector.

collective bargaining
for federal employees

The federal government occupies a unique position in the American system of government. It is big, regardless of what measure is used. Of a total gross national product of $860.6 billion in 1968, the federal government's net purchases of goods and services amounted to $100 billion. Almost eleven million persons were employed in the federal government's share of the national product. Of these, 4.6 million were employed in private industry, 3.4 million were military personnel, and 2.9 million were civilians employed in government enterprises and the operations of the feaeral government.[1] The civilian employees of the federal government are the focus of this chapter. The federal government is widespread, in both geographic and functional terms. Because of the federal government's position in the system of government as well as the factors noted previously, its actions set precedents and influence the conduct of government at state and local levels. Therefore, understanding the changing policy and present operation of collective bargaining for federal government employees has significance beyond the groups immediately affected.

The year 1962 marked a decisive turning point in the policy of the federal government toward collective bargaining by its employees. Although the government had supported employee organizations and collective bargaining in the private sector since 1935, it had taken no similar stand with respect to its own employees. In fact, Congress had explicitly excluded federal employees from the various labor relations acts. Nevertheless, collective bargaining and more particularly employee organizations were not unknown in the federal government. Since 1962 the federal government has embarked on an official program of collective bargaining by federal workers. This program, though expanding and changing, is unique to the federal government.

Federal Employment

CHARACTERISTICS

The federal government is the nation's largest single employer. It employs four of every one hundred nonagricultural workers in the labor force and one-fourth of all public employees.

The federal labor force has grown in absolute and relative terms since 1932, when the 559,000 federal employees represented but 2.4 percent of employees on nonagricultural payrolls.[2] The most rapid increase occurred during World War II; in fact, federal government employment levels did not match the 1945 peak in any of the following 24 years. In the 1947–1966 period, nonagricultural employment increased at a more rapid rate than did employment in the federal government.

Projected employment levels for the federal government are moderate. In the 1965–1975 decade, an increase of 10.8 percent in federal government employment has been forecast, compared to an increase of 24.9 percent in total nonagricultural workers and 47.8 percent in state and local government employment.[3]

The growth of federal employment can be attributed largely to the role of the country in international relations, to consequence of war, to increase in population, to economic crisis and hardship, and to technological change.[4] In 1934 the Post Office Department employed 270,000 persons; by 1968 the number of employees had increased to 730,977. Despite more than doubling in size, the department's relative share in total federal employment had decreased from 40 percent to 24 percent in the same period. The biggest federal agency in terms of civilian employment continues to be the Department of Defense, with 43 percent of the total in 1968. Following the Department of Defense and the Post Office Department are the Veteran's Administration, with 6 percent; the Department of Agriculture, with 4 percent; and the Department of Health, Education and Welfare, with 3.8 percent. Each of the other individual segments (departments, commissions, councils, boards and other sections) of the federal government employed less than 100,000 persons, and together they constituted less than one-fourth of all federal employees. A complete distribution of federal civilian employment, by agency, as of June 1968, is shown below.

Federal government employees are engaged in approximately 15,000 separate occupations.[5] Almost any kind of work done in the private sector is performed by government employees as well; some jobs in government have no counterparts elsewhere. Compared to private industry, government has greater demand for professional, scientific, clerical, and service workers, and less for managerial, skilled, and semiskilled workers.[6] One-fourth of all employees in the federal government are designated blue-collar workers, and about three-fourths of these are in the Department of Defense. Post Office employees are not included in this category. In 1956 the proportion of blue-collar workers in the federal government amounted to 34 percent. This decline in blue-collar employment is expected to continue in absolute numbers as well as in relative terms.[7] The occupational composition of the federal labor force suggests that federal government employees have a higher average level of education than workers in private industry.

Federal government employees are as widespread geographically as they are occupationally. Only 11 percent of federal employees works in the Washington, D.C., area. Five-sixths are in the fifty states, with the largest concentrations in California (10 percent of the total), New York (7 percent), Pennsylvania (5 percent), Texas (5 percent), Illinois (4 percent), and Ohio (4 percent). Five percent of civilian employees are located in foreign countries, and the remaining 1 percent in territories of the United States. The largest groups of federal employees outside the United States are the personnel of the Departments of State and Defense and workers employed in Panama Canal Zone activities.

The number of employees in any given location may be related

Federal Civilian Employment, By Agency (June 30, 1968)°

Total, All Agencies†	3,049,190
Legislative Branch	28,675
Judicial Branch	6,561
Executive Branch	
Executive Office of the President	5,310
Executive Departments	
State‡	46,761
Treasury	89,116
Defense:	
Office of the Secretary	2,731
Department of the Army	486,859
Department of the Navy	430,205
Department of the Air Force	316,230
Other	74,521
Justice	35,811
Post Office	730,977
Interior	77,534
Agriculture	122,715
Commerce§	38,619
Labor	10,594
Health, Education and Welfare	117,113
Housing and Urban Development	15,686
Transportation	61,972
Independent Agencies	
Atomic Energy Commission	7,665
Canal Zone Government	3,459
Civil Service Commission	5,577
General Services Administration	39,925
Information Agency	11,603
National Aeronautics & Space Administration	34,641
Panama Canal Company	13,018
Selective Service System	9,027
Small Business Administration	4,667
Tennessee Valley Authority	19,958
Veterans Administration	175,668
Other Independent Agencies	25,992

° Includes all paid employees of agencies listed; excludes employees of the Central Agency and of the National Security Agency and uncompensated employees.

† Includes 61,952 employees hired in the President's Youth Opportunity Campaign Program.

to several factors, including population, defense installations, and resources. The Department of Defense accounts for 82 percent of federal government employees in Hawaii but only 2 percent of those in Vermont; similarly the Post Office Department accounts for 54 percent of federal government employees in Connecticut and only 5 percent of those in Alaska.[8]

Although the federal government has been regarded by some as a single monolithic organization, federal pay scales are multiple and until recent years have been close to chaotic. In 1958 there were seventy-seven separate compensation systems for civilian employees. Civil Service employees under the Classification Act of 1949, as amended, have the best-known system, but they represent only 46 percent of regular full-time employees. Another major group, 22 percent of the total, are covered by the Postal Field Service Compensation Act of 1955, as amended. About 1 percent each are included in the Foreign Service Schedules and the Veterans Administration Department of Medicine and Surgery Schedules. The wages of about 4 percent of employees are administratively determined; included are those working for the Atomic Energy Commission, the Canal Zone Government, the U.S. Information Agency, the Federal Deposit Insurance Corporation, and the Selective Service System. The remaining 26 percent of the full-time employees are wage-board employees whose wages have been fixed by agency boards on the basis of prevailing wage rates in their area of employment. The concept of applying prevailing wages and hours to federal employees was recognized for Navy shipyard workers in 1862.

Wage-board employees are blue-collar manual workers whose skills are sought by and available in the private labor market. While the wage rates of other federal employees are fixed throughout the world, those of wage-board employees vary from area to area, depending on local conditions. The largest group of wage-board employees work for the Navy Department; the next in sizes are those working for the Army and the Air Force. These three departments employ almost four-fifths of all wage-board workers.

‡ Includes 1,570 employees in the Peace Corps and 18,030 employees in the Agency for International Development.

§ Includes 6,475 seamen employed by the Maritime Administration.

SOURCE: U.S. Civil Service Commission, *Annual Report 1968*, Table A–1, pp. 66–67.

Table II-1

Federal Full-Time Employment by Agency and Pay System, All Areas, June 30, 1967

Agency	TOTAL	GENERAL SCHEDULE	WAGE BOARD	POSTAL FIELD SERVICE	OTHER ACTS AND ADMINISTRATIVE DETERMINATION
Total, all agencies[a]	2,809,105	1,251,603	764,579	605,125	187,798
Legislative branch	27,020	7,756	6,486		12,778
Judicial branch	6,158	163	14		5,981
Executive branch					
Executive Office of the President	4,538	4,252	93		193
State Department[b]	45,865	5,974	391		39,500
Treasury Department	88,061	79,133	5,074		3,854
Defense Department					
Office of the Secretary	2,713	2,540	36		137
Army	478,806	249,689	218,571		10,546
Navy	400,051	154,854	230,778		14,419
Air Force[c]	318,081	157,007	157,164		3,910
Other	73,777	57,622	14,399		1,756
Justice Department	33,712	31,241	1,379		1,092
Post Office Department	607,312	2,089	74	605,125	24
Interior Department	72,748	51,383	15,672		5,693
Agriculture Department	103,882	90,407	10,018		3,457

Commerce Department[a]	35,742	23,315	9,508	2,919
Labor Department	9,843	9,596	103	144
Health, Education and Welfare	102,617	87,115	6,795	8,707
Housing and Urban Development	14,618	14,200	89	329
Transportation	57,241	49,127	6,535	1,579
Atomic Energy Commission	7,370	2	95	7,237
Civil Service Commission	5,306	5,162	50	94
General Services Admin.	39,207	18,208	19,919	1,080
Information Agency	11,982	2,332	401	9,249
National Aeronautics and Space	35,703	29,685	5,234	784
Panama Canal Company	12,057		8,799	3,258
Selective Service System	7,085	1,138	22	5,925
Small Business Administration	4,279	4,195	17	67
Tennessee Valley Authority	18,426		11,006	7,420
Veterans Administration[e]	157,576	94,796	33,714	29,066
Other Independent Agencies	27,329	18,622	2,143	6,564

[a] Excludes Central Intelligence Agency and National Security Agency.
[b] Includes 1,351 employees in the Peace Corps and 17,055 employees in the Agency for International Development.
[c] The Department of the Air Force reported as of August 31, 1967.
[d] Includes 7,464 seamen employed by the Maritime Administration.
[e] Includes 2,751 resident physicians and interns.

SOURCE: U.S. Civil Service Commission, *Annual Report, 1967* (Washington, D.C.) Table A–3.

Other significant groups of wage-board employees are found in the Government Printing Office, the Department of Interior, the Department of Agriculture, the Veterans Administration, the Tennessee Valley Authority, and the General Services Administration. Table II–1 shows a distribution of full-time federal employees by agency and pay system.

With all the various wage schedules and systems, it is not surprising that inequities occurred among groups of employees. Not until the Salary Reform Act was passed in 1962 were the schedules coordinated. The wage-board system must, of course, steer an independent and not necessarily a related course.

The method of determining wages has helped blue-collar workers in general to maintain parity with their private industry counterparts. Clerical workers were also considered to be paid in accordance with labor market standards. Executive, managerial, and advanced professional and technical personnel, however, were underpaid.[9] One objective of wage legislation passed by Congress in 1967 was to establish by 1969 wage comparability between federal employees and their private industry counterparts.

To determine pay of employees the various pay schedules group job positions into a number of grades. The General Schedule for the Classification Act of 1949, as amended, includes eighteen grades. A distribution of employees in 1967 showed a broad if uneven pattern, with a median grade of 7 and over 20 percent of the employees at grade 12 or higher. A distribution of full-time employees among the twenty grades of postal field service revealed over 70 percent at grade 4 (comparable in pay to the General Schedule grade 5) and less than 1 percent at grade 12 or higher.[10]

DEVELOPMENT OF PERSONNEL ADMINISTRATION

The personnel system affecting present-day employees of the federal government has developed piecemeal since 1880. It reflects the growth, complexity, and problems of government in a modern society.

Employees of the federal government have traditionally been under the jurisdiction of the Congress and the President. The former, with authority to pass appropriations, could control the activities and the programs of government. For much of the nineteenth century, members of Congress regarded employment in the federal service as suitable for patronage and as an appropriate source of political funds. This view was shared, and in some cases even more zealously promoted, by the President. Changes in political administration were likely to produce wholesale changes in federal employees. A president could defend this action by showing a need to control and have confidence in the employees of the Executive branch of government.

The intrusion of politics into the civil service was far-reaching and notorious by the second half of the nineteenth century. Civil service reformers sought to introduce the concept of merit in employment and promotion and to exclude political ties and pressures. The assassination of President James A. Garfield by a disappointed job seeker provided the impetus necessary for passage of an effective measure. The result was the Civil Service Act of 1883, which established the Civil Service Commission, provided for competitive examinations to rate applicants (with positions awarded to the highest ranking), and prohibited contributions to political funds as a condition of employment.

The act was not an immediate cure for the ills of the spoils system; only 10.5 percent of federal government employees were enrolled in civil service by 1884 and 45 percent by 1903. Exemptions and the creation of new agencies and positions outside the jurisdiction of the act could lower the proportion under classified civil service, as evidenced by the drop from 80 percent in 1932 to 60.5 percent in 1936. By the 1960s the percentage had reached an all-time high of 86 percent; those not covered included cases where competitive examinations were not practical or customary (e.g., lawyers) and cases of foreign nationals serving outside the United States. Also exempt were jobs in Schedule C, high-ranking positions in the Executive branch filled by Presidential appointment. The designation of Schedule C positions has been closely watched by supporters of a career civil service. Personnel of some agencies, such as the Tennessee Valley Authority, the Federal Bureau of Investigation, and the Atomic Energy Commission, have been employed under merit systems outside the jurisdiction of the Civil Service Commission; the principles of these merit systems are basically identical with those followed by the Civil Service Commission.[11]

The criteria used in civil service appointments and political appointments are not always clearly distinguishable.[12] Exempt or political positions may be filled by careful consideration of an applicant's job qualifications. At the same time, appointment to certain post office jobs, which are part of the competitive civil service system, have required political clearance as well as examinations.

Moreover, merit concepts are affected by other parts of the personnel framework. Veterans' preference provisions give an advantage in appointment and layoffs to those who have served in the armed forces. In December 1965, more than one-half of all federal employees had veteran preference.[13]

Additional insulation between civil servants and the political system was provided by the Hatch Act of 1939, which prohibits federal employees from active involvement with political parties, candidates, and campaigns.

A second major change in the federal personnel system occurred in 1923 when the Civil Service Commission began to classify jobs on the basis of requisite preparation and difficulty and scope of duties. The classification system affects appointments, promotions, and pay.

The Classification Act of 1949 delegated responsibility for classifying jobs to the personnel divisions of each department, following guidelines of the Civil Service Commission and subject to checks by the commission. Departments and agencies assumed larger roles in examining and appointing candidates, as well as in classifying positions. Employing departments and agencies recruited and examined over 85 percent of those appointed to competitive civil service jobs in 1962.[14] One critic has charged that by 1964 decentralization of the personnel function had "ended up essentially as delegation of detail, but not of control to the line administrators."[15]

Despite the delegation of functions and the establishment of the civil service and classification systems, Congress retains control over important personnel matters with its "power of the purse," which determines rates of pay, pay levels and steps, classification systems, number of positions, retirement age, and the entire package of "fringe benefits" (holidays, vacations, sick leave, insurance, pensions). Nor need Congress act with one policy for all employees; in 1967, Congress attempted to withhold general pay increases from employees of the Office of Economic Opportunity as an indication of Congressional displeasure with that agency. The significance of the Congressional role in personnel matters has long been understood by the federal employees and their organizations.

EMPLOYEE ORGANIZATIONS

TYPES AND NUMBERS OF ORGANIZATIONS

As in private industry, employee organizations interested in improving working conditions of federal employees started among skilled workers. As early as 1836, workers of the Philadelphia Navy Shipyard conducted a strike.[16] The printers and the bookbinders of the Government Printing Office also became well organized in the nineteenth century.[17] In 1904, the International Association of Machinists established District 44 for machinists employed in government shipyards and arsenals.[18] These and other skilled employees working for the federal government joined traditional craft unions. There was a natural affinity among skilled craftsmen employed in the private and public sectors. They received the same training, associated socially, and moved interchangeably among private and public sector jobs.

The earliest attempts at organizing noncraft employees of the federal government occurred among postal workers.[19] Several groups of postal workers affiliated with the Knights of Labor in the late 1880s. The first national organization of postal employees was established in 1890 with the formation of the National Association of Letter Carriers. The National Association of Rural Letter Carriers followed in 1903. Various attempts to organize postal clerks into a national association foundered on internal dissension until the National Federation of Post Office Clerks was formed in 1906; it was the first national union composed solely of government employees to receive a charter from the American Federation of Labor (AFL). The railway postal clerks and the city letter carriers affiliated with AFL in 1917, and other craft unions of postal workers eventually followed suit.

The formation and affiliation of these unions was not uncontested. At times rival craft postal unions or groups did not wish to affiliate. The National Rural Letter Carriers Association is the oldest continuous organization not affiliated with AFL-CIO. There are also separate organizations for postal supervisors and postmasters.

At least three attempts have been made to form a single union for all postal employees: in 1917 by the clerks, in the mid-1930s by the Postal Workers of America, and in 1959 by the National Postal Union (NPU). NPU has been successful in organizing some of the big city post offices. The Congress of Industrial Organizations (CIO) through its United Public Workers of America made the only significant effort at integrating post office employees with other government workers. Post office employees have, in general, been unwilling to join general labor organizations.

The relatively long history and the number of organizations among postal employees suggest that such workers have much in common with other groups who joined labor organizations in the early part of the twentieth century. For the most part, the hiring standards of post office workers are similar to those of workers entering apprenticeship programs. They develop limited, specialized skills. The "flatness" of the grade structure offers limited chance for promotions and increases interest in existing jobs and working conditions. Finally, the work site and the jobs provide opportunities for close and frequent communication.

Activity among white-collar federal government workers outside the Post Office started in 1896 with the formation of the National Civil Service Association. Even concentration on a single issue, retirement, brought forth only limited response, however. One of the first successful organizations was the National Association of United States Customs Inspectors, organized in 1916.[20] Only one year later AFL chartered the National Federation of Federal Employees (NFFE), whose jurisdiction included all federal employees except those in the postal service and those within the jurisdiction of other affiliated organizations. In 1931 NFFE withdrew from AFL when craft unions with government employees objected to the general classification system being promoted by NFFE, and feared its threat of industrial unionism; at the time NFFE had about 50,000 members.[21] The AFL reacted by chartering the American Federation of Government Employees (AFGE) in the next year, and CIO added its union for federal government employees, the United Federal Workers of America, in 1937.

The membership of these general government work organizations fluctuated, depending upon the temper of the times, the policies and politics of the individual organizations, and the personnel issues before Congress. They never represented more than a small proportion of the total eligible employee force. This is not surprising, considering the wide distribution of employees in function, grade classification, geographic area, and attitudes. The only thing shared by many of these workers was their common employer. Unions have long had difficulty with organizing white-collar professional workers, and many of these employees fit that category.

Other organizations have been formed to represent employees of one department or function in an agency. Examples of such organizations on a national level are the National Association of Internal Revenue Employees, National Association of Government Inspectors, Patent Office Professional Association, and National Association of Federal Veterinarians.

Still more numerous and beyond cataloguing are the local organizations, whose functions vary from providing recreational facilities to protecting members with insurance benefits to improving employee morale and working conditions. Such organizations exist in many agencies and locations and for many different groups of workers. No census of these organizations is available. In some cases, the local organizations have challenged successfully the entry or the existence of a national group and have been designated a local independent union. On other occasions, they manage to coexist by serving complementary purposes. In still other cases, they have organized and then have disappeared. By late 1968 the federal government recognized a total of 130 different employee organizations as representing federal employees: 48 AFL-CIO national and international unions, 31 national independent unions, 9 AFL-CIO directly affiliated councils and locals, and 42 local independent unions.[22] Ninety-five of these organizations represented groups of employees in bargaining matters.

MEMBERSHIP IN EMPLOYEE ORGANIZATIONS

The number of federal workers who are members of federal employee organizations is unclear. Until recent years insufficient interest in such figures has made a historical analysis difficult. Large groups of federal employees have been part of general employee or labor organizations that have not classified separately their government members. The bienniel survey of the Bureau of Labor Statistics estimated that 1,349,000 employees of the federal government were members of national and international unions in 1968. Despite these limitations, a number of conclusions can be set forth about membership in employee organizations in the federal government.

Until 1961 the proportion of federal government workers who were members of employee organizations was roughly parallel to that of private industry workers.[23] At that time, one-third of federal government employees were estimated to be members of employee organizations, compared to over 30 percent of all civilian nonagricultural employees in the labor force. In 1964 the gap had widened, as 39 percent of government employees were members of national unions compared to 29 percent of non-agricultural employees.[24] By 1966, over 41 percent of federal government employees were members of unions, while member-ship among nonagricultural employees had slipped to 28 percent.[25]

Organization has been consistently strongest among workers in the Post Office Department. The twelve national organizations of postal workers reported a total membership of 539,337 in 1964, representing a six-year increase of over 130,000 members among postal employee organizations. Three of the twelve or-ganizations represented 57,000 supervisors and postmasters. A high proportion of all employees in the department and about 90 percent of those covered by the Postal Field Service Com-pensation Act are members of employee organizations.

As in private industry, blue-collar workers are more likely to be members of employee organizations than are white-collar workers. Although no exact membership data are available, an approximation can be obtained from the number of employees represented by organizations with exclusive recognition. In late 1968, 67 percent of blue-collar wage-board employees and 87 percent of postal employees were in exclusive units compared to 28 percent of white-collar employees. The majority of wage-board employees who were members of employee organizations belonged to organizations consisting entirely of federal govern-ment employees. The largest such group held membership in the American Federation of Government Employees, which repre-sented over 190,000 wage-board employees, or 48 percent of all wage-board employees in exclusive units. The National Federation of Federal Employees and the National Association of Government Employees together represented almost 47,000 wage-board employees. About 30 percent of wage-board employees were represented by traditional craft and industrial labor unions. The International Association of Machinists and Aerospace Workers and the Metal Trades Councils had the largest number of members among such unions.

Some of the highest proportionate gains in membership in recent years among federal government employees have been made in the white-collar classified ranks. Major organizational drives have been successful in the Departments of Health, Education and Welfare; Labor; and Treasury, as well as in the Veterans Administration and the Smithsonian Institution. While some organizational activity has led to shifts of members among unions, there can be little question that it has raised the total level of membership among classified employees. The rise in membership among such employees largely accounts for the increase of total membership of the American Federation of Government Employees from 60,000 in 1958 to 290,000 in 1968.

Unions affiliated with AFL-CIO had the largest number of members among federal government employees. Most postal and wage-board employees, who form the largest part of union membership among federal workers, have favored AFL-CIO unions. It is likely that some of the independent organizations of government workers have been losing membership ground in absolute and relative terms in recent years.

Despite the increasing interest of traditional unions in organizing federal government employees, government workers favor organizations composed solely of government workers; 90 percent of union members employed by the federal government are in organizations composed overwhelmingly of government employees.

CHARACTER AND SERVICES OF EMPLOYEE ORGANIZATIONS

The personalities of the employee organizations vary widely, depending upon the occupational nature of the membership, the proportion of nongovernment workers in the organization, the degree of affiliation with organized labor, and the tenor of the times. The introduction of collective bargaining policy by the federal government seems to have clarified differences among groups. For instance, the National Federation of Federal Employees has chosen to emphasize a professional character. In general, organizations of blue-collar employees and those affiliated with AFL-CIO have appeared more militant than white-collar and independent groups. There are important exceptions, however; the independent National Postal Union has charged the dominant postal craft unions, most of which are affiliated with AFL-CIO, with being conservative and slow-moving.

The employee organizations may offer a number of services for members, in addition to representing them to the employer in grievances and for improvement of working conditions. Probably the most notable such service is the provision of medical insurance plans. Several large government organizations, including the postal unions and AFGE, sponsor insurance programs which compete with other programs made available by the federal government. The employee organizations must report to the Civil Service Commission the operations of these programs, for which the government pays part of the cost. For example, membership in the Letter Carriers' Health Benefits Plan in October 1967 was 133,130 and its investment portfolio totaled $6.7 million.[26] Employee organizations may also offer life insurance, retirement income, and other forms of insurance.

BACKGROUND OF COLLECTIVE BARGAINING

The existence for over a century of employee organizations in the federal government, many of them affiliated with the AFL-CIO, suggests that employees believed they could derive benefits from joining associations. The problem for the organizations was that, generally, there were no authorized procedures by which they could represent their members in traditional union fashion.

LEGAL FRAMEWORK

The limited and changing role of employee organizations has been determined by Presidential executive orders and by legislation passed by Congress. The President's "Gag Rule" of 1902 forbade employees and their associations from petitioning Congress for wage increases or other improvements except through department channels. The Lloyd-La Follette Act of 1912 reversed this rule, permitting employees to petition Congress individually or collectively, and provided further that postal employees had the right to join organizations that did not authorize the use of strikes. The statute was broadened to include other federal workers when they showed an interest in joining organizations. Since 1912 employee organizations of federal employees have been free to lobby.

Other forms of employee-management relations were not provided for federal employees, even though the government's policy toward labor relations generally was revised over time. The National Labor Relations Act of 1935, the War Labor Disputes Act of 1943, and all but one section of the 1947 amendments to the National Labor Relations Act specifically exclude government employees from coverage of the legislation. In short, Congress did not wish to provide for collective bargaining for government workers.

The one exception in the legislation just mentioned is Section 305 of the 1947 amendments, which forbids employees of the federal government from participating in any strike. An employee who does "shall be discharged immediately from his employment, and shall forfeit his civil service status, if any, and shall not be eligible for reemployment for three years by the United States. . . ." The motivation for this provision was a policy of CIO-affiliated United Public Workers of America requiring consent of the union president before any local could strike.[27] The union has since disappeared, but the intent of Section 305 remains. Indeed it was strengthened in 1955 by Public Law 330, which makes the act of striking or of asserting the right to strike a felony and requires new employees to sign affidavits certifying compliance.[28]

ADMINISTRATIVE FRAMEWORK

The attitudes and policies of public administrators toward employee organizations have varied widely; these factors naturally affected the role and the status of the organizations. Perhaps the most antagonistic opponent of unions in federal service was Albert Burleson, who served as postmaster general from 1913 to 1921.[29] A more common attitude has been one of virtual ignorance and unwillingness to deal with employee organizations. Even in the late 1940s the "conventional approach" to relations with employee organizations was for management to be neutral about organizations and to consult occasionally with representatives of all groups.[30]

LOBBYING

The legal and administrative frameworks encouraged most organizations of federal employees to turn their primary efforts to lobbying. This approach was reinforced by Congressional control over the economic benefits and by the willingness of congressmen to welcome strong union support. Because the postal employees were well organized and strategically located throughout the country, the postal unions became the acknowledged masters among government unions in the art of lobbying. The larger postal unions have been among the top-ranking lobbyists in terms of annual expenditures. The United Federation of Postal Clerks was the leading lobbyist in 1966, spending $287,000 for the purpose.[31] Much effort for promoting pay raises and other benefits for federal workers has been undertaken by the postal unions year after year. Although all workers have benefited from these efforts the postal workers have probably benefited most of all.

COLLECTIVE BARGAINING

Notwithstanding the restrictions noted, collective bargaining did exist in the federal government prior to 1962. In 1948, the Department of Interior provided a labor relations program for its employees, including selection of bargaining representatives, collective bargaining resulting in written agreements, and advisory arbitration in grievance procedures.[32] The postmaster in Boston signed a collective bargaining agreement in the mid-1940s on the matters of seniority and procedures for settlement of disputes.[33] Other agencies having collective bargaining, as it is traditionally known, were the Government Printing Office, the Alaska Railroad, and the Tennessee Valley Authority. These cases are few and exceptional; the important thing is that they existed at all.

The most remarkable instance of collective bargaining occurred in the Tennessee Valley Authority (TVA), because bargaining agreements included white-collar as well as blue-collar workers. In establishing TVA as a separate government corporation, Congress exempted its employees from civil service regulations concerning appointment, wages, and duties but did insist on applying the merit principle in personnel actions and on the prevailing-rate method of setting wages.[34] In 1935 the board of directors issued an Employee Relationship Policy, giving employees the right to join unions and to choose representatives for bargaining; the policy included procedures for implementing these rights. The management of TVA has gone further. It recommends to new employees that they join their respective unions, and it trains supervisors to support collective bargaining. Twelve craft unions, all affiliated with AFL, formed the Tennessee Valley and Trades Council and negotiated a general agreement for blue-collar workers in 1940. The issues for bargaining have included wages, job classification, training, adverse actions, and grievance procedures. In 1943, five organizations of salaried employees, two of which were independent, organized a joint panel; engineers, chemists, clerks, administrators, custodians, and public safety workers are represented by this joint body. Since 1950, the panel, which represents about 75 percent of all salaried employees, has bargained for written agreements, covering many of the same topics as those negotiated with blue-collar workers. Perhaps the most outstanding instance of union-management cooperation has been the eighty joint cooperative committees which have been credited with promoting safety and efficiency at TVA.

The TVA experience proved to employee organizations and other supporters of collective bargaining in public employment that collective bargaining for federal employees could be effective. At the same time it destroyed many of the shibboleths of the opponents to the wide-scale introduction of collective bargaining in the federal service. More than practical demonstrations would be necessary to change long-entrenched patterns.

MOVES TO A NEW POLICY

LEGISLATION

From 1949 to 1961, Representative George Milton Rhodes of Pennsylvania sponsored in each session of the Congress a bill providing that employee organizations have the right to represent employees in grievances and to confer with departments; that disputes go to binding arbitration; and that administrators violating the act be subject to penalties up to and including removal. The bill was never voted on.

While he was member of the Senate, John F. Kennedy had supported legislation for recognition of federal employee organizations. In June 1961 when he was president, he named a task force of top-appointed officials of the Executive branch to study employee-management relations in the federal service. The task force was to make recommendations within five months on such subjects as "appropriate employee organizations, standards for recognition . . . matters upon which employee organizations may be appropriately consulted, and the participation of employees and employee representatives in grievances and appeals."[35]

The task force report of November 1961 acknowledged the absence of any policy and the existence of widely varying practices. It recommended "a governmentwide Presidential policy which acknowledges the legitimate role which these organizations should have in the formulation and implementation of Federal personnel policies and practices." The report proposed details to effect the policy, including forms of recognition, scope of negotiations, impasse procedures, union security, and grievance procedures. These recommendations were the essence of Executive Order 10988 signed by President Kennedy on January 17, 1962, which led into a new era of employee-management relations in the federal government.

Executive Order 10988

Executive Order 10988 resembled in some ways legislation implementing national labor relations policy for persons employed in most private industries. It gave the right to employees of the federal government to organize or to refrain from organizing for employee representation; employees may always elect to bring matters on an individual basis to their supervisors. The bases of unit determination were essentially similar to those employed by the National Labor Relations Board. Organizations representing a majority of employees were entitled to bargain with management on "personnel policy and practices and matters affecting working conditions" and to have the results of negotiations appear in written agreements. The essence of representation and collective bargaining as they are generally known were thus incorporated in the Executive Order.

In other regards, however, the Executive Order departed radically from the established course of labor legislation. First, the role and the authority of management were explicitly preserved. Agencies determined appropriate units and, if the agency or the employee organization desired, it requested advisory arbitration. Similarly, grievance procedures were negotiable, but final-step arbitration was limited to advisory arbitration. Negotiated agreements were subject to the approval of agency heads. Section 7 of Executive Order 10988 specified that all agreements include a management-rights clause:

> In the administration of all matters covered by the agreement officials and employees are governed by the provisions of any existing or future laws and regulations, including policies set forth in the Federal Personnel Manual and agency regulations, which may be applicable, and the agreement shall at all times be applied subject to such laws, regulations and policies; . . .
>
> Management officials of the agency retain the right, in accordance with applicable laws and regulations, (a) to direct employees of the agency, (b) to hire, promote, transfer, assign, and retain employees in positions within the agency, and to suspend, demote, discharge, or take other disciplinary action against employees, (c) to relieve employees from duties because of lack of work or for other legitimate reasons, (d) to maintain the efficiency of the Government operations entrusted to them, (e) to determine the methods, means and personnel by which such operations are to be conducted; and (f) to take whatever actions may be necessary to carry out the mission of the agency in situations of emergency.

Second, employee organizations had certain limitations placed on them by the Executive Order. Organizations were not recognized if they discriminated in membership because of race, creed, color, or national origin, or if they "assert the right to strike against the Government of the United States . . . or assist or participate in any such strike." Matters pertaining to internal organizations operations, such as dues collection or membership solicitation, had to be conducted off duty.

Third, in addition to exclusive recognition, the Executive

Order introduced two other forms of recognition previously unknown. These forms may be described as follows:

1. Exclusive recognition was accorded to organizations that met the requirements for formal recognition and were also chosen by a majority of employees in the unit as their exclusive representative. Such recognition gave the organization the right to negotiate agreements on behalf of all employees and the duty to represent all employees in the unit. It thus corresponded to recognition in terms of the Labor Management Relations Act. The Executive Order contained no provision for exclusive recognition at the national level.

2. Formal recognition was granted to organizations with "a substantial and stable membership" of at least 10 percent of employees in a unit in which there was no exclusive recognition. Organizations with formal recognition would be consulted "in the formulation and implementation of personnel policies and practices, and matters affecting working conditions that are of concern to its members." Formal recognition at the national (agency) level was granted to an employee organization at the discretion of the agency head on the basis of the union's representation of local units or members within the agency. The Executive Order provided no specific numerical guidelines to determine granting of national formal recognition.

3. Informal recognition was available to employee organizations ineligible for other forms of recognition and entitled the organization "to present to appropriate officials its views on matters of concern to its members."

Fourth, the area of bargaining was restricted by law and established regulations, by the management rights clause, and by specific exemption from negotiation of "the mission of any agency, its budget, its organization and the assignment of its personnel, or the technology of performing its work."

Fifth, the Executive Order left implementation of the Order largely within the Executive branch of government, specifically to individual department heads. As discussed in more detail below, the Secretary of Labor assisted department heads in contested unit determinations with rules for advisory arbitration and selection of arbitrators. The Civil Service Commission provided departments with advice, information, and feedback on their employee-management relations programs. The Department of Labor and the Civil Service Commission were to prepare standards of conduct for employee organizations and a code of fair labor practices.

Sixth, unlike legislation passed by Congress, the Executive Order was an administrative law. As such, it could be revoked or altered at any time at the discretion of the President. As long as a President friendly to employee organizations and the concept of collective bargaining was in office, there would be no significant difference in the labor relations policy for federal employees. However, lobbying efforts by employee organizations are less effective in changing Executive Orders than in affecting Congressional legislation.

Despite the differences noted, Executive Order 10988 marked a significant departure in labor relations for federal employees. These differences may be attributed to the uncertainty of developing labor relations in unchartered areas and to the desire to retain sovereignty of the state in employee relations. The fact remains that by issuing the order the government for the first time officially opened the door to employee organizations and to collective bargaining.

MANAGEMENT ORGANIZATION

The issuance of Executive Order 10988 affected the structure and the operations of management and of employee organizations. Management had to reorganize itself to establish continuing relations with employee organizations, to administer labor relations consistently within its own area of authority, and to develop communications with other parts of the federal service on matters of employee relations. The employee organizations, too, had to accommodate themselves to the new situation.

CIVIL SERVICE COMMISSION

The Civil Service Commission has been the key agency in developing and coordinating the employee relations program in the federal service. The Executive Order gave to the Civil Service Commission the staff functions of guiding agencies in their employee relations programs and in reviewing these programs. The commission, together with the Department of Labor, was directed to prepare standards of conduct for employee organizations and a code of fair labor practices. Civil Service Commission guidance of agency programs consists of conducting training programs, developing and issuing guidelines and standards, reporting on the overall program, and consulting regularly with agency personnel responsible for labor relations programs.

The Civil Service Commission also provided guidance to unions on implementation of the Executive Order. For instance, five maritime unions appealed to the Civil Service Commission when they felt that the Navy was not bargaining in good faith on union security for personnel on ships. The commission staff could not change agency action but did spend sufficient time in explaining the reasons for the action to close the matter.

The importance of the labor relations role of the Civil Service Commission was recognized in the creation of an Office of Labor-Management Relations in 1966. The staff of this office is small, thus limiting the possibility of extensive day-to-day involvement in the labor relations of any particular agency.

The responsibility for reviewing programs lies with the Bureau of Inspections of the Civil Service Commission. The annual inspection reports provide agencies with information on specific problems and the commission with information requiring policy changes or more general corrective action.

DEPARTMENT OF LABOR

In addition to its joint duties with the Civil Service Commission, the Department of Labor was assigned the continuing function of assisting in representation procedures and in nominating arbitrators to advise agency heads in disputes about unit determinations and recognition procedures. A one-man office was established for this purpose. By early 1968 the Department of Labor had issued twenty-five administrative rulings and had nominated several dozen arbitrators. In fact, the influence of the department was more widespread as unions and agencies requested the office to mediate informally not only disputes about representation but also impasses on other matters. Moreover, the office has participated in many training and coordinating activities of the Civil Service Commission.

INTERAGENCY COORDINATION

Besides the formal letters of the Civil Service Commission and the informal activities of both the commission and the Department of Labor, interagency meetings have been held periodically. Their purpose has been to provide federal managers with information on developments in labor relations, to discuss common problems and consult on possible changes, and to meet informally with their counterparts in other agencies. The main group of this kind has been a Civil Service Commission Interagency Advisory Group on Employee-Management Cooperation (IAG-190), composed of over twenty chief staff persons responsible for labor relations in federal agencies. The problems discussed at these monthly meetings reflect the current status of labor relations at the federal level. At first, discussion centered on unit and recognition problems; more recently the problems have concerned competing unions and negotiations. Another group with similar purposes is the Federal Conference on Employee-Management Relations, an ad hoc discussion group of operating personnel.

AGENCY

Collective bargaining and administration of agreements occur within each agency, because each agency has its own functions, budget, and regulations. Agencies set policies and administer the Executive Order within the guidelines established by the Civil Service Commission. Each agency, however, has ultimate responsibility for implementing the order and conforming to its standards, for negotiating and administering agreements, and for regulating the climate of employee-management relations.

In some ways the agency labor relations staff serves its operating divisions much as the Civil Service Commission does the agency. It establishes policies, conducts training programs, advises on questions, and reviews program effectiveness. The staff has a more direct role, however, in determining the substance of agreements and the settlement of disputes.

There is little uniformity among agencies in organizing for labor relations. The central labor relations staff of individual agencies depends on the agency's size, the extent of organization, and the number of exclusive bargaining relationships. In small agencies, a personnel specialist may be responsible for everything from recruiting to labor relations. The Navy Department, on the other hand, has a separate Employee-Management Relations Division with three branches and four sections. Agencies with extensive field operations may also assign labor relations specialists to field staffs, especially if negotiations or grievance administration is handled through field offices.

Two trends have appeared in agency organization for labor relations. Agencies have increased their staff of labor relations specialists and have separated labor relations from personnel functions. Both trends reflect an increasing importance of union-management relations in the federal government.

EMPLOYEE ORGANIZATIONS

Executive Order 10988 had an impact on employee organizations as well as on management. Although employee organizations were common in government prior to the Executive Order, their size and function changed after 1962. Organizations composed entirely of government workers were skilled in lobbying but knew little of collective bargaining or representing workers covered by a negotiated agreement. Unions with labor relations experience in private industry had more resources in staff and knowledge but had to adjust to the special nature of collective bargaining in the federal government. Unlike the private sector, for instance, labor relations under the Executive Order limited the scope of bargaining and provided employees with dual grievance procedures. All organizations had to cope with the rapidly increasing number of members who needed servicing and representation.

Unions increased their staffs and adapted to the newly developing relationships. They coordinated efforts where there was no jurisdictional competition. The seven craft unions with exclusive recognition in the Post Office Department agreed to bargain jointly for a major national agreement, a move that has undoubtedly facilitated consideration of merger by some of the unions involved. The National Association of Post Office Mail Handlers agreed to merge with the Laborers' International Union in the spring of 1968 to provide better service to members. The Government Employees Council, AFL-CIO, founded in 1945, expanded its activities to include training in collective bargaining and periodic assessment of the functioning of the Executive Order.

IMPLEMENTING DIRECTIVES

Sixteen months after Executive Order 10988 was issued, President Kennedy prescribed two additional directives "to
assist in securing the uniform and effective implementation of the
policies, rights, and responsibilities described in the Order."[36]
These were the Standards of Conduct for Employee Organizations
and the Code of Fair Labor Practices.

STANDARDS OF CONDUCT FOR EMPLOYEE ORGANIZATIONS

The Standards of Conduct established requirements for organizations representing federal employees. In particular, organizations had to ensure democratic procedures, exclude from office
persons identified with corruption or totalitarian movements,
prohibit conflict of interest on the part of officers or agents, and
maintain fiscal integrity. Agencies suspecting organizations of
violating the code held hearings to provide the organization an
opportunity to present its case, but the determination of the
agency head was final. Violations of the Standards could
result in denial, suspension, or withdrawal of an organization's
recognition. The purposes and many of the provisions of the
Standards of Conduct were the same as those of the Labor-Management Reporting and Disclosure Act of 1959; their methods of
enforcement and penalties were quite different. As of 1968, no
cases had been filed formally for violation of the Standards of
Conduct.

CODE OF FAIR LABOR PRACTICES

The Code of Fair Labor Practices was similar to the unfair
labor practices in the Labor Management Relations Act governing
private employers and unions. The code prohibited agency management from interfering with employees in exercising rights
granted by the Executive Order, controlling any employee organization, refusing to accord proper recognition to organizations or
to accord them the rights of such recognition, and encouraging or
discouraging membership in employee organizations. Unfair labor
practices for employee organizations included interference with

employees in exercising rights granted by the Executive Order; discrimination against any employee with regard to membership because of race, creed, color, or national origin; coercion of members such as by interfering with their duties as public employees; participation in a strike, slowdown, or related picketing; and attempts at inducing an agency to coerce employees in exercising their rights under the order. Moreover, organizations with exclusive recognition could not deny membership to persons except for failure to "meet reasonable occupational standards uniformly required for admission, or . . . to tender initiation fees and dues uniformly required as a condition of acquiring and retaining membership." The principal differences between the code and the unfair labor practices found in Section 8 of the Labor-Management Relations Act relate to matters illegal in the federal government, such as union security, strike, and boycott.

Except for strikes and slowdowns, which were subject to legal sanctions as determined by the agency head, each agency was to establish procedures for investigating and processing alleged violations of the code. These procedures included hearings with "impartial hearing officer(s)"; hearing officers were responsible to the agency head. The hearings could range from informal proceedings to fact-finding, with recommendations. The code provided that agencies or employee organizations found in violation of the code were to take corrective action. If employee organizations did not comply, the agency head might withhold or withdraw recognition.

Almost all the complaints filed under the Code of Fair Labor Practices have charged agency violations of the code. Complaints have included discrimination against union members, interference with organizing, and refusal to accord proper recognition to employee organizations. In general the charges have been rejected by the agencies. In at least one case, an employee organization has been charged with a code violation for encouraging members to picket.

Since the Code was issued, employee organizations have repeatedly complained about the unilateral procedure for processing and judging alleged code violations. They contend that the system was inherently inequitable if the accused determined and administered violation procedures and also decided whether or not to accept the verdict. The denial of alleged violations by agencies had convinced the organizations that management could not be judge and defendant simultaneously.

DUES DEDUCTION

Payroll withholding for organization dues deduction was authorized by President Kennedy and permitted by Civil Service Commission regulations on January 1, 1964. Dues deduction was permitted only for organizations with formal or exclusive recognition. The withholding had to be voluntary on the part of individual employees and revocable at six-month intervals. The cost of withholding, at a rate of two cents a deduction, was to be paid by the organization.

A Civil Service Commission study reported that in January 1968 a total of 811,366 federal employees had requested that union dues be withheld from their pay and transmitted to 76 unions. More than three-fifths of these employees were members of the American Federation of Government Employees, the National Association of Letter Carriers, and the United Federation of Postal Clerks.

AGENCY IMPLEMENTATION

Each agency must implement Presidential Executive Orders and Civil Service Commission regulations. In some cases, as in hearings procedures of the Code of Fair Labor Practices, the initiating directive provided latitude in implementation. In all cases, agencies had to issue their own rules and regulations to carry out the order and its offsprings. For instance, the Department of Defense issued a twenty-six-page directive in August 1964 providing standards for recognition, criteria for establishing new units, and rights of employee organizations.[37]

Collective Bargaining

UNIT DETERMINATION AND REPRESENTATION PROCEDURES

Section 6 of the Executive Order spelled out the main criteria of unit determination: (1) a unit must have a community of interest; (2) professionals must consent to be included in units with exclusive recognition; (3) supervisors cannot be in the same units as subordinates. These guidelines required interpretation. Much of the early effort in implementing the government's labor relations program was devoted to the definition of appropriate units.

Part of the problem of defining appropriate units resulted from delegating to agencies the responsibility for unit determination. Because they were the employers, agencies could be considered to be prejudiced in deciding unit composition. In addition, agencies had neither knowledge nor experience in unit determinations, especially in the early years of the Executive Order. The absence of rules and case-by-case determinations made the matter seem more complex and consistency more difficult. An employee organization dissatisfied with an agency ruling on unit determination could request advisory arbitration, but it had no assurance of uniform rulings from such quarters nor any guarantee that the agency would abide by the advisory opinion.

The types of unit determination difficulties changed since the early days of the Executive Order. Initial controversy centered on size of units, for example, whether a unit should consist of a single installation or an entire agency. Later, problems in unit determination centered on functional units, especially where functions do not fit into traditional craft lines. For example, a union requested representation rights for all employees working in heating tunnels, rather than have steam fitters join other craft members in the geographic area. Requests for carving out certain groups of workers as an appropriate unit may be heightened by the increasing competition among employee organizations as the unorganized area is reduced.

The parties may sometimes recommend unit size on the basis of pragmatic self-interest. For instance, an agency may prefer a larger unit because of administrative efficiency or because of the likelihood that the union could not win an election in such a unit. Similarly, extent of organization may be the raison d'être for unit requests by employee organizations. Especially in the first years of the Executive Order, when unorganized areas were common, employee organizations were willing to establish units wherever they had sufficient membership strength.

A continuing recognition problem concerned units of supervisors. Although units composed of supervisors were permitted under Executive Order 10988, the Civil Service Commission had discouraged recognition of such units where the organization representing supervisors also represented subordinates in the same agency. The commission's policy was based on identical negotiating teams representing the separate units, thus obviating the distinction required by the order. The problem was significant only in the Internal Revenue Service, where the National Association of Internal Revenue Employees (NAIRE) was the representative of about eighty units composed solely of supervisors.

A sure sign of developing labor relations and organizational rivalry was the introduction of procedures to permit employees to change organizations having exclusive recognition.[38] These provisions protected existing representative organizations by a contract bar until the terminal date of the agreement or for two years, whichever was earlier, or, in the absence of an agreement, for a minimum of twelve months following the granting of exclusive recognition. The challenging organization had to prove that it represented at least 30 percent of the employees in the unit and also met the requirements for formal recognition noted previously.

Questions were also raised about methods used to select organizational representatives. Employee organizations had protested administrative decisions to grant recognition by counting membership cards rather than by conducting secret-ballot elections. They had also criticized the definition of majority required in elections to determine an exclusive representative. Protests were filed about management interference in representation elections by favoring one organization over another, usually by permitting the use of facilities to the favored organization. Recently, however, challenges have been directed more by one employee organization against another than by an organization against an agency. This trend reflects both resolution of and experience with agency procedures, as well as interorganizational rivalry for additional areas.

ADVISORY ARBITRATION

Requests for advisory arbitration in disputes on unit determinations and representation procedures were submitted by any interested party to the Secretary of Labor.[39] By early 1967 the secretary had received over two hundred requests for the nomination of arbitrators.[40] The Division of Federal Employee-

Management Relations determined the validity of the request. The requests were denied in forty-nine cases. For instance, a claim made by one organization that another had used unfair propaganda during an election was ruled irrelevant to the outcome, because the claimant had ample time to refute the charges. In another case, the request for arbitration by an organization objecting to a representation election because it claimed proof of majority approval was denied on grounds that the elimination of dual memberships did not leave the organization with a majority. The requests for the nomination of arbitrators were withdrawn in fifty-five cases.

When the request for advisory arbitration was granted, each party was sent a list of three names chosen by the Secretary of Labor from a federal panel of arbitrators, generally on the basis of geographic proximity to the hearing site. After the parties had registered their preference, the Secretary of Labor selected the arbitrator to hear the case. The agency paid the arbitrator's entire fee, but the employee organization paid the cost of presenting its case.

The cases brought to arbitration have been concerned primarily with the size of the appropriate unit and with representation election practices. In a study of the first thirty-four determinations referred to arbitration, it was found that agencies generally wanted larger units than did the employee organizations but that arbitrators favored units smaller than agency-wide or installation-wide.[41] Moreover, arbitrators usually supported the petitioning requests of employee organizations. The types of cases reflect the operations of an agency. The Internal Revenue Service, for instance, was repeatedly challenged in the geographic scope of its units (zone office versus regional office). The armed services agencies and the General Service Administration have had problems with grouping of craft employees. In one case the arbitrator agreed with the Navy that two occupational groups could be taken out of two bargaining units accorded exclusive recognition to form another appropriate bargaining unit.[42]

When more than one employee organization is involved in a unit determination or representation dispute submitted to arbitration, the agency is likely to find itself in the middle of a dispute among employee organizations. This is particularly evident in charges of alleged unfair campaign practices by rival employee organizations. In almost every case decided in 1967, one or more employee organizations intervened to support the agency's position. An arbitrator's ruling affirming the agency decision in these cases was as much a victory for the nonpetitioning employee organization(s) as it was for the agency.

Federal agencies accepted the arbitrators' decisions in all sixty-one advisory decisions issued in the first five years of the Executive Order.

CASES UNDER AFL-CIO ARTICLE XXI

Another channel for resolving some interunion disputes is available to affiliates of AFL-CIO. The federation's internal disputes plan provided by Article XXI of the constitution affords affiliates an opportunity to resolve jurisdictional disputes before an impartial umpire. When AFL and CIO merged in 1955, few jurisdictional problems existed in the federal government. After the issuance of Executive Order 10988, numerous appeals were made to the disputes machinery. Three reasons accounted for the increase. (1) The rise in union membership among federal employees caused more unions to be interested in organizing these workers. (2) The largest union of federal employees, AFGE, is an industrial union, while many other affiliates of AFL-CIO interested in organizing federal employees are nominally craft unions. (3) The Excutive Order permitted various forms of recognition, and the resulting situation was not covered by guidelines established under the federation's no-raiding agreement.

The key criterion in deciding AFL-CIO jurisdictional disputes is whether an established relationship exists between union and management. Where such a relationship exists, the union has a protected interest as far as other affiliates are concerned. In a case involving an election challenge by the National Maritime Union in a unit for which AFGE had been given exclusive recognition, umpire David L. Cole ruled that there was no established collective bargaining relationship, because the exclusive recognition had existed for less than one year and had not been certified.[43] Evidence of an established collective bargaining relationship could presumably be a signed collective bargaining agreement. Under this interpretation, a union with formal recognition which therefore could not qualify for agreement negotiations would be left open to raiding. The AFL-CIO Executive Council subsequently ruled that Article XXI applies to unions holding or seeking exclusive recognition at the federal level. At the same time it agreed that a union seeking to organize and gain formal or informal recognition for employees already members of a union holding informal or formal recognition violates Article XXI.[44] Even decertification and hence the end of an established collective bargaining relationship does not necessarily permit other affiliates to organize at once.[45] Certainly some of this confusion would be eliminated with restrictions in the types of recognition at the federal level.

RECOGNITION

Despite occasional problems, collective bargaining units have been established steadily and with startling rapidity. Between 1962 and the end of 1968, almost 2,300 units with 52 percent of executive branch employees had been granted exclusive recognition (see Table II–2). Exclusive recognition at the national level

Table II–2
Increase in Collective Bargaining Units with Exclusive Recognition

YEAR	TOTAL NUMBER OF UNITS	EMPLOYEES REPRESENTED
Prior to 1962	26	19,000
1962	61	
1963*	470	670,000
1964*	630	730,000
1965*	830	835,000
1966*	1,174	1,054,000
1967*	1,813	1,239,000
1968*	2,305	1,416,073

* Figure for number of units includes only seven national postal units; there are also 24,500 exclusive local units in the Post Office Department.

SOURCE: U.S. Civil Service Commission, *Report to the President on the Status of Implementing Executive Order 10988* (Washington, D.C.: 1963, 1964, 1965), and U.S. Civil Service Commission, Office of Labor-Management Relations, *Union Recognition in the Federal Government* (Washington, D.C.: November 1967, November 1968).

had been granted in a few cases by the Post Office Department, the Department of Agriculture, the Department of Justice, and the Railroad Retirement Board. There were also 1,087 units with formal recognition, 83 national units with formal recognition, and, in 1967, 1,031 units with informal recognition.

The AFL-CIO unions had clearly forged into a commanding lead in gaining recognition (see Tables II–3 and II–4). Significantly the federation affiliates showed greatest relative strength in exclusive recognitions and in the units with large numbers of employees. Among AFL-CIO unions, AFGE had emerged as the most

Table II–3
Government-wide Recognition of Labor Unions, by
Affiliation, November 1968

Union affiliation	Units by Type of Recognition				Employees in Exclusive Units	
	FORMALS		EXCLUSIVES			
	NUMBER	%	NUMBER	%	NUMBER	%
AFL-CIO	617	57%	1,503	65%	1,219,236	86%
National independent	420	39	783	34	192,052	14
Local independent	50	5	19	1	4,785	0
Total	1,087		2,305		1,416,073	

SOURCE: U.S. Civil Service Commission, Office of Labor-Management Relations, *Union Recognition in the Federal Government* (Washington, D.C.: November 1968), Table F.

formidable power. In 1967 it became the largest exclusive representative in the federal government, thereby eclipsing the former leader, the United Federation of Postal Clerks. The AFGE represented 453,155 federal employees under exclusive recognition in November 1968. Of greater relevance, however, was the widening margin in employees represented by exclusive recognition that AFGE enjoyed over its most direct rival, the Metal Trades Council; this edge increased from 3 to 1 in August 1966 to 4 to 1 in November 1967 to 6 to 1 in November 1968.

Despite the trend to increasing recognition of all federal em-

Table II-4
Unions Representing More Than 10,000 Federal Employees with Exclusive Recognition and Under Agreements, November 1968

Unions	Number of Employees		PERCENT OF EMPLOYEES WITH EXCLUSIVE RECOGNITION UNDER AGREEMENT
	UNDER EXCLUSIVE RECOGNITION	UNDER AGREEMENT	
American Federation of Government Employees (AFL-CIO)	453,155	304,256	67%
International Association of Machinists and Aerospace Workers (AFL-CIO)	33,552	29,415	88
Metal Trades Council (AFL-CIO)	77,180	75,737	98
National Association of Government Employees (Ind.)	51,519	34,590	67
National Association of Internal Revenue Employees (Ind.)	39,145	8,498	22
National Association of Letter Carriers of the U.S.A. (AFL-CIO)	196,416	196,416	100
National Federation of Federal Employees (Ind.)	51,518	27,879	54
National Association of Post Office and General Service Maintenance Employees (AFL-CIO)	24,963	24,504	98
National Association of Post Office Mail Handlers, Watchmen, Messengers, and Group Leaders (AFL-CIO)	45,966	45,966	100
National Federation of Post Office Motor Vehicle Employees (AFL-CIO)	11,915	11,915	100
National Rural Letter Carriers Association (Ind.)	30,906	30,906	100
United Federation of Postal Clerks (AFL-CIO)	304,026	304,026	100
Total of all Unions	1,416,073	1,175,524	83

SOURCE: U.S. Civil Service Commission, Office of Labor-Management Relations, *Union Recognition in the Federal Government* (Washington, D.C.: November 1968), Table C.

ployees, there remains considerable variation among occupations (see Table II–5). For all intents and purposes postal workers have been in exclusive units since 1963. The increasing proportion of workers in units with exclusive recognition is thus due to the organization of nonpostal employees. Although less than one-third of white-collar employees were in exclusive units in 1968, they represented the most rapidly increasing sector of federal employment to gain exclusive recognition. Approximately two-thirds of

Table II–5
Federal Employees Covered by Exclusive Recognition, November 1968

	NUMBER OF EMPLOYEES	PERCENT OF EMPLOYEES COVERED
Postal	618,562	87%
Blue collar	400,669	67
White collar	396,842	28
Total	1,416,073	52

SOURCE: U.S. Civil Service Commission, Office of Labor-Management Relations, *Analysis of Data on Union Recognition in the Federal Service,* Bulletin No. 711–16 (Washington, D.C.: May 15, 1969), Table A.

Table II–6
Exclusive Units by Type, November 1968

1. Activity-wide	684
2. Activity-wide except professionals	266
3. Activity-wide except guards/fire fighters	15
4. Wage board	210
5. Classification Act employees	83
6. Professional employees	68
7. Supervisors	109
8. Craft	70
9. Guards	70
10. Fire fighters	106
11. Other occupations (inspectors, nurses, etc.)	221
12. Functional (maintenance, printing, etc.)	85
13. Organizational (carpentry shop, motor pool, etc.)	318
Total	2,305

SOURCE: U.S. Civil Service Commission, Office of Labor-Management Relations, *Union Recognition in the Federal Government,* (Washington, D.C.: November 1968), Table H.

the white-collar employees in exclusive units were represented by AFGE.

Of 2,305 'units with exclusive recognition, over two-fifths were activity-wide or installation-wide, although one-third of these excluded certain groups, in addition to managerial executives, supervisors, and nonclerical employees engaged in personnel work (see Table II–6). Of the 109 units composed of supervisors, sixty-eight were in the Treasury Department and 21 in the Department of Defense.

SCOPE OF BARGAINING

A significant feature of labor relations in the federal government is the limited scope of negotiations. Many matters common to bargaining—sometimes considered central to bargaining—are not bargainable, because authority for decision making on these matters has been placed elsewhere or because the Executive Order excluded them from negotiation.

Congress has jurisdiction over many personnel policies and conditions of employment. For instance, Congress establishes levels of pay for classified employees, hours of work, and supplementary benefits, including time off and insurance benefits. Congress also prescribes the merit principle in hiring and promotion, compulsory retirement age, and preference for veterans in certain personnel actions. The implementation of Congressional legislation by the Civil Service Commission takes on the force of law. Thus job classification and performance-rating regulations are inviolate and nonbargainable. Union security provisions were limited by the ruling that union membership as a condition of employment was incompatible with the merit principle.

Executive Order 10988 further limited the scope for joint union-management determination. Reserved for management were "the mission of an agency, its budget, its organizations and the assignment of its personnel, [and] the technology of performing its work."[46] Moreover, management retained the right to hire, promote, transfer, suspend, demote, discharge, and discipline employees and to decide the "means and personnel by which . . . operations are to be conducted."[47] Agency regulations were beyond the scope of negotiations and had precedence over any contradictory provisions that might be negotiated.

The limitations just noted contained some leeway. For instance,

Congressional determination of wage levels for classified employees does not determine the classification of a particular job. Nor does the setting of overtime rates determine how overtime will be allocated. Similarly, the merit principle in promotions leaves some room for administering a promotion program and for interpreting criteria used to measure merit.

The structure of bargaining further limits the scope of negotiations. Since most units with exclusive recognition are at the local level, meaningful negotiations are restricted to matters within the authority of management at that level. Many policies of concern to employees are not formulated at the local level, however, and cannot therefore be negotiated, even though they formally fall within the scope of negotiations permitted by the Executive Order. This problem does not exist if an organization has exclusive recognition at the national level, but such recognition was common only in the Post Office Department.

The items contained in any agreement depend upon the level of the bargaining unit and the sophistication of the parties. The Department of the Army estimated that there were one hundred different substantive negotiable items, but most agreements contained only from three to thirty-six items.[48] The more commonly covered items included work scheduling, working conditions (rest periods, parking), work clothing, safety, personnel practices (promotion, training, discipline), grievance procedure, resolution of impasses, and union activities.

A survey of fifty-five agreements in effect in the General Services Administration in 1967 found that eighteen contained one or two substantive items, twenty-two contained three to four substantive items, and fifteen contained five or more substantive items.[49] The most frequently negotiated items were meetings for union-management activities, resolution of negotiation impasses, and grievance procedures.

At times agreements were little more than restatements of agency policy prefaced with standard recognition and other contract provisions. Local agreements supplementing national agreements might likewise consist primarily of a reaffirmation of the national agreement. Two local postal contracts contained only the additional provisions for time off during the deer-hunting season or the baseball World Series if a series game was played in the city of the local agreement.

Wage-board employees have looked with particular interest to collective bargaining for resolving their complaints about inequities in surveys that determine their wage rates. Unilateral rate determinations at the agency level precluded negotiations with organizations recognized exclusively only at the local level. As a result of collective bargaining in one case, three employees were appointed to the wage survey team from a list submitted by the employee organization.[50] Most wage-board employees, however, found little satisfaction through direct collective bargaining. In 1968 a change was instituted with the establishment of the Coordinated Federal Wage System to fix rates of wage-board employees. The system provides for active union participation at all levels of the system in channels outside collective bargaining.

WRITTEN AGREEMENTS

Formal and informal recognitions provided limited representational rights to employee organizations; only exclusive recognition permitted negotiations for agreements. In 1968, 1,181 collective bargaining agreements covered 1,175,524 employees, or 43 percent of all federal employees.[51] Agreements had been negotiated in only one-half the units with exclusive recognition, but these agreements covered 83 percent of employees in exclusive units. Thus, agreements were concentrated in larger units.

The proportion of employees covered by a negotiated agreement varied widely among agencies (see Table II–7). Only in the Post Office Department and in TVA were all employees in exclusive units under negotiated agreements. At the other end of the scale, one-fifth of Defense Supply employees in exclusive units and one-third of Treasury employees in such units were under agreement. In general, a correlation existed between the proportion of an agency's employees in exclusive units and the proportion of employees in exclusive units who were under agreement.

The distribution of agreements among unions reflected the strength of organizations and of the employees they represented (see Tables II–4 and II–8). Unions with membership exclusively in the Post Office Department had agreements for all represented employees. In general, unions affiliated with AFL-CIO had negoti-

Table II–7

Agencies and Collective Bargaining Agreements (agencies with more than 10,000 employees with exclusive recognition), November 1968

	Number of Employees		Percentage of Employees in Agency	
Agency	IN EXCLUSIVE UNITS	UNDER AGREEMENT	IN EXCLUSIVE UNITS	UNDER AGREEMENT
Treasury	54,913	16,775	65%	20%
Army	151,837	101,009	39	26
Navy	206,213	178,796	53	46
Air Force	123,669	68,958	44	25
Defense Supply	24,118	5,285	42	9
Post Office	618,562	618,562	87	87
Justice	13,340	7,089	69	37
Health, Education and Welfare	35,086	28,128	32	26
Agriculture	10,821	9,838	10	9
General Services	15,746	12,649	41	27
Transportation	12,367	5,030	21	8
Tennessee Valley Authority	18,150	18,150	91	91
Veterans Administration	89,934	76,228	53	45
Overall federal government total	1,416,073	1,175,524	52	43

SOURCE: U.S. Civil Service Commission, Office of Labor-Management Relations, *Union Recognition in the Federal Government* (Washington, D.C.: November 1968), Table A.

ated agreements for a higher proportion of represented employees in exclusive units than did independent organizations. The success of AFL-CIO unions was due to their more abundant experience with negotiations and the over-all higher proportion of blue-collar workers among their membership. A lag may occur between a unit's gaining exclusive recognition and its negotiating an agreement, but time cannot fully account for the smaller number of agreements than units. For example, no negotiations for agreement had been started in 35 percent of the nonpostal units with exclusive recognition. The absence of negotiations was attributed to the absence of a request for negotiations by the employee organization or to a preference of the organization to exist without an agreement.[52]

Table II–8
Negotiated Agreements by Union Affiliation, November 1968

Union Affiliation	Agreements		Employees Under Agreement		
	NUMBER	%	NUMBER	%	PERCENT IN EXCLUSIVE UNITS
AFL-CIO	918	78%	1,055,552	90%	87%
National independent	255	22	116,416	10	61
Local independent	8	1	3,556	—	75
Total	1,181		1,175,524		

SOURCE: U.S. Civil Service Commission, Office of Labor-Management Relations, *Union Recognition in the Federal Government* (Washington, D.C.: November 1968), Table F.

CONDUCT OF NEGOTIATIONS

The newness of collective bargaining in the federal sector has at times caused difficulties in the negotiating process. Initial awkwardness and unprofitable negotiations have resulted when both parties have little previous experience. When the situation has involved unions experienced in collective bargaining in the private sector of the economy, the imbalance in experience has led federal-government managers to fear collective bargaining and to realize a need for labor relations training.

Management has usually been willing to negotiate. Sometimes a manager has refused to negotiate anything substantive for fear of undermining management rights or of giving credit to the union for employee gains. Recognition of the labor relations policy by top management and reinforcement from persons and groups within government to further collective bargaining convinced most managers that outright obstinacy was ineffective as well as unpolitical. Agency training programs promote the manager's role and authority in employee-management relations. A highly regarded program is that of the Navy Department, which, since 1963, has conducted semiannual courses in Washington for facility military and civilian personnel who are involved in negotiations.

Breakdowns in negotiations may be due to the conduct of negotiations. One of the chief stumbling blocks in the 1968 negotiations in the Post Office Department was the insistence of postmasters that a number of items, some of which had been part of collective bargaining agreements at the local level, were no longer negotiable. More than 8,500 items had been unresolved at the local level, 3,800 of which remained unsettled after negotiations at the regional and the national levels. The change in the department's attitude was attributed to management training programs. The impasse was resolved only when the Postmaster General issued a policy statement permitting the negotiation of many issues at the local level and requiring the review of all local issues in light of the new policy.[53]

The formality of negotiations depends on their level and on their relationship to other negotiations. The most formal procedures for both national and local negotiations are those detailed in the national agreement of the Post Office Department. These procedures provide for time, place, and scope of negotiations; conduct of "good faith" bargaining; and resolution of impasses. The seven unions with exclusive recognition at the national level bargain jointly with the department for a master agreement. In the 1967 national agreement negotiations, the postal employee unions presented over one hundred proposals and the Post Office Department contributed more than forty items. All negotiators met on items of interest to all employees, and craft representatives negotiated separately on items of concern to their particular employees. Following conclusion of negotiations at the national level, local negotiations take place. The local affiliate of the national exclusive organization must be invited to attend all local negotiations, even if it has only informal local recognition.

The absence of national exclusive recognition in other agencies makes the negotiation pattern more chaotic. In an effort to systematize bargaining and to facilitate uniformity in results, the Federal Aviation Agency (FAA) and NAGE have agreed to negotiate on a regional basis rather than on a facility basis.[54] In the spring of 1968, negotiations took place for two master agreements, one for employees at airway facilities and one for employees at air traffic control installations. Supplementary negotiations dealt with local facility matters.

Each agency is responsible for its own employee-management relations. Although the Civil Service Commission does not suggest model provisions, agreements are shared between and within agencies and by employee organizations. Prior to agreement expirations agency employee relations staffs may also work closely with local management to develop management proposals and alternatives. Uniformity within an agency has been encouraged when an employee organization works with management at the national level on local contract items. When the Bureau of Ships disapproved twenty-seven contract provisions negotiated at the local level within a short period, the Metal Trades Department and the bureau together devised satisfactory terms, which became standard provisions in local agreements. The Metal Trades Department also proposed to the Department of the Navy for review a dues-deduction provision, which subsequently became the pattern in local collective bargaining agreements.

The national office of the agency may play two roles, one during negotiations and one following negotiations. First, a representative of the national office has sometimes been a member of the local management's negotiating team. On occasion, the national office also has insisted on submission of all proposals before negotiations. Some agencies have preferred to delegate this responsibility to regional offices, particularly if they have instituted training programs.

A second role of the national office in negotiations has been to review and approve the content of local negotiations. No local negotiation is completed until such approval is secured, even though the local parties are satisfied with the agreement. Approval may be withheld pending the clarification of ambiguous language or the resolving of contradictory provisions. Agreements may also be vetoed and changed unilaterally by the national office if they conflict with regulations. The General Services Administration, for instance, has refused to approve a provision for equipment and uniform allowances, because no agency authority existed for granting such allowances.

Employee organizations have been experimenting with tactics to influence negotiations and to pressure management. One that has disturbed management has been public criticism of management's operation of the agency. For instance, the organization representing air traffic controllers conducted a survey on airway safety and

agency equipment and staffing as it affected safety. The organization issued the results simultaneously to Congress and to the press
to call the public's attention to the absence of air safety. Agency
management cried "foul," believing that the charges about program operation were not germane to union-management matters
and impaired union-management relations. Whether the particular
charges, which involved maintenance of professional standards,
were within the scope of personnel matters may be debatable. It
is clear, however, that exposure of an agency to Congress and to
the public, whether or not warranted or legal, is a pressure weapon
that employee organizations may utilize if other means are not
available.

GRIEVANCES

President John F. Kennedy issued Executive Order 10987
and Executive Order 10988 at the same time. These two orders
provided the bases for grievance procedures in the federal government. Executive Order 10987 required each agency to establish an
appeals system for adverse personnel action, which includes discharge and suspensions for over thirty days. Advisory arbitration
might be a step in the system, although the final appeal for adverse
actions remained with the Civil Service Commission. Employees
had the right to a representative of their own choosing in the
appeals process. Executive Order 10988, Section 8, allowed employee representatives with exclusive recognition to negotiate a
grievance procedure with advisory arbitration, but such a procedure could not supersede existing appeals systems, including
those established under Executive Order 10987. Excluded from the
negotiated grievance procedures were such subjects as wage determination, position classification, performance ratings, and reductions in force. At the agency's discretion, adverse actions might be
processed under existing grievance systems or under a separate
procedure. If an agency had two grievance systems, an employee
could elect the system under which he wished to process his
grievance.

Most grievances were settled at the local level, although appeals
were common. In the fiscal year ended June 1967, regional offices
of the Post Office Department received more than 1,000 grievance
appeals and upheld about 30 percent of the grievances they re-

viewed. The Department Board of Appeals and Review received 246 grievances and upheld 20 percent in its decisions.

More than one-half of federal agreements provided for advisory arbitration in the grievance procedure, and the trend was upward. In January 1969 the Civil Service Commission reported on 62 advisory arbitration decisions in grievances.[55] This represented a three-fold increase in advisory arbitrations since the previous report issued in 1967. The principal subjects at issue included discipline (eleven cases), promotion procedures (eleven cases), and overtime matters (nine cases). Management was sustained in 36 cases, while the claims of grievants were upheld in the other 26 cases. Grievance arbitration has been used more by unions experienced in the private sector because of their familiarity with the process and their willingness to spend money on arbitration; the Metal Trades Council and the International Association of Machinists filed 46 of the 62 cases. Not all issues could be placed in the grievance procedure. In at least one case, however, the Civil Service Commission found that refusal by an agency to arbitrate an adverse action was a violation of the collective bargaining agreement.[56]

For the most part, management has been willing to accept the arbitration decisions. In the first twenty cases, three advisory decisions were rejected by agency management on the grounds that the arbitrator had ruled in violation of agency regulations. More recently a Coast Guard commander refused to accept an arbitrator's recommendation that employees be paid at a higher rate for time in which they temporarily work in a higher classification, because of an unpublished ruling by the Comptroller General that employees may be paid only at the rate of the position to which they are appointed.[57] Sometimes agencies have accepted an arbitrator decision that subsequently has been overruled. In one case the Comptroller General refused to issue money for holiday pay recommended by the arbitrator. Another authorization for overtime proved meaningless when no funds were made available to pay for such overtime.

Unions objected to the grievance system permitted by the Executive Order.[58] They felt the negotiated grievance system was impaired by the existence of a dual grievance system, the exclusion of certain subjects from the negotiation procedure, and the limitations on arbitration as a final step in the grievance procedure.

STRIKES

The prohibition against strikes by federal employees preceded Executive Order 10988. Legislated strike prohibitions date back to the Lloyd-LaFollette Act of 1912. The most recent statute, Public Law 330 enacted in 1955, requires individual employee affidavits renouncing the right to strike at the time of hiring and makes striking against the government a felony. Employees who strike or assert the right to strike must be discharged and are subject to a year in jail and/or a fine of $1,000. No person has ever been brought to trial under this law.

In recent years strikes by federal government workers have been almost unknown. In 1962, eighty-five sheet-metal workers staged a wildcat strike against TVA. The strikers were immediately dismissed, and their union helped the government find replacements.[59] Teachers in military dependents' schools threatened a strike in December 1964, and Brooklyn letter carriers did likewise in August 1967. In both cases the Civil Service Commission and the agency convinced the unions that the government would dismiss all workers who participated in the walkout. In March 1968, members of the National Association of Government Employees who were employees of the Weather Bureau demonstrated during off-duty hours at Rockefeller Center in New York City. The Department of Commerce claimed that picketing during negotiations violated Executive Order 10988 and the negotiated agreement; it revoked exclusive recognition and dues checkoff privileges granted to the employee organization.[60] In the last decade the Bureau of Labor Statistics has recorded eight stoppages involving 5,870 federal employees.

Union leaders and members have grown increasingly restive with the no-strike policy, especially because of no provision for third-party determination of disputes. Unions would jeopardize recognition by the government if they advocated strikes. Yet three national unions composed entirely of federal employees eliminated the no-strike provisions from their constitutions in conventions held in 1968: the United Federation of Postal Clerks, the National Postal Union, and the National Association of Government Employees.[61] The convention of the National Association of Letter Carriers directed its officers to study ways that would grant federal employees the right to strike. The implication of these actions is that unions believe there can be no true collective bargaining without granting employees the right to strike. There is no indication that the present government prohibition of strikes will be changed.

IMPASSE PROCEDURES

The Executive Order did not provide for third-party intervention in the case of negotiation impasses. Advisory arbitration could be used only in cases of disputes on unit determination and majority representation and in the interpretation of agreement. The designers of the order hoped that the absence of an outside resource would help to establish a meaningful direct relationship between the negotiating parties and would encourage them to bargain in good faith. It was left to the parties to develop techniques other than arbitartion for resolution of impasses.

The search for suitable methods to end impasses proved difficult. The lack of satisfactory impasse resolution procedures constituted "one of the principal complaints by leaders of employee organizations."[62] The three most common impasse procedures that have evolved are fact-finding, mediation, and referral to higher authority in the agency. By 1966 about one-fourth of the agreements in the federal service provided for fact-finding, and over one-tenth for mediation. In 1967, forty-five of fifty-five agreements in the General Services Administration contained provision for resolving impasses. Of these forty-five agreements, all permitted referral to higher authority, about half provided for fact-finding, and only two included mediation as an impasse procedure.

Fact-finding in the federal service is not a disguise for advisory arbitration. Many agreements providing for fact-finding specify that members of the fact-finding committee be employees of the facility in which the impasse has occurred, and that the report of findings be given only to the negotiating parties.

Mediation has been advocated by the Civil Service Commission as "probably the most appropriate method for dealing with important and difficult issues that remain unresolved."[63] In several major agreements, including those involving the Department of

Labor and the Post Office Department, the Federal Mediation and Conciliation Service (FMCS) is designated as the source for mediators. Other agreements, however, mention only an impartial third party to be named by the negotiating parties. Normally the cost of the mediator's services is shared equally. The mediator serves as an internal catalyst to clarify the issues and to bring the parties together. To emphasize the mediator's role, the Post Office Department agreement states: "The mediator shall use his best efforts to bring the parties to an agreement on any and all impasses without taking sides. This will include any and all means he deems advisable providing he makes no public report or evaluation on the issues nor any public statement of findings of fact." On the other hand, the policy of some federal agencies such as the Department of Defense barred any outsider, including mediators, from participating in negotiations.

Impasses have occurred in the federal service. In 1966, 790 of the 3,000 agreement negotiations in the Post Office Department resulted in impasses. Of these, 653 were referred to and resolved at the regional level; the remaining 137 were forwarded to the department level where an additional 39 were resolved. The disputes in the other 98 negotiations concerned negotiability of items, such as assignment of employees and work scheduling.[64] Over one-third of the impasses found in nonpostal negotiations in 1967 were likewise due to negotiability of issues, while about one-half dealt with such substantive issues as seniority in promotion and method of work scheduling.

Without announcing the availability of its services, FMCS assigned mediators to 34 negotiation impasses at the federal level prior to July 1968 and helped to resolve fifteen cases.[65] A major test of its value in resolving impasses occurred in the 1967 negotiation for a national Post Office Department agreement. The department sought changes in the procedure for employee appeals of short-term suspensions and reassignments. Eleven days of mediation by an FMCS mediator brought no settlement, but the mediator privately recommended to the Postmaster General that no change be made in the existing provisions. The acceptance of these recommendations ended the dispute.

Regardless of the resolution technique used, final authority rested in the hands of agency management. Employee organizations have been unable to strike legally and third-party interveners could not announce their findings publicly and thereby attempt to influence public opinion. If the management of an agency chose to remaintain its position and ignore impasse procedures, the employee organization could do little that was permissible and effective.

NONBARGAINING METHODS

The limited scope and means of collective bargaining in the federal service ensure that employee organizations continue to use other channels to secure the goals and interests of their members. Dealing with Congress and with the Civil Service Commission has been a favored method.

Congress remains responsible for establishing employee compensation, including supplementary benefits. The larger and older organizations composed entirely of federal employees have accumulated much skill in lobbying for improvements in the compensation package, and other employee organizations are learning the techniques quickly. Agency administrators have also found that organizational lobbying at Congress can be used to circumvent or to continue the collective bargaining process. When the Post Office Department and the postal unions could not agree on a uniform reimbursement plan, the unions successfully lobbied at Congress for the desired changes.

Lobbying may help to alleviate organizational frustration with the existing process. At the same time it poses a dilemma for federal agencies. A strong "management stand" on a given demand may cause employee organizations to by-pass the agency and to press their case in Congress. Agreeing to the demand at the outset may avoid possible wasted effort and ultimate embarrassment, on the other hand it may weaken the agency. The issue is sometimes complicated by management uncertainty about its authority and its scope of bargaining.

The Civil Service Commission represents another channel of relief for employee organizations in matters that individual agencies cannot negotiate, because these matters are considered part of management's authority or are outside the agency's authority. The Civil Service Commission is responsible for interpreting Congressional legislation and Executive Orders affecting personnel in the federal service, and consultation with employee organizations has become part of the normal process. The organizations have raised issues with the commission to determine if administrative changes of existing procedures will make lobbying for legislative changes unnecessary. The AFL-CIO Government Employees Council has worked with members of the Civil Service Commission to change administrative rulings on laws governing pay for hazardous jobs. Employee organizations have also claimed success in pressuring the commission to change adverse action decisions. The organizations initiated the suggestion issued by the commission to agencies that advisory arbitration awards of grievances be accepted or denied by a management level above that involved in the grievance step preceding arbitration.

The organizations' dealings with the Civil Service Commission probably have been most clear-cut and significant in the wage-board system of pay administration. Under statutory authority, each agency with wage-board employees determines the prevailing wage rate for comparable jobs in the area and sets its wages accordingly. This practice led to discrepancies in wages among agencies for the same job in the same area. After a proposed revision of the system by the Civil Service Commission proved unsatisfactory to employee organizations, a team of three civil service representatives and three union representatives met at length to work out an acceptable compromise. The final plan, implemented in July 1968, provides for participation of employee representatives at all levels and for a uniform rate schedule within an area. The new program is essentially the product of extralegal negotiations between the Civil Service Commission and union representatives. It illustrates how bargaining is adjusted to reach a mutually desirable goal.

Pressures for Change

Dissatisfaction with Executive Order 10988 and its interpretations by federal agencies increased as collective bargaining units and agreements spread among federal employees. The problems had become aggravated over time, because some measures had become outmoded and others had proved more confining as employee organizations and employee-management relations developed.

One method of reforming the existing system has been the continued attempt by some employee organizations, especially the postal unions, to urge Congress to enact legislation.[66] Such legislation would not only incorporate features altering the existing labor-management relations in the federal service but also remove control of the system from the executive branch to the legislative branch of the federal government. The lobbying for such legislation by employee organizations has been no more successful since Executive Order 10988 was issued than it was before. Such lobbying may encourage the president to revise the order, just as previous lobbying efforts called attention to the need for a system of employee-management relations in the federal service and influenced President Kennedy's decision in 1962.

In September 1967, President Lyndon B. Johnson appointed a panel to study the operations of Executive Order 10988. "The time has come for a public review of our five years of experience under Executive Order 10988—what the program has accomplished and where it is deficient—and for consideration of any adjustments needed now to ensure its continued vitality in the public interest."[67] The members of the panel consisted of the Secretary of Labor, the Secretary of Defense, the Postmaster General, the Director of the Budget, the Chairman of the Civil Service Commission, and a Special Assistant to the President. The Review Committee later named an advisory panel of neutrals familiar with collective bargaining in the public sector and held public hearings in October 1967 for testimony by representatives of employee organizations, government agencies, and interested groups. Differences occurred between the recommendations of employee organizations and those of government groups, as well as among some of the employee organizations. It was generally recognized, however, that modification of the Executive Order was needed to rationalize and strengthen employee-management relations. The areas receiving principal attention were forms of recognition, dispute settlement, neutral agency to administer the order, and scope and process of agreement negotiations.

The three official forms of recognition established by the Executive Order were long regarded by many working with the order as a transitional step in the early stages of labor-management relations. They argued that since the transition had been made, it was time to reduce the kinds of recognition. Some agencies and many employee organizations advocated the abolition of informal recognition, because it offered organizations no meaningful role and could impede the relations between an agency and an organization with exclusive recognition. There was less agreement on the future of formal recognition. Some unions with primary experience in the private sector, such as the International Association of Machinists, urged the abolition of formal recognition. Other AFL-CIO unions, especially those composed primarily of government employees, such as AFGE, wanted to maintain formal recognition for communication and check-off purposes. If formal recognition were retained, the unions requested a clarification of the circumstances under which such recognition could be obtained, and of the rights of an organization having the recognition. Some organizations complained that consultation meant little more than notification of executed action.

A major criticism of Executive Order 10988 was that it did not provide a mechanism for resolving disputes. The available impasse resolutions required management consent before they became part of any agreement or before they could be implemented effectively. Unions felt that the ban on the right to strike and on recourse to the binding decision of a third-party deprived them of effective countervailing power. Only Congress could grant federal employees the right to strike, and such action was highly unlikely at the time. The AFL-CIO had advocated a tripartite board to make final, binding decisions in the case of impasses. Others interested in revising the Executive Order had advocated the availability of an arsenal of techniques, including fact-finding with public recommendations, mediation, and arbitration.

An unusual feature of the Executive Order was the provision permitting each agency to determine representation procedures, to conduct elections, to rule on the eligibility of employee organizations, and to interpret the order and the attendant Code of Fair Labor Practices. Invariably unions would accuse the agencies of bias and of operating "star chamber" investigations. Even agency officials conceded that a party to the proceedings could never be regarded as impartial. Moreover, the fifty-eight agencies were bound to interpret the order and Civil Service Commission suggestions differently, thus leading to confusion and sometimes contradiction. All organization and many agency personnel believed a single, independent impartial board was needed to interpret and implement the Executive Order, much as the National Labor Relations Board interprets and administers labor legislation in the private sector. The creation of such a board would consolidate the functions of the Civil Service Commission and the Department of Labor as well as those delegated to the agencies in establishing collective bargaining relationships.

A final major area of dissatisfaction with the Executive Order was the agreement itself. Unions desired to widen the scope of negotiations and to limit the agency's right to review agreements negotiated at lower levels. Recognizing that the President could not make bargainable matters controlled by Congress, the unions requested that all other personnel items be negotiable, including matters covered in agency regulations. Other newly bargainable subjects could include union security and an all-inclusive grievance procedure with binding arbitration as a final step.

The report of the Review Committee, though never released officially by President Johnson, was issued in draft form as part of the 1968 annual report of the U.S. Department of Labor. The report contained nineteen recommendations designed to respond to complaints raised during the public hearings and to affect the course of the federal labor relations program. While the report of the Review Committee contained no official sanction for the Nixon administration, the existence of the recommendation strengthened the demand for change. Indeed, most of the recommendations were accepted by a cabinet-level group established by President Nixon and were eventually incorporated into Executive Order No. 11491.

Executive Order No. 11491

On October 29, 1969, with little publicity or warning, President Nixon issued Executive Order No. 11491, thereby revoking Executive Order 10988 as well as the Standards of Conduct for Employee Organizations and the Code of Fair Labor Practices.

The purposes of the new Executive Order were: to strengthen the existing labor-management relations system in the federal government, to revise policies and procedures that had led to confusion or difficulty, and to standardize certain practices and terminology in the federal program with those in the private sector. The major changes introduced by the new Executive Order were the following:

1. Establishment of the Federal Labor Relations Council.

   a. The Council . . . consists of the Chairman of the Civil Service Commission, who shall be chairman of the Council, the Secretary of Labor, an official of the Executive Office of the President, and other such officials of the executive branch as the President may designate from time to time . . .

   b. The Council shall administer and interpret this Order, decide major policy issues, prescribe regulations, and from time to time, report and make recommendations to the President.

   The Council may consider, subject to its regulations

   (1) appeals from decisions of the Assistant Secretary of Labor . . . ;
   (2) appeals on negotiability of issues . . . ;
   (3) exceptions to arbitration awards; and
   (4) other matters it deems appropriate to assure the effectuation of this Order. (Sec. 4.)

The Council thus becomes the key group to set the guidelines and oversee the implementation of the federal labor-management relations program. It is the single, central authority that permits uniform, government wide interpretations and rulings. Although the Council's activities include some matters that concern the National Labor Relations Board in the private sector, its charge is broader.

2. Expansion of the duties of the Assistant Secretary of Labor for Labor-Management Relations. These duties include determining appropriate bargaining units, supervising elections to determine exclusive representation, deciding on questions of eligibility of labor organizations and their compliance with the standards of conduct for labor organizations, and ruling on complaints of alleged unfair labor practices. These functions had been assigned to agency heads under Executive Order No. 10988, although questions of appropriate units could be brought to advisory

arbitration. The Assistant Secretary now performs much of the work in the federal sector that he and the National Labor Relations Board perform in the private sector.

3. Alteration in unit determination and membership. The main criterion in Executive Order No. 10988 for establishing a unit was to "ensure a clear and identifiable community of interest among the employees concerned." Another criterion is added in the new Executive Order—to "promote effective dealings and efficiency of agency operations." (Sec. 10(b).) Changes in unit membership bring the executive order into closer conformity with the existing law and practice in the private sector. Guards cannot be in the same negotiating unit as other employees, and supervisors are excluded from negotiating units altogether.

> "Supervisor" means an employee having authority, in the interest of an agency, to hire, transfer, suspend, lay off, recall, promote, discharge, assign, reward, or discipline other employees, or responsibly to direct them, or to evaluate their performance, or to adjust their grievances, or effectively to recommend such action, if in connection with the foregoing the exercise of authority is not of a merely routine or clerical nature, but requires the use of independent judgment. (Sec. 2(c).)

> This Order does not preclude . . . recognition for units of management officials or supervisors represented by labor organizations which historically or traditionally represent the management officials or supervisors in private industry and which hold exclusive recognition for units of such officials or supervisors in any agency on the date of this Order. (Sec. 24(a) (2).)

4. Reduction and changes in forms of recognition. Executive Order No. 11491 ends informal and formal recognition. No new recognitions of these types are accorded after the date of the order. All informal recognitions expire July 1, 1970. The process for terminating local formal recognition is to be established by the Federal Labor Relations Council prior to October 1, 1970. National consultation rights replace national formal recognition for "the representative of a substantial number of employees of the agency." The rights of an organization with national consultation rights are spelled out in greater detail than had been the case of an organization with national formal recognition.

When a labor organization has been accorded national consultation rights, the agency through appropriate officials, shall notify representatives of the organization of proposed substantive changes in personnel policies that affect employees it represents and provide an opportunity for the organization to comment on the proposed changes. The labor organization may suggest changes in the agency's personnel policies and have its views carefully considered. It may confer in person at reasonable times, on request, with appropriate officials on personnel policy matters, and at all times present its views thereon in writing. An agency is not required to consult with a labor organization on any matter on which it would not be required to meet and confer if the organization were entitled to exclusive recognition. (Sec. 9(b).)

Exclusive recognition is given to a labor organization "selected, in a secret ballot election, by a majority of the employees in an appropriate unit as their representative." Exclusive recognition at the national level precludes recognition of other labor organizations at lower levels.

When a labor organization has been accorded exclusive recognition, it is the exclusive representative of employees in the unit and is entitled to act for and to negotiate agreements covering all employees in the unit. It is responsible for representing the interests of all employees in the unit without discrimination and without regard to labor organization membership. The labor organization shall be given the opportunity to be represented at formal discussions between management and employees or employee representatives concerning grievances, personnel policies and practices, or other matters affecting general working conditions of employees in the unit. (See. 10(e).)

The simplified forms of recognition emphasize the importance of exclusive representation and negotiation to the federal labor-management relations system. They strengthen the relative position of organizations with exclusive representation while further weakening other employee organizations. The concept of national consultation rights reflects the continuing difficulty most organizations have in gaining exclusive representation of employees in an entire agency.

5. Redefinition of the scope of negotiations. Several subjects are now specifically negotiable, thus broadening the scope of negotiations:

a. Technological change. The parties may negotiate ". . . agreements providing appropriate arrangements for employees adversely affected by the impact of realignment of work forces or technological change." (Sec. 11(b).)

b. Grievance procedure. "A negotiated employee grievance procedure . . . is the exclusive procedure available to employees in the unit when the agreement so provides." (Sec. 13.)

c. Grievance arbitration. "Negotiated procedures may provide for the arbitration of employee grievances and of disputes over the interpretation or application of existing agreements . . . Either party may file exceptions to an arbitrator's award with the Council . . ." (Sec. 14.)

At the same time, the proposal of the Review Committee for a limited expansion of union security is specifically denied. "Nothing in the agreement shall require an employee to become or to remain a member of a labor organization, or to pay money to the organization . . ." (Sec. 12(c).)

To clarify the role of agency regulations in the negotiation and administration of labor-management relations issues, the new order specifies that such issues are governed

by published agencies policies and regulations in existence at the time the agreement was approved; and by subsequently published agency policies and regulations required by law or by the regulations of appropriate authorities, or authorized by the terms of a controlling agreement at a higher agency level. (Sec. 12(a).)

Perhaps of greatest significance in the area of scope of negotiations is the introduction of a procedure and appeals process to resolve questions of negotiability.

(1) An issue which involves interpretation of a controlling agreement at a higher agency level is resolved under the procedures of the controlling agreement, or, if none, under agency regulations;

(2) An issue [other than above] which arises at a local level may be referred by either party to the head of the agency for determination;

(3) An agency head's determination as to the interpretation of the agency's regulations with respect to a proposal is final;

(4) A labor organization may appeal to the Council for a decision when—

(i) it disagrees with an agency head's determination that a proposal would violate applicable law, regulation of appropriate authority outside the agency, or this Order, or

(ii) it believes that an agency's regulations, as interpreted by the agency head, violate applicable law, regulation of appropriate authority outside the agency, or this Order. (Sec. 11(c).)

6. Specification of impasse handling. Executive Order 11491 authorizes the Federal Mediation and Conciliation Service to assist in resolving negotiation disputes. This authorization makes official a practice already undertaken reluctantly by the federal service. If mediation or other "voluntary arrangements" fail, the parties may turn to the Federal Service Impasses Panel, an agency within the Council consisting of three members appointed by the President.

either party may request the Federal Service Impasses Panel to consider the matter. The Panel . . . may recommend procedures to the parties for the resolution of the impasse or may settle the impasse by appropriate action. Arbitration or third-party fact finding with recommendations to assist in the resolution of an impasse may be used by the parties only when authorized or directed by the Panel. (Sec. 17.)

The Panel thus has broad, indefinite powers, and the parties cannot know which procedures the Panel will use in a given case.

7. Restrictions on labor organizations. In addition to the requirements for employee organizations under Executive Order 10988, organizations seeking exclusive representation "shall file financial and other reports, provide for bonding of officials and employees of the organization, and comply with trusteeship and election standards." (Sec. 18 (c).) In addition, a new unfair labor practice for labor organizations to parallel one existing for management is to "refuse to consult, confer, or negotiate with an agency as required by this Order." (Sec. 19 (b) (6).) These restrictions

are identical to provisions applicable to unions in the private sector of the economy. Interestingly and perhaps significantly, the new Executive Order uses the designation "labor organization" instead of the earlier term "employee organization."

The main changes in Executive Order 11491 appear to be a removal of authority from the agency head, an attempt to standardize the federal labor-management relations system, and a closer conformity of the system to that in the private sector. The extent to which these goals are met will be determined by the implementation of the order, especially the role played by the central authorities.

Executive Order 11491 maintains some of the basic foundations and concepts of Executive Order 10988. The Executive Branch continues to be responsible for implementing and controlling the order. Management retains considerable authority, including a mandatory management rights' clause in each agreement and approval of the agreement by the agency head. The scope of negotiations remains far narrower than in the rest of the public sector, let alone than in the private sector. Labor organizations are forbidden to strike. Finally, the new Executive Order is a continuation of the tradition that federal labor-relations programs are issued administratively rather than determined by Congress.

Conclusion

The problems and the limitations of employee-management relations in the federal service should not obscure the achievements. First, as it stands, the system has expanded rapidly. Membership in employee organizations grew by approximately one-third in six years; the number of collective bargaining agreements increased in the same period from a handful to over one thousand. To be sure, collective bargaining in some cases is limited to management's recognition that an employee organization represents employees exclusively and has the right to bargain with agency management. In other cases, issues that were previously decided unilaterally have been determined jointly. Second, collective bargaining progressed to the point where inadequacies in the system were widely recognized and the framework for collective bargaining was revised. Third, collective bargaining has been introduced into a vast public organization without violence. Whether credit is due to the framers and amenders of Executive Order 10988, to the absence of widespread determined opposition by federal managers, or to the conditioned restraint of employees is a moot point. The fact remains that the basis for collective bargaining in the federal service is now a reality.

Equally important is the effect of the Executive Order and its implementation outside the federal government. Federal agencies have recognized collective bargaining for nonfederal employees with whom they have some relations. For instance, the Secretary of Agriculture adopted the Executive Order concepts for dealing with county employees of the Agricultural Stabilization and Conservation Service. Nonfederal employees without direct relation to federal authorities have also felt the impact of Executive Order 10988. In the summer of 1962 the commissioners of the District of Columbia chose to extend collective bargaining privileges to district employees. Public officials at state, county, and local levels of government have found the federal example a compelling reason for reviewing their own programs of employee relations. Certainly employee organizations have had a stronger case for demanding some form of recognition and bargaining; public officials, one less good reason for denying collective bargaining; and the public at large, reassuring knowledge that employee organizations could function reasonably in the public sector.

collective bargaining for state, county, and municipal employees

Organization of State and Local Government

Over 75 percent of all public employees work for the approximately 90,000 separate state or local governments in the United States. Collective bargaining activities in this sector are extremely difficult to describe, no less analyze, because of the large number of different widely dispersed individual employers and the diversity among the 8.6 million employees. Chapters IV and V separate respectively teachers, policemen, and fire fighters because of the special characteristics of these groups and their conditions of employment. This chapter discusses all other state and local employees.

Table III–1, shows that the United States has about 3,000 counties, 18,000 municipalities, 17,000 townships and towns, and 18,000 special districts. Since 1942, special districts have more than double, in number, and municipalities have increased by about 1,700, while townships have decreased by almost the same number because of reclassification. The number of counties has remained almost constant, and that of states, of course, has increased from forty-eight to fifty. The major change has been the decrease in the number of school districts, a matter that will be discussed in the following chapter.

Table III–1
Employment and Payrolls of State and Local Governments, by Type of Government, October 1968

Government		Number of Employees (thousands)			Total October Payroll (thousands of dollars)
LEVEL	NUMBER OF UNITS	TOTAL (FULL TIME AND PART TIME)	FULL-TIME ONLY	FULL-TIME EQUIV-ALENT	
Total State and Local Governments in United States	91,235	9,358	7,414	7,879	4,751,995
State	50	2,495	1,953	2,085	1,256,690
Local, total	91,185	6,864	5,460	5,795	3,495,297
Counties	3043	1,151	987	1,034	531,725
Municipalities	17,979	2,112	1,744	1,813	1,097,129
Townships	17,144	315	166	185	107,191
School districts	34,678	3,028	2,367	2,555	1,643,980
Special districts	18,323	258	196	207	115,206

SOURCE: U.S. Bureau of the Census, *Public Employment in 1968,* GE68, No. 1 (Washington, D.C.: 1969), p. 8.

The numbers of counties and municipalities vary greatly among states. For example, Texas has 243 counties, more than any other state, whereas Rhode Island has five, Delaware three, and Connecticut none. Larger cities such as the following are sometimes also coterminus with the county in which they are located and thus assume county functions: New York, Philadelphia, Baltimore, St. Louis, Boston, San Francisco, New Orleans, Honolulu, Denver, and Baton Rouge. A similar situation can be found in many cities in Rhode Island and Virginia. These cities either are completely or substantially consolidated with county governments, overlap county boundaries, or for other reasons have no county governmental operations in the area of the city. Washington, D.C. is unique in that it performs functions usually handled by a state government.

The population of the United States is concentrated heavily in a small group of states and of local governments. More than one-fifth of the population is concentrated in sixteen counties, while 3.5 percent of the population is served by 1,500 counties. Similarly, one-third of the nation's population lives in fewer than 2 percent of the municipalities, and almost one-half of the population lives in 10 percent of the municipalities.

EMPLOYMENT IN STATE AND LOCAL GOVERNMENT

Total employment by state and local government is shown in Tables III–1 and III–2—table III–1 shows such employment by level of government; table III–2, by function. Approximately 25 percent of all state and local workers are employed by the state, 13 percent by the counties, and 23 percent by the municipalities. The remainder work in special districts and school districts. The total number of employees in these sectors has increased rapidly since World War II. The largest increase (71 percent) has occurred among municipal employees.

Employment on the state level is concentrated mostly in higher education, hospitals, highways, and natural resources; and that on the county level is concentrated in hospitals, highways, police protection, and correction. Employment in special districts varies greatly among the states, but most employees work in hospitals, transit, and housing and urban renewal. Aside from those employed by the education department, the largest groups of municipal and town employees in order of importance work for the police department, the fire department, local utilities (water, electric, transit, and gas), hospitals, and the sanitation department.

The above categories are broad generalizations and vary widely among state and local governments. In one state, hospitals may be operated as a state function; in other states, most hospitals may be operated by the county or the municipality. In many states, all three levels of government operate hospitals. Moreover, in some localities private firms often own and operate utilities such as transit and electric power, while municipalities operate these utilities elsewhere.

Function	All Employees (Full time and Part time) (thousands)†							Full time Equivalent Employment (thousands)		
			Local Governments†							
	TOTAL	STATE GOVERNMENTS*	ALL LOCAL GOVERNMENTS	COUNTIES	MUNICIPALITIES	TOWNSHIPS	SPECIAL DISTRICTS	TOTAL	STATE GOVERNMENTS	LOCAL GOVERNMENTS
Hospitals	821	420	401	191	130	3	76	781	407	375
Health	116	44	71	38	30	2	.7	106	42	64
Police protection	463	52	412	73	314	25	.009	408	51	357
Local fire protection	255	—	255	8	202	26	19	179	—	179
Sewerage	60	—	60	4	43	2	10	56	—	56
Sanitation other than sewerage	125	—	125	5	115	5	7	118	—	118
Local parks and recreation	153	—	153	19	110	6	18	111	—	111
Natural resources	178	142	35	14	1	.5	19	149	123	26
Housing and urban renewal	48	—	47	.9	23	.08	23	45	—	45
Airports	11	—	11	3	7	.07	2	11	—	11
Water transport and terminals	17	5	12	.5	3	.03	9	15	4	11
Correction	131	81	51	38	13	.003	—	127	79	48
Local libraries	75	—	75	15	47	5	7	54	—	54
Financial administration	233	90	142	60	60	22	.017	202	88	114
General control	339	40	299	120	129	50	.039	229	33	196
Local utilities	268	—	268	4	197	3	63	258	—	258
Water supply	114	—	114	3	92	3	17	107	—	107
Electric power	58	—	58	.3	46	.7	10	56	—	56
Transit	88	—	88	1	53	—	34	87	—	87
Gas Supply	8	—	8	.09	6	—	3	8	—	8
Other and unallocable	326	117	209	59	128	19	3	269	107	162

* —Represents zero.

† Statistics for local governments are subject to sampling variation. Because of rounding, detail may not add to totals.

SOURCE: U.S. Bureau of the Census, **Public Employment in 1968**, GE 68, No. 1 (Washington, D.C. 1969).

83

STRUCTURE AND FINANCING

Organizational structure also varies extensively both among and within levels of government.

STATE

Most states still have a "weak governor" structure, under which the governor has very limited power. Governors usually do not possess sufficient legal authority or administrative power to control the activities of many persons considered their subordinates, but they must "supervise" state functions. Many state officials are elected by the people, not appointed by the governor. State agencies frequently are controlled by boards or commissions whose members are almost unremovable by the governor or, in practice, by anyone else. State personnel systems are based either on patronage or on civil service procedures outside the control of the governor.[1] Under this structure, the governor's principal powers and only means of influencing policies of state agencies are the recommendation of a budget and a veto or threat of a veto of legislative appropriation. To carry out his program, the governor often must resort to "coordination by persuasion."[2]

Since 1909 several states have adopted a "strong governor" structure. Under this plan, the governor can appoint and remove from office agency heads, thus giving him extensive administrative power and control over state agencies. Although details of the "strong governor" structure differ widely, the plan is found in Alaska, California, Idaho, Kentucky, New York, Ohio, Pennsylvania, Rhode Island, Virginia, and Washington. Other states have adopted parts of the plan.

COUNTY

Counties generally have no chief executive similar to a governor or a mayor. Instead, the executive powers are vested in a governing board, which is known by various titles including board of commissioners, board of supervisors, board of freeholders, or merely county board. In most states, these boards consist of three to five members, but an individual or as many as eighty persons occasionally may carry out the duties of a county board.

The composition of the governing board can be classified into four major categories:

1. Commissioners or supervisors, who are elected specifically to perform county duties and typically hold no other public office. About two-thirds of all county governing boards are in this category.

2. Township supervisors, who have responsibilities as officers of townships as well as of counties.

3. One judge plus commissioners, the latter being similar to the commissioners in the first category.

4. One judge plus justices of the peace, all of whom have public responsibilities other than governing the county.[3]

Members of county governing boards are almost always popularly elected for four-year terms. Annual salaries range from about $100 to $2,000 or $3,000. In most cases, the county boards meet once a month; those in highly populated areas often meet more frequently.

Most county boards may levy taxes, appropriate funds, and borrow money, but these powers are subject to state constitutional and statutory limitations. In only about 270 counties is financial control lodged in an agency other than the county governing board.[4]

CITY

Cities in the United States have three different basic forms of government structure: mayor-council, commission, and council-manager.

Over one-half the cities use some variation of the mayor-council plan. The two major variations are the weak mayor-council plan and the strong mayor-council plan. The former plan, found mainly in small cities and villages, is in many respects similar to the organization of the weak governor plan operating in many state governments of the United States. Several major city offices are filled by direct election, and there are a large number of boards and commissions beyond the control of the mayor. The council is both a legislative and an executive organization. It makes policy and appoints administrative officers. The mayor can recommend legislation to the council, has veto power over council actions, and sometimes even presides over sessions of the council. Neither the mayor nor any other individual, however, is charged with the responsibility of seeing that laws and ordinances are properly carried out or that the city administration proceeds according to the overall plan. Even when the mayor appoints officials, he cannot remove them from office; thus he has no control over, or responsibility for, them.

The distinguishing characteristic of the strong mayor-council plan is its integrated structure with administrative authority and responsibility vested in an individual or a body. Theoretically each employee or officer is formally responsible to a supervisor, who in turn must answer to his supervisor, until ultimately department heads are each responsible to a single chief executive. Under this plan, policy making is a joint responsibility of the council and the mayor. Administration is the responsibility of the mayor, who appoints and dismisses department heads usually without council approval. Under a variation of this plan, the mayor appoints a chief officer, who is delegated many administrative and supervisory responsibilities of the mayor. Most large cities in the United States use some version of the strong mayor-council plan.

A second form of government structure for cities is the commission plan, found in less than 300 cities with more than 5,000 population. Under this plan, a five-man commission is elected for a four-year term. Each commissioner serves as head of one of the city's administrative departments. Collectively the commissioners form the city's policy-making council, thus performing both legislative and executive functions.

The council-manager plan, the third type of governmental structure, has become increasingly popular since 1915. By 1969, managers were used in approximately 50 percent of all cities with populations between 10,000 and 500,000. The manager works under the direction of an elected council of laymen, which is responsible for policy. In practice, the city manager becomes a major community leader, and

> . . . the manager's job in the complex affairs of tomorrow will probably not be vastly different from that of the elected executive. Like the mayor, he too must court favor with his council, and like the mayor, he can be far more effective if he has a strong following of civic groups, newspapers, and the public to support him. . . . If he serves the community as prime mover and star salesman of

forceful governmental action, he will build up his own clientele—
a clientele which the council will antagonize only at its peril.[5]

State and local governments have adopted various taxes to
finance the increasing costs of government operations. The sales
tax is the most common tax for state governments, although the
state income tax is increasing in popularity.

The county's main source of tax revenue is the property tax.
Attempts at introducing other taxes have not been successful. In
1963 the property tax was responsible for over 93 percent of all
county tax revenue. Tax revenue, however, is responsible for only
one-half the total revenue of the county. The remainder comes
from state and federal aid and direct charges for county services.[6]

The municipalities derive about 72 percent of their tax revenues
from the property tax, which contributes 42.8 percent of the total
general revenue of the cities. The remainder of tax receipts are
made up of income and sales taxes. State and federal aid also
contribute to the cities' general revenue.[7]

Government structure and financing has many implications for
labor relations at the state and local government levels. The
relative powers of elected officials and government administrators
affects the strength of the employer side at the bargaining table.
Similarly, placing fiscal authority in a separate governmental
agency makes it difficult for government negotiators to make binding agreements in collective bargaining. These and other implications will be discussed later in this chapter and in Chapter VIII.

CIVIL SERVICE SYSTEMS

Civil service systems developed as a reaction to political
favoritism and patronage. Employees working for state and local
governments frequently were dependent for their jobs upon
electing the right man to office. Today, civil service systems are
widespread for state and local employees. Over one-half the states
have some form of merit or civil service system covering most
employees in state agencies. An additional sixteen states cover
employees engaged in activities aided by grant-in-aid programs
administered by the United States Department of Health, Education and Welfare. Civil service and personnel boards, which are

usually appointed by the governor, attempt to determine promotions and discipline by equitable criteria such as examinations, efficiency ratings, seniority, and administrative judgment.

Almost all cities of 100,000 or more have an independent civil service commission or personnel board. Boards and commissions in larger cities are more likely to classify positions and to recommend salary levels for various groups of workers than their counterparts in smaller cities. These boards and commissions prepare salary surveys, conduct entrance examinations, and hear appeals on dismissals and suspensions.[8]

The salaries of the civil service board members are usually paid by the city for which the board functions. In smaller communities, however, membership on the civil service board is sometimes an unpaid position. The work is then done by part-time nonprofessionals who feel an obligation to serve in such a capacity.

Not all city employees are covered by civil service; the extent of coverage varies among cities. In many communities, the department head and his immediate assistants are appointed by the mayor; in other communities, the department head may be the only individual exempt from coverage.

Fewer than 10 percent of the counties have a merit system. Most of these counties are located in California, New York, and Ohio; only a few of the more populous counties in other states have merit systems. As with state employees, county employees administering welfare programs work under a merit system because of federal requirements accompanying grant-in-aid programs. Only a minority of county employees are covered by job classification, well-developed pay plans, organized training programs, and adequate retirement systems. Because of job insecurity, the major objective of county organized employees is job security. The belief that advancement comes through the political machine, however, makes county employees more difficult targets for unionization than city employees.[9]

Even in jurisdictions where civil service systems are well established, employees have joined unions and pressed for collective bargaining rights. One reason is that union leaders and, apparently, many union members consider civil service commissions to be oriented to management's point of view. They claim that employees are not protected against arbitrary and capricious actions

by management. Although it is difficult to evaluate these asser-
tions, the fact that they are widespread accounts in part for the
growth of union membership among state and local employees.
Because civil service systems do not give the employee a voice in
the determination of his wages and conditions of employment,
the desire for such participation by employees frequently is another important reason for joining unions. Other reasons for the
growth of unions and collective bargaining will be analyzed in
Chapter VI.[10]

Employee Organizations

State and local governments have dealt with two types of employee organizations: unions and employee associations. Each
will be discussed below.

UNIONS

The American Federation of State County and Municipal
Employees (AFSCME), the Laborers International Union (LIU),
and the Service Employees International Union (SEIU) represent
the largest number of state and local employees. All three unions
are affiliated with AFL-CIO. The AFSCME alone enrolls only government employees.

AMERICAN FEDERATION OF STATE,
COUNTY, AND MUNICIPAL EMPLOYEES

The AFSCME initially evolved from the Wisconsin State Employees Association (WSEA). Arnold Zander, a leader of WSEA, became
interested in organizing municipal employees, and, in 1933, Bill
Green, president of the AFL, encouraged AFSCME toward this goal.
At first AFSCME was an autonomous union operating within the
American Federation of Government Employees (AFGE), whose
leaders were primarily interested in organizing federal employees.
The AFGE agreed to AFSCME's becoming an independent international with jurisdiction over employees of state and local governments. There is some question over whether AFGE's decision
resulted from noninterest in state and local organization or from
fear that AFSCME would become strong enough to take over AFGE.[11]

By early 1969, AFSCME had approximately 400,000 members, compared to 235,000 members in 1964. During this period AFSCME was one of the fastest growing unions in AFL-CIO. City employees accounted for nearly one-half the membership; state employees, over one-fourth; county employees, a little over 9 percent; and employees of academic and nonprofit organizations, the remainder.

The AFSCME has 1,700 locals, a very large number for a union its size. The United Automobile Workers has the same number of locals, but three times as many members. In part, the large number of AFSCME locals is a result of the attempt of the previous union administration to control the 1963 convention through the votes of newly chartered locals. The union also has been historically quick to charter locals regardless of actual membership. This practice is now being modified, and a move is under way to consolidate some of the smaller locals for administrative and bargaining efficiency.

An important change in the leadership of AFSCME occurred in 1964, when Jerry Wurf, former head of the New York City District Council 37, was elected international president in a bitterly fought contest with Arnold Zander. Since that time, the goals and the image of AFSCME have changed drastically. Wurf established collective bargaining as the major objective of AFSCME, whereas Zander had accepted the civil service system and relied heavily on lobbying and other political activity. The AFSCME continues to lobby actively but its primary goal now is state legislation guaranteeing collective bargaining rights to government employees. It also has increased greatly the number of collective bargaining agreements with state and local governments. By 1969, union headquarters had records of over 700 written agreements negotiated by 420 locals in thirty-six states and the District of Columbia.

LABORERS INTERNATIONAL UNION

The LIU, the sixth largest AFL-CIO affiliate, has approximately 550,000 members. The LIU consists mainly of semiskilled and unskilled construction workers who perform tasks such as digging ditches and pushing wheelbarrows. Technological changes have eliminated many jobs formerly held by members of LIU. Membership in the union dipped from 477,000 in 1958 to 421,000 in

1963. As a result, the union has initiated aggressive organizing efforts in other fields and sought mergers with other unions. Approximately 73 percent of its members work in construction, compared with 91 percent in 1962.

Lately, public employees have been the primary target of LIU. Public employees now constitute about 10 percent of the union's membership. In 1968 the union completed mergers with the 60,000 member Post Office Mail Handlers Union, which enrolls unskilled postal employees, and with an independent union representing about 2,000 city employees in Miami. Future mergers are planned with an independent union representing Oakland, California policemen and with other postal unions. In 1967, LIU organized a separate department for public employees called the Public Service Division; it enrolls all federal public employees in the union. The division issues separate publications for public employees to supplement the publications distributed to all union members.

The organizing efforts of LIU among public employees have caused jurisdictional conflicts with AFSCME over municipal employees in Baltimore and other localities. The LIU has also vied with AFGE and the National Postal Union for units of federal employees. The union recently won a major victory in ousting AFSCME in Providence, Rhode Island and it also made significant inroads in other cities.

SERVICE EMPLOYEES INTERNATIONAL UNION

The SEIU is one of the fastest growing unions in the AFL-CIO. Between 1964 and 1967 membership in SEIU increased from about 320,000 to 400,000. It is estimated that approximately 24 percent of the union's members are employed by government. The SEIU claims that it has made "sizable gains" in public employment in the past few years. The union has met strong challenges in some cases, however, and it has lost representation rights for public employees in a number of elections. The union's main success has been in organizing municipal workers on the west coast.

In some cities SEIU is the second strongest municipal union, ranking behind AFSCME. In Boston, for instance, SEIU represents 2,500 employees, primarily white-collar city hall employees and hospital and public works employees. The union local in Boston, which is organized primarily along departmental lines, represents many of the same job classifications as the dominant AFSCME.

Prior to 1968, SEIU was known as the Building Service Employees International (BSEIU). In order to attract additional groups of workers, BSEIU became SEIU in 1968. Public employees, of course, were one group the union was attempting to attract.

OTHER UNIONS

Other unions active in organizing public employees include the building trades (e.g., carpenters, plumbers), the International Brotherhood of Teamsters, Chauffeurs, Warehousemen and Helpers (Teamsters), the International Brotherhood of Electrical Workers (IBEW), and the International Brotherhood of Electrical Radio and Machine Workers (IUE).

The building trades, which are affiliated with AFL-CIO, play a significant role in municipal employment, but, unfortunately, no data are available on how many municipal employees are represented by the trades. The AFL-CIO's Building and Construction Trades Department is composed of nineteen international unions, and local councils are located in almost every city of any importance throughout the United States

The building trades unions were often the first municipal employee organizations recognized by city governments. Once adjustments were made for seasonality and fringe benefits the trade unions were able to attain pay rates similar to those in the private sector.

In some cities conflict has occurred between AFSCME and the building trades unions. Historically, the building trades gave minimal service to city employees, who represented a small portion of their total membership. Once or twice a year the business agents would notify the city office of the prevailing wage rates for the trades. With the growth in size and aggressiveness of AFSCME, building trades members have complained about the service they receive compared with AFSCME members. On the other hand, cases have also been reported of AFSCME members requesting building trade representation because they felt that the trades constituted a more powerful organization and could attain higher wages. The AFSCME takes a liberal industrial union stand on many issues, whereas the trades are craft oriented and are usually more conservative.

The Teamsters, an independent union, have directed most of

their activity toward public employees at the municipal level. Over one-hundred municipalities, thirty-five counties, and nine state agencies have signed collective bargaining agreements with the Teamsters covering a wide range of diverse occupational groups. With few exceptions, the Teamsters enroll public-employee members in the same locals as members working in private employment. In some instances membership in the union local includes private employees, employees in various levels of government, and employees of different cities. For example, Local 2 of the Teamsters includes Silver Bow County employees and has separate agreements covering city drivers of Butte, Montana; maintenance workers, machine operators and truck drivers of Helena, Montana; and engineers, laborers, painters, and carpenters of the Montana State Highway Commission.

PUBLIC-EMPLOYEE ASSOCIATIONS

Employee associations, the second type of organization, are primarily oriented to their own state or locality and have a very loose relationship with other associations. Although accurate data are not available, membership in public-employee associations has increased in recent years. Many of the associations are allied with the Assembly of Governmental Employees (AGE), a loosely knit federation of associations without full-time officers or staff. In 1967, AGE reported affiliates in twenty-six states and 429,692 members among state employees. As shown in Table III–3 AGE gained a little more than 66,000 members of state employee associations since 1964; no AGE data are available for municipal employee associations.

Employee associations were often formed to take advantage of group insurance benefits. Some associations served as cooperatives, establishing stores where members could purchase goods at a discount. Other groups were formed as social organizations. In almost all cases, association dues are much lower than dues for unions affiliated with AFL-CIO.[12]

Associations usually support the merit system for efficiency in government, encourage high standards of conduct, advance the image of the public servant, exchange information, conduct research, process grievances through established civil service procedures, and act as lobbyists for public employees. They rarely

Table III–3
Membership—Assembly of Governmental Employees, by State, November 1, 1967

STATE ASSOCIATION	YEAR FOUNDED	1964 MEMBERSHIP	1967 MEMBERSHIP	PERCENTAGE GROWTH IN 3 YEARS
Alaska	1962	1,100	1,600	45.4%
California	1931	101,439	115,053	13.4
Colorado	1928	7,675	10,309	34.3
Connecticut	1938	12,300	17,310	40.7
Florida	1959	900	450	−100.0
Hawaii	1934	10,849	14,734	35.7
Idaho	1959	2,424	3,346	38.0
Illinois	1921	9,478	8,560	−10.7
Indiana	1953	842	1,780	111.4
Louisiana	1966	New	1,200	New
Maine	1943	7,100	8,500	19.8
Maryland	1936	13,220	16,960	28.3
Michigan	1950	13,000	17,000	30.7
Montana	1945	3,285	2,833	−0.01
Nevada	1950	600	1,600	166.6
New Hampshire	1940	3,242	3,356	0.003
New York	1910	90,399	104,000	15.0
North Carolina (highways and prisons)	1947	9,338	9,984	0.06
North Carolina* (other state employees)	—	11,345	12,864	13.4
Ohio	1938	16,890	23,973	41.9
Oregon	1943	12,000	15,748	32.0
Rhode Island	1945	3,700	4,300	16.2
Texas	1946	21,886	20,488	−0.06
Utah	1959	3,450	4,700	36.2
Vermont	1944	3,500	3,900	11.4
Washington	1956	2,700	3,500	29.6
Wyoming	1962	403	1,644	307.9
		363,065	429,692	18+

* As of 1967 the North Carolina State Employees Association was not affiliated with AGE; it is included because the North Carolina Highway and Prison Employees Association is a member and works jointly with NCSEA.

SOURCE: Association of Governmental Employees.

negotiate collective bargaining agreements, but they often favor discussion looking to consensus.

In recent years, some associations have changed their traditional roles and have acted as bargaining agents in states with public employee bargaining laws. Many associations still oppose bargaining, and prefer to rely on lobbying or discussions with agency heads. Some small associations, of course, are still primarily social clubs or exist only because they offer group insurance plans or other benefits to their members. On the other hand, the New York Civil Service Employees Association and the Hudson Council of the New Jersey CSEA dropped their no-strike pledges in 1967. To a great extent, the degree of success enjoyed by public-employee organizations has been determined by the amount of political pressure they wield. In some cases these associations have become so effective politically that their cooperation is solicited by local officials desiring approval of referendums.

Very little information is available on municipal employee associations. A 1961 study of state employee associations found that twenty-five associations claimed a membership of 355,000, only 37,000 of which were local employees. The study concluded that independent associations had made little headway in organizing municipal employees. Only seven of the twenty-five state associations admitted local employees to membership, and only five of these seven reported any local members. Moreover, the proportion of local membership varied among associations. About three-fourths of the members of the New Jersey Civil Service Employees' Association were local government employees. Slightly over one-half of the Hawaiian Government Employees' Association and about one-third of the Montana membership were composed of local government employees. In New York State 15 percent, and in Ohio only 5 percent, of the association's members constitute local government employees.[13]

Employee associations are more likely to exist in larger cities. In 1967, nearly 70 percent of cities with over one-half million population reported the presence of employee associations. In cities with a population between 250,000 and 500,000, the incidence of employee association amounted to 59 percent; in cities with populations between 25,000 to 50,000, only 30 percent; and in cities with populations between 10,000 and 25,000, only 15 percent.[14] One-half the central cities reported a municipal employee association, while only one out of four suburban cities reported an association.

Employee associations are most common in Western municipalities; 70 percent report active associations. Associations are most rare in the South, where less than 10 percent of the cities report such associations.[15]

California probably has the most public-employee association activity. One study of California showed that 250 out of 373 city governments had independent employee associations. In fact, independent public-employee associations in California were more numerous than unions in representing employees in every city job classification in the state.[16] The original purpose of California associations was the same as that of unions—to correct employee dissatisfaction with terms and conditions of work. Once these organizations accomplished their goal of improved working conditions, however, they ceased to exist, lapsed into relative inactivity, or became social and benevolent associations. If the associations fail to accomplish their goals over a long period, they also cease to be active organizations.[17]

A more recent study of associations in California focused on 187 groups representing city employees. In December 1963, 63,900 city employees, or about 50 percent of California municipal employment, were members of associations. The largest organization was the All-City Employees Association in Los Angeles, with 9,600 members in all departments except schools and the uniformed services. San Francisco's Civil Service Association was the second largest, with 8,000 members. One hundred and three independent local associations with 18,200 members formed the California League of City Employee Associations to coordinate legislative informational and other programs.[18]

Employee associations represent various groups of public employees. They may represent all employees in a city, all employees in a particular department, or a particular group of employees within a department or a city. Employee associations also enroll professionals—for example, attorneys employed in the Milwaukee City Attorney's Office are allowed to join the Association of Municipal Attorneys.

Collective Bargaining

Collective bargaining activity among employees of state and local governments has increased rapidly in recent years. Prior to 1962, no state had passed a law permitting or requiring government agencies to bargain with employee organizations. During that period, state attorney general orders and judicial decisions generally opposed the concept of collective bargaining by government agencies. Employees of such agencies were specifically excluded from federal and state labor statutes requiring private-sector employers to bargain with their employees.

Despite the lack of statutory support, unions used their political power to persuade cities to bargain voluntarily; in some cases the persuasion was effective. New York City, Cincinnati, and Philadelphia are frequently cited as examples of cities with long-standing collective bargaining relationships with representatives of municipal employees.

LEGAL FRAMEWORK

Since 1962, however, many states have passed laws requiring municipalities to recognize and bargain with employee organizations; fewer statutes require state agencies to bargain. Under these laws, unions and employee associations have increased greatly their membership and collective-bargaining relationships with government agencies. Table III–4 lists the states and summarizes their laws requiring or permitting collective bargaining with state and local employees.

RECOGNITION

All the statutes provide for exclusive recognition under which the employees in an appropriate unit of representation choose a single organization to represent them in collective bargaining with their employing agency. The only slight modification of the principle of exclusive recognition occurs in New York State, where the parties can voluntarily establish other recognition procedures, such as proportional or dual recognition, as long as no one objects. If a minority organization objects to a

Table III-4
State Public-Employee Laws—Aspects of Recent Enactments, Selected States

STATE	COVERAGE	ADMINISTRATIVE MACHINERY	BARGAINING	REPRESENTATION	DISPUTE PROVISIONS	STRIKES *
California	State and local	Governmental subdivisions	Required to "meet and confer."	Rules left to subdivisions.	None specified	
Connecticut	Local	State Labor Relations Board (SLRB); Board of Mediation and Arbitration (BMA)	Duty to negotiate	SLRB determines representative. Exclusive representation.	BMA mediates, and factfinding	Prohibited
Delaware	All except teachers	State Department of Labor and Industrial Relations (SDLIR); State Mediation Service (SMS)	State and county—duty to negotiate. Municipalities—independent decision.	SDLIR determines. Exclusive representation.	SMS mediates	Prohibited
Massachusetts	All local	State Labor Relations Commission (SLRC); State Board of Conciliation and Arbitrators (SBCA)	Duty to negotiate.	SLRC determines. Exclusive representation.	SBCA factfinding	Prohibited
	State	State Director of Personnel (SDP)	Duty to negotiate.	Rules for determination by SDP. Exclusive representation.		Prohibited
Michigan	All local	State Labor Mediation Board (SLMB) (separate administration of the labor relations and mediation function)	Duty to negotiate.	SLMB determines. Exclusive representation.	SLMB mediates grievance	Prohibited; sanctions against strikes subject to appeal and court review
Minnesota	State and local	Division of Labor Conciliation (DLC)	Required to "meet and confer."	DLC determines. Formal recognition to majority organization; informal to others.	DLC mediates. Then adjustment panel for findings	Prohibited
Missouri	State and local except teachers, police, state police	State Board of Mediation (SBM)	Required to negotiate.	SBM determines. Exclusive representation.		Prohibited

State	Coverage	Agency	Authorized to negotiate	Subject to study	Adjudication by	
Nebraska	All state and local	Court of Industrial Relations (CIR)	Authorized to negotiate.	Subject to study by CIR.	Adjudication by CIR	Prohibited; striking organization subject to loss of certification rights and fine
New York	All state and local	Public Employment Relations Board (PERB) (autonomous in State Department of Civil Service)	Required to bargain.	Exclusive representation subject to study by PERB.	Parties establish own procedures of recourse to mediation and factfinding through PERB	Prohibited
New Jersey	All state and local	Public Employment Relations Commission (PERC)	Required to bargain.	Exclusive representation.	Mediation and fact-finding	Prohibited
Oregon	State and local	Civil Service Boards, State Conciliation Service (SCL)	Requires bargaining.	Individual agencies to establish procedures.	Mediation SCL	Prohibited
Rhode Island	Local	State Labor Relations Board (SLRB)	Required to bargain.	SLRB determines. Exclusive representation.	Mediation by SDL, with arbitration on request of either party	Prohibited
Vermont	State / State Employees	State agencies / State Employee Labor Relations Board	Required to bargain. Duty to negotiate.	Represents members. Exclusive recognition.	Mediation and fact-finding	Prohibited / Prohibited
	Local employees, excludes "professional employees"	State Labor Relations Board (SLRB); Department of Industrial Relations (DIR)	Authorized to bargain.	SLRB determines. Exclusive representation.	Mediation by DIR and governor, effort to have parties agree to arbitration, otherwise factfinding by labor emergency board.	Prohibited; states right of public employer to petition for injunction
Washington	Local	Department of Labor and Industries (DLI)	Required to bargain.	DLI determines, exclusive representation.	Mediation	Prohibited
Wisconsin	Local	Wisconsin Employment Relations Board (WERB)	Required to bargain.	WERB determines, exclusive representation.	WERB factfinding; unless local authorities have established comparable procedures.	Prohibited
	State	WERB	Required to bargain.	WERB determines, exclusive representation.	WERB factfinding	Prohibited

* Refers only to statutory provisions and not to decisions of the courts and attorney generals.

NOTE: The table is based on the study of the statutes.

SOURCE: Joseph P. Goldberg, "Labor-Management Relations Laws in Public Service," Monthly Labor Review Vol. 91, no. 6 (Washington, D.C.: June 1968). Updated by Authors.

recognition procedure, the dispute is submitted to the Public Employment Relations Board (PERB), the agency established to administer the statute. The New York State act also requires PERB to conduct studies of alternative recognition procedures and to recommend future action on this problem.

Most state laws empower a state administrative agency to certify organizations and to conduct representation elections when necessary. Even though election and certification procedures exist, the employer may extend recognition informally by agreement with the employee organization. The administrative agency will not usually investigate informal recognitions unless complaints are filed by minority organizations or by individuals. Some administrative agencies may request a show of membership cards as assurance that the union is the majority choice in a new bargaining unit.

Some local governments voluntarily recognize employee organizations although they are not required to do so by statute. Two decades prior to the passage of state legislation, several Wisconsin unions achieved recognition in small towns because of the personal relationships between union members and community leaders in decision-making positions on the town council. Except for state highway departments, very few state agencies voluntarily recognized employee organizations. The large percentage of state employees covered by classified civil service partially accounts for the relatively little pressure brought by state employees for recognition of employee organizations.

Some cities extend formal recognition for negotiations only to limited groups of employees. Akron, Ohio recognizes formally nonuniformed nonsupervisory personnel, but only informally public health nurses and uniformed personnel.

In a recent study of council-manager cities, only 220 (20 percent) of the municipalities reported that they have local laws or policies which permit recognition of the union representing the majority of city employees. Seven hundred four cities (64 percent) have no policy. The most frequent first step in gaining recognition is for the union to request an appointment with the city manager (44 percent). One-third of the cities have no specific procedure. Seven percent of the cities require that the request for recognition be heard before the city council, and 6 percent of the cities require that the employee organization first submit its bylaws and its list of officers.[19] The city may agree to recognition by consent or if there is proof of support for the union by a majority of the employees in the bargaining unit.

DETERMINATION OF BARGAINING UNITS

Prior to legislation and in state and local governments not covered by state legislation, collective bargaining units were for the most part determined by the persuasive powers of the union and the extent of organization. Most state statutes establish some criteria for unit determination and give administrative agencies the responsibility to determine appropriate units. These agencies usually elaborate on the statutory criteria or establish their own criteria for unit determinations, if criteria are not established by statute. Before a representation election is held, the agency must decide which groups of employees will be represented by the organization, and who, therefore, are eligible to vote.

The statutory and administrative agency criteria for unit determination vary widely. In fact, no two state statutes or agencies have established exactly the same set of criteria. As an example of the differences among states, the Appendix at the end of this book lists the criteria for nine different states. "Community of interest" frequently is one of the criteria used for unit determinations. The term usually refers to a common work site, common supervisor, common skill or educational requirements, or other working conditions.

Two frequently contradictory criteria often used for unit determination are "effective representation" and "employer efficiency." If effective representation were the only criterion to be considered, the unit or units would be coterminous with the wishes of the employees. Frequently many small units would be created to assure effective representation of separate crafts or groups of employees. On the other hand, "employer efficiency" usually means as few units as possible, so the employer will not have to bargain with many different employee organizations.

Most administrative agencies usually attempt to reach a balance between the two criteria in determining and in carving out units. On the other hand, the statutes in Minnesota and New York stress "employer efficiency," while the Wisconsin statute takes the opposite approach by giving employees the right to vote on the unit being established. In 1966, the Committee on Government Employee Relations of the American Bar Association claimed that the Wisconsin statutory provisions on unit determination "resulted in the fragmentation of some bargaining units which would probably not have resulted if the Board were permitted to establish units based upon the criteria found in the National Labor Relations Act."[20] Aside from Wisconsin, the statutes of most of the other states are too new to evaluate the impact of the criteria on unit determination.

Larger cities often have highly fragmented bargaining units. For example, New York City has over 200 units; Detroit, 78 units; Boston, 22 units; and Minneapolis, 20 units.

Under Executive Order 49, issued by former Mayor Robert F. Wagner of New York City, unions could organize and receive certificates issued by the City Department of Labor if they represented a majority of city employees in a unit. A majority could be secured within a department, or a majority could be defined by job title on a city-wide basis. This method of unit determination has resulted in annual negotiations of more than two hundred separate contracts between New York City and various unions. The AFSCME negotiates for fifty of these contracts whose expiration dates vary. The Teamsters also have numerous negotiations because they represent employees in courts, the housing authority, and other departments.

The proliferation of units frequently results from the absence of legislative guidelines and of foresight by management. If there is no state legislation, cities recognize employee organizations when they file a petition and show majority support among a group of employees. Few city administrators think of the effect the new unit will have on labor relations; nor do they attempt to change the unit requested by the organization.

Philadelphia and Cincinnati gave more careful thought to bargaining units. These cities have city-wide bargaining units, which originated in the absence of statutory guidelines. Under a 1961 ordinance, Philadelphia accepted as the bargaining agent a union that had enrolled as members the majority of permanent, full-time, nonuniformed city employees. The city has warded off attempts by unions to establish separate units for nurses and engineers.

Both Philadelphia and Cincinnati brought in labor relations experts to help formulate a management position *prior* to recognition of the employee representative. The experience of these experts, though restricted to labor relations in the private sector, proved valuable in guiding the public employer in the formative stages of the bargaining relationship. For instance, the experts could advise the employers on the repercussions of granting recognition along departmental, craft, or other lines that would result in the formation of many units. The public employer would certainly have an easier time negotiating and administering a collective bargaining agreement if most municipal employees belonged to only one unit. The formation of a single city-wide bargaining unit, as well as subsequent labor relations dealings, was a conscious management decision and was not left to chance.

Even though bargaining by state employees is in its early stages, bargaining-unit disputes have already arisen. Job classifications frequently determine the wages of state employees with the same wage rates paid to all employees in a single classification. Job classifications, however, cross department lines. Naturally, a state would not want to bargain separately with unions representing employees in the same classification but in different departments. At the same time, unions often organize employees by departments or installations, not by classification.

A related unit determination problem recently arose among state employees in New York State. In 1967, the New York State Civil Service Employees Association petitioned for representation rights for all state employees except state policemen. Subsequently AFSCME petitioned to represent groups of employees working for some of the separate state agencies, but the state accepted the association's request for one statewide bargaining unit. The New York Public Employment Relations Board (PERB) took jurisdiction and overturned the agreed-upon unit. The association appealed PERB's action to a lower court in New York, which overruled PERB. The court reasoned that a unit determination by PERB would preclude bargaining on wages that year, because there was not enough time to make the unit determination before the deadline for budget submission. Both PERB and AFSCME appealed the decision to a higher court in New York which, in 1969, reversed the lower court's decision.

Cities also have had to decide whether appropriate units should be determined by department or by job title. In most cases, the unit is based on departmental lines. For instance, both sanitation workers and street and sidewalk employees have separate units.

A troublesome issue is whether supervisors should be included in units with other employees. In some cases this matter is spelled out by law; in others it is an administrative decision. "Function" rather than "title" has been the criterion used in deciding this issue. Persons enjoying the title of supervisor have not been precluded from rank-and-file bargaining units as long as they do not have the power to hire, to fire, or to effect change in employee status.

Michigan's Labor Mediation Board held that units of supervisory employees are not prohibited by the Public Employee Relations Act, nor are the units contrary to public policy. The board has not decided whether the supervisory unit may be represented by a bargaining agent that also represents nonsupervisory employees.[21] The Wisconsin Employee Relations Board found that attorneys employed in the City Attorney's Office, Milwaukee, do not participate as managerial employees and may decide if they desire representation. The attorney who advises the city labor negotiator was excluded from the unit.[22]

UNION SECURITY

State laws have not specifically authorized municipalities to negotiate public union security clauses. However, by being silent on this point most of these laws do not prohibit such clauses. Of course, states with right-to-work legislation prohibit the union shop in the public as well as in the private sector. In a study of municipalities, only nineteen, amounting to 5 percent of those with union organizations, reported that the union shop covers some segment of their labor force. The study also revealed that the union shop is most common in public works, although it is also found in utilities, sanitation, and fire departments. Two-thirds of the agreements are with nationally affiliated unions, and one-third of the cities have agreements with both national unions and local nonaffiliated organizations.[23]

The fair-share agreement, a form of the agency shop, has been considered in two states. The agency shop was declared a mandatory subject of collective bargaining in Michigan. Proposed amendments to the Wisconsin municipal employer relations law define a fair-share agreement as follows:

> Fair share agreement means an agreement between a municipal employer and a labor organization under which all or any of the employees represented by that organization but not members thereof are required to pay their proportionate share of the cost of the collective bargaining process, measured by the amount of dues paid by members of said labor organization, with the option of the employee to require that any portion of his payment to the labor organization which the latter might otherwise use for political activities, be paid by it to a recognized charity. . . . An employee desiring to exercise such option shall do so by written notice by registered mail addressed to the secretary treasurer of the labor organization.[24]

In spring 1969 two major cities in other states agreed to fair-share, or agency shop, provisions. The New York City clause covering 12,000 municipal hospital workers could not be implemented until the state legislature approved it. The Massachusetts legislature authorized Boston to start payroll deductions for union fees—amounts equivalent to monthly dues for union members and service charges for union representation for the 8,000 nonunion workers.

Attainment of organizational security clauses in the near future similar to those negotiated in the private sector is doubtful. Supporters of the merit system maintain that ability instead of union membership should be the key to municipal employment.

The New York Governor's Committee has suggested that an employee organization which is granted recognition be allowed to have the checkoff upon presentation of dues-deduction authorization cards.[25] Though the legality of the checkoff has been questioned, even areas unsympathetic to public unionism have seen widespread use of the checkoff.[26]

The checkoff exists where legislation permits collective bargaining and where no legislation exists. Geographically, the checkoff is most common in the West and least common in the South. Metropolitan central cities and suburbs are most likely to have such arrangements.[27] All cities with populations over 1,000,000 provide for dues checkoff. Seventeen of the twenty-two cities with populations between 500,000 and 1,000,000 have checkoffs. Of the other cities with populations over 100,000, 66 percent report checkoffs.

The scope of bargaining differs among and within state and local governments. In general, employee organizations wish to broaden the scope of bargaining, while managers wish to retain unilateral authority over as many areas as possible.

On the other hand, the scope of bargaining for local governments is sometimes limited by state statutes. For example, the retirement or the longevity-stipends program may be under the jurisdiction of the state rather than the city or the county. Salaries and many working conditions for state employees are usually set by the legislature. In some states, for example Minnesota, the "bargaining" on salaries that takes place by state employees is very similar to "lobbying." Even in these cases, however, employee organizations bargain on other items, such as job classifications and tests for hiring.

Some states have attempted to limit the scope of bargaining by encouraging agencies to recognize and negotiate management-rights clauses. The Oregon State Board of Control issued the following statement listing rights retained by management:

> Institutions and agencies retain the right, in accordance with applicable laws and administrative rules
> (a) To direct employees of the activity or institution;
> (b) To hire, promote, transfer, assign and retain employees in positions within the agency, and to suspend, demote, discharge, or take other disciplinary action against employees;
> (c) To relieve employees from duties because of lack of work or for other legitimate reasons;
> (d) To maintain the efficiency of the operations entrusted to them;
> (e) To determine the methods, means, and personnel by which such operations are to be conducted; and
> (f) To take whatever actions may be necessary to carry out the mission of the agency in situations of emergency.

These limitations do not prohibit "administrators from administering the manner in which these rights will be administered."[28]

Municipalities have attempted to limit the scope of negotiations by legislating certain issues; such issues cannot therefore be bargained. For example, some city attorneys have ruled that certain issues cannot be bargained because the law demands that public officials carry out specific obligations. Moreover, the city and the union may negotiate a management-rights clause that specifies nonnegotiable issues.

The Milwaukee-AFSCME agreement gives the city rights to establish work rules, to schedule overtime work, to define job content, to discipline, to contract, and to subcontract. Other contract clauses specifically define management's rights to hire, to promote, and to carry out agency policies.

Comprehensive collective bargaining agreements are still relatively rare in state governments, although the number of such agreements has increased in recent years. Comprehensive agreements are much more prevalent in municipalities; almost 40 percent of the council-manager cities report having signed such agreements.

Written but unsigned agreements also exist between cities and unions. Management officials sometimes think the signing of an agreement is illegal or subject to legal challenge by citizens. Furthermore, some unions prefer to have a flexible, rather than a formal, understanding with politicians. They feel they can gain more through pressure tactics than they can under a formal agreement.

The written agreement may be of secondary importance. For example, getting a contract signed in New York City is not so significant as getting a monetary agreement implemented by a personnel order. The personnel order is what puts the union municipal wage agreement into effect.

State laws providing for negotiations are apparently related to a larger scope of bargaining in local governments. In a study of 193 public sector contracts, Gerhart found that collective bargaining agreements tended to be more comprehensive in non-Southern states with negotiations statutes than in non-Southern states with no explicit public policy.[29]

CONDUCT OF NEGOTIATIONS

Collective bargaining among state employees is too new to detect patterns for negotiation procedures. The experience of two states illustrates different approaches to bargaining. In Minnesota, the Civil Service Commission rules constitute, in a sense, the collective bargaining contract for state employees, so the procedure for "negotiations" is similar to that required in the passage of a law. Department heads and representatives of employee organizations make proposals to the commission. In some cases the department's proposals are based on recommendations of employee organization representatives. Proposals approved by the commission are submitted to the applicable legislative committee for refinement and then to the state legislature. This negotiating procedure makes political lobbying between legislative sessions the primary negotiating tool of the union.

The Governor of New York State established, in 1968, an employee relations division to conduct negotiations with organizations of state employees. Between 1965 and 1968 the bargaining team consisted of the budget director, a professional negotiator, and the chief of the Civil Service Commission. The professional negotiator acted as spokesman for the team.

In bargaining at the local government level, the composition of the management bargaining team varies according to the size of the city. The roles played by members of the management team are determined by the power of the departments and the department heads, the history of participation, and the relative strength of the chief official, of the department heads, and of the legislative body.

It is becoming more common for the management team in a large city to be headed by an individual with the primary responsibility for conducting negotiations. He is given various titles—labor negotiator, director of labor relations, or labor relations negotiator. These chief negotiators have diverse backgrounds—the city's law department, the labor movement, the city council, or labor relations in the private sector.

Representatives from the finance, the legal, and the personnel departments usually support the chief negotiator. These persons provide information on cost, legality, and civil service rules. Representatives from operating departments, including the department head, sometimes also play a role in negotiations. If a department representative is not present, the negotiator is often ignorant of problems faced by the department in its day-to-day operations. The chief negotiator cannot be expected to know the details of department operations, as informal practices frequently differ from written policies. Discussion of these topics without the presence of the department head gives the employee organization a definite advantage. In New York City, however, department heads are not on the negotiating team because they are frequently organized.

In council-manager cities, the city manager usually represents the municipality in negotiations. In 7 percent of the cities unions negotiate with the city council or with a committee of the council. The civil service commission has negotiated with the employee organization in only three percent of council-manager cities. These cities rarely use a professional negotiator.

Small cities are still experimenting with the composition of their negotiating teams. Eau Claire, Wisconsin, for instance, has tried three variations in negotiations: the entire city council, a committee of its council, and one member of the council. In other small towns, the mayor or the city manager has negotiated with the union.

The mayor of a city is rarely on the municipal bargaining team, but he may have a significant effect on negotiations. Besides being chief executive of the city, the mayor is also a politician. The dual nature of the job often leads mayors to undercut the position of their own bargaining team; their political interests may be completely divorced from the interests of their constituents. For example, in one city the mayor unilaterally reopened contract negotiations prior to a mayoralty election and gave city workers one of the best public employee pension plans in the nation. The mayor was reelected by a small plurality, thanks to union assistance in his election campaign. Another common occurrence in municipalities, is for unions to go through the motions of collective bargaining knowing that the mayor will enter negotiations just before the strike deadline and give the union a favorable settlement.

Where weak mayors prevail and city council committees are responsible for bargaining, unions place political pressures on council members by withholding political endorsements and contributions. Appointed representatives on negotiating teams may also be subject to union pressures.

Governors sometimes enter municipal bargaining situations in order to help settle disputes between municipal authorities and local unions. In some cases, the governor is able to provide additional funds; in others, he acts as mediator. Involvement in a municipal bargaining dispute has obvious political advantages to the governor who frequently ends up as the "hero." Such involvement, however, may complicate the city's bargaining position; the mayor will be under increased pressure to settle, especially if the governor is a political rival.

The lesson to be learned from these examples is that pressures often force elected officials to become involved in bargaining, despite their intentions to leave collective bargaining in the hands of experts. In fact, it is extremely difficult in municipalities to insulate collective bargaining from political pressures. As a result, the bargaining power of municipal unions is greatly enhanced.

The employee organization bargaining team varies on the basis of size of city and number of locals represented. In major negotiations involving a number of local unions, the AFSCME team, composed of representatives of the local unions, is often headed by the district council president or the staff director. If the negotiations involve one local, the president of the local will usually be the major spokesman for the union team. Assistance in preparing for negotiations will be given by the professional staff of the district council and by the international union.

In suburban communities, negotiations are led by the local president. The staff of one of AFSCME's joint district councils assists and may even take over the negotiations on behalf of the local. The council president does not play a role unless an impasse develops.

The AFSCME sometimes engages in joint negotiations. In Cincinnati six locals of AFSCME representing clerks, and employees of the municipal garage, the waterworks, the highway maintenance department, and the general hospital, as well as foremen and supervisors, negotiate jointly with representatives of the Operating Engineers Union and the Firemen and Oilers Union.

In 31 percent of council-manager cities, the employee spokesmen are organization officers. Both business agents and officers negotiate in 18 percent of the municipalities, while business agents alone negotiate in 10 percent of the cities. Employee councils negotiate with city officials in 6 percent of the municipalities, and various teams of business agents, employee councils, and organization officers negotiate with city officials in the remainder of the cities.

Prior to negotiations, taxpayer groups frequently testify on the cost of government before the city council. In some cities, for example Milwaukee, the quality of the arguments has been so high that one or both of the parties (usually management) use taxpayer testimony in bargaining sessions. The public, however, has little if any say while negotiations are proceeding.

The city negotiator or the negotiating team is often limited by the council, the finance committee, or the chief executive in the extent of the union demands to which it may accede. If the union remains adamant in its demands, which exceed the limit imposed on the city negotiator(s), the negotiator(s) may request higher limits and warn the union of a possible impasse.

The demands of the employee organizations are usually made and approved by the membership. The leadership is empowered to make concessions in the original demands in order to achieve a favorable contract. Contract ratification used to be a matter of form; with increased membership militancy, it no longer is in some cities.

Ratification may also be a problem for state and local government. In the case of "weak mayor" and "weak governor" political structures, the top elected official cannot be confident that other political bodies will accept tentatively negotiated agreements. The requirement of fiscal approval by completely separate governmental bodies prevents a unified management approach to negotiations. The extreme case of this problem probably occurs in New England towns where the town meeting must approve the tentatively negotiated agreements. "Strong governor" and "strong mayor" political structures, on the other hand, are less likely to experience problems in contract ratification.

Although municipal negotiations cover many issues, the most important items are usually wages and fringe benefits. During negotiations various arguments are used by both sides to support their positions. The relevance of such arguments to any particular settlement is a controversial point.

Typical arguments made by unions and rebutted by cities are (1) increase in the cost of living, (2) increase in productivity, (3) maintenance of pay in the face of a shorter workweek, (4) ability of the employer to pay higher wages, (5) wages paid for comparable work in private industry and in other agencies. The number and importance of the arguments are tailored to local circumstances.

The employer's ability to pay is often the key dispute in negotiations. Generally, cities do not argue that they are *unwilling* to pay, but rather that they are *unable* to pay. In commenting on the 1967 agreement between the city of Detroit and AFSCME, the City Controller stated that the union "agreed to the city's present inability to grant a pay raise and agreed to work with us on formulating the raise for next year."[30]

Comparative wage data can also be a major and confusing factor employed in municipal wage negotiations. In Philadelphia the city supports its bargaining position by undertaking massive wage surveys of employees in similar jobs in other municipalities. The union attempts to gain greater leverage in negotiations by using the highest comparative wage data.

In Milwaukee, the city and the union use all the traditional arguments employed in private bargaining. Particularly stressed are the ability to pay and comparative wages. The AFSCME representatives feel that the final outcome of bargaining has little to do with the arguments employed. Instead they believe that the final agreement reflects the relative power positions of the parties. Milwaukee's labor negotiator feels that arguments do play an important role but not the determining one. The traditional arguments provide a starting point for negotiations and establish limits to the wage settlement.

Budget deadlines frequently affect the bargaining process in state and local government jurisdictions. Some state constitutions or statutes list specific dates for budget submission. According to a New York State statute, an impasse is automatically declared if the parties do not reach an agreement by sixty days prior to the budget submission date. Mediation and fact-finding procedures must then be initiated. This type of deadline puts different kinds of pressures on the parties than do strike deadlines. If the parties are anxious to initiate mediation or fact finding, the deadline provides very little pressure. But if the government employer fears loss of political support, the deadline places considerable pressure on him to settle.

Yet budget deadlines sometimes have little noticeable effect on municipal bargaining. For example, bargaining continued on a year-round basis in one city because of the large number of different unions of municipal employees. Bargaining with influential or strategic unions set patterns, but these patterns were modified as the city negotiated with subsequent unions, and retroactive changes were made in the earlier settlements. The city frequently found extra funds regardless of previous statements about budget deficits, a fact that further encouraged the unions to increase the size of their demands. This cycle of bargaining produces conflicting pressures. Political leaders become increasingly aware of the public's annoyance with the chaotic bargaining and budget-making. City negotiators and personnel directors become more experienced and sophisticated in collective bargaining and attempt to persuade elected officials to maintain predetermined bargaining limits regardless of union strikes and strike threats. At the same time, elected officials may cringe at the thought of a strike especially when it affects large or politically important groups of voters. Government officials may also use union strike threats as a means of persuading the public to accept increased taxes. In general, it is extremely difficult for a government to break a cycle of year-round bargaining and to integrate bargaining with budget deadlines without accepting a strike. Breaking the cycle, however, could improve labor relations and decrease strikes in the long run.

GRIEVANCES

Grievance procedures have been established by some Civil Service Commissions prior to the negotiation of grievance procedures by employers and employee organizations. Therefore, even though a grievance procedure has not been mutually determined, it can be pursued by an employee with the assistance of the union or the association. In some jurisdictions, both procedures exist and the employee has the option as to which procedure he will use.

Negotiated grievance procedures consist of four to seven steps. The initial steps resemble private-employment procedures, the first step being the registering of a complaint by the worker or a group of workers and the discussion of the complaint with the supervisor. If the matter is not resolved, the employee or the representative of the employee organization, often called the shop steward, puts the complaint in writing and submits it to the supervisor. (The steward is sometimes allowed time off his job to investigate and process the grievance.) The supervisor submits a written answer to the steward, and, if the matter is still not settled, the employee may appeal to the bureau, department, or agency head. The head may consult with the union and must submit his written answer within a specified period.

The mechanics of the procedure in the next stages vary among jurisdictions. In Milwaukee, if the union is not satisfied with the answer of the department head, it may submit a written appeal to the department head, asking him to review the decision. In Detroit, the union may appeal the grievance to the bureau head, or may refer the grievance to the joint district council. The grievance is then presented to a city-wide union committee for consideration.

Impasse procedures for disputes involving interpretation and implementation of the agreement are formally being included in municipal collective agreements; and either advisory or binding arbitration is increasingly used as the terminal point in municipal grievance procedures.

Some question still exists whether a municipality can agree to binding arbitration. Critics of the practice have said that cities cannot delegate such responsibility to a third party. In 1967, courts in Michigan and Wisconsin ruled that it is not unlawful for cities to agree to binding arbitration.[31]

The Milwaukee-AFSCME agreements exclude certain grievances from final and binding arbitration: provisions of the contract that affect the obligation of the city, obligations which by law evolve upon the common council, matters covered by Wisconsin statutes and relating to the operation and jurisdiction of the City Service Commission, discontinuance of any job with certain exceptions provided by contracting and subcontracting provisions, and any pension matter.[32]

Under the Detroit agreement the arbitrator is not allowed to grant wage increases or to order wage decreases. In decisions about back pay, the arbitrator can only allow back pay minus any compensation received by the worker for temporary employment subsequent to his removal from the city payroll.[33]

Many municipal grievances arise because supervisory personnel are not accustomed to working under a collective agreement. One union official has stated: "Supervisors have had the keys to the kingdom. Now since the contract spells out job assignments, the worker can say he doesn't have to do what the supervisor says. The supervisor still hasn't accepted the union."

In some cities, supervisors have been enforcing technical work rules that were not enforced prior to collective bargaining. City officials as well as union leaders complain about the number of petty grievances caused by strict interpretation of rules by intermediate supervisors. Some supervisors are receiving special training in human relations and labor relations in order to facilitate more harmonious labor-management relations.

Specific problem areas in grievances include sick leave, overtime, shift assignments, and job reclassifications. Grievances about reclassification are the most complex, because civil service enters the picture. Relatively few grievances about wage payments have been filed.

Although the grievance procedure is intended to police the contract, it has been used for other purposes as well. City officials have complained that unions overuse the procedure to show non-union employees the value of the union. Where a union has just been granted recognition, a grievance demonstrates to the union member that he is getting something for his dues and helps to establish greater group cohesiveness.

Unions have also processed grievances as a tactical weapon to harass municipal employers into making contract changes. In some instances, grievances have been taken through the preliminary steps and then dropped, because the union knew it would lose if the grievance went to arbitration.

The number of grievances filed by any city department is not necessarily indicative of the state of labor relations in the department. Municipal employers as well as union leaders have admitted that the frequency of grievances depends more on the temperament and courage of the steward than on the harmony or the disharmony in labor relations. Unions have found it difficult to get stewards to file their first grievances, because the stewards fear retaliation by the supervisor.

UNFAIR LABOR PRACTICES

Some state statutes which guarantee the right of municipal employees to organize and to engage in collective bargaining specify unfair labor practices. The following prohibited employer practices are stated in the amended Wisconsin municipal employee statute: (1) to interfere, coerce or restrain municipal employees in the exercise of rights guaranteed in the legislation; (2) to initiate, create, dominate or interfere with the formation or administration of any employee organization; (3) to encourage or discourage membership in an employee organization through hiring, tenure, or other terms and conditions of employment; (4) to refuse to bargain in good faith; (5) to violate the collective agreement; (6) to deduct dues without a signed authorization from the municipal employee.

Prohibited employee practices consist of (1) coercing or intimidating municipal employees; (2) coercing, intimidating or inducing any officer or agent of a municipal employer; (3) refusing to bargain collectively; (4) violating the collective agreement; (5) engaging in, inducing or encouraging any municipal employee to engage in a strike; (6) coercing or intimidating a municipal officer, agent or supervisor to become a member of a labor organization; (7) doing or causing to be done any act prohibited in (5) or (6) on behalf of or in the interest of municipal employees, or in connection with or to influence the outcome of any controversy as to employment relations.[34]

Seven states have followed Wisconsin's lead in specifying unfair practices for both employee organizations and municipalities. In Washington, the legislation contains only a general noninterference clause. The New York law is silent on the subject of unfair practices. Delaware and Michigan legislation resemble the original Wagner Act rather than current federal law in that only employer unfair practices are specified.

No early cases were decided by WERB or the courts on unfair labor practices in Wisconsin.[35] A number of charges have recently been filed, however, involving refusal to bargain and discrimination against union members.[36] A few unfair labor practice cases have appeared in Massachusetts, but only one case concerns refusal to bargain.

In Connecticut, a number of cases have been filed with the state administrative agency. The charge of refusal to bargain is generally made by the union, but in one case the city of New Haven accused the union of not bargaining. It was found, however, that many of the charges resulted from legitimate impasses. In the first year of operation under Connecticut legislation, twenty-one unfair labor cases were filed by employee organizations. Sixteen were filed by AFSCME and three by SEIU.[37]

The first charge of an unfair labor practice under the New York City collective bargaining law was filed in early 1969. Three employee organizations representing superior police officers charged that New York City was not bargaining in good faith because it used the agreement reached with the Patrolmen's Benevolent Association, which represents the lower ranks of policemen, as the basis for determining officers' pay and ignored the higher wages recommended by a special panel.

STRIKES

Strikes have occurred with increasing frequency in disputes involving state, county, and municipal employees. Strikes against municipal governments are often prohibited by state legislation. Eighteen states have laws prohibiting public-employee strikes, and numerous state attorneys general orders and court decisions have declared strikes illegal. (See below.)

List of states having State Laws, Attorneys General Opinions, or Court Decisions Prohibiting Strikes

STATUTES	ATTORNEYS GENERAL OPINIONS	COURT DECISIONS
Connecticut	Alabama	California
Delaware	New Mexico	Illinois
Florida	New York	New Hampshire
Hawaii	South Carolina	New Jersey
Massachusetts	Utah	North Dakota
Michigan	West Virginia	Tennessee
Minnesota		
Missouri		
New York		
Ohio		
Oregon		
Pennsylvania		
Rhode Island		
Texas		
Vermont		
Virginia		
Washington		
Wisconsin		

Table III–5
Work Stoppages in Government by Type of Work, 1958–68°

Year	Number of stoppages	Workers involved	Man-days idle during year	Number of stoppages	Workers involved	Man-days idle during year
	SANITATION SERVICES			ADMINISTRATION AND SERVICES		PROTECTION
1958	7	950	4,890	3	620	2,230
1959	7	390	1,020	3	130	1,560
1960	12	8,180	21,400	2	130	760
1961	12	1,390	3,550	2	40	1,000
1962	5	850	4,100	—	—	—
1963	8	1,760	7,720	2	120	240
1964	5	700	1,550	1	30	30
1965	16	1,750	8,030	3	6,620	114,000
1966	36	7,500	24,700	19	9,360	50,300
1967	23	3,100	17,300	24	22,200	197,000
1968	63	27,500	200,100	28	10,600	44,300
Year	STREET AND HIGHWAY DEPARTMENTS			HOSPITALS AND OTHER HEALTH SERVICES†		
1958	1	10	40	—	—	—
1959	6	660	5,310	—	—	—
1960	11	920	2,310	—	—	—
1961	3	150	1,170	—	—	—
1962	4	140	390	—	—	—
1963	6	260	1,580	1	10	30
1964	9	560	4,250	—	—	—
1965	6	650	3,700	1	160	1,120
1966	2	60	210	17	7,760	23,400
1967	5	1,330	3,030	19	1,200	26,800
1968	5	100	1,000	21	11,000	85,500
	PUBLICLY OWNED TRANSPORTATION			PUBLIC SCHOOLS AND LIBRARIES		
1958	—	—	—	—	—	—
1959	—	—	—	4	220	440
1960	2	8,340	16,100	5	10,200	17,000
1961	2	4,520	4,520	2	90	180
1962	4	1,700	2,340	6	23,900	37,700
1963	—	—	—	7	2,540	5,080
1964	4	3,840	18,300	18	17,100	40,600
1965	1	180	4,620	9	1,930	13,800
1966	2	34,900	275,000	54	44,800	78,300
1967	6	1,530	5,360	89	96,200	983,000
1968	1	10	30	112	148,000	2,193,800

Most municipal strikes now occur because of a breakdown in contract negotiations; many such strikes previously resulted from management's refusal to recognize and bargain with the union. In 1968, over 200,000 employees struck against state and local governments. Of the 254 government work stoppages, 235 involved local employees and 16 involved state employees. Ninety-eight out of each one hundred days lost because of government employee work stoppages occurred at the local level.

In 1968, approximately 10 days were lost because of work stoppages by government workers for each 10,000 days worked; in private industry about 20 days were lost for each 10,000 days worked. In spite of the relatively fewer days lost for stoppages by government employees, strikes by the government sector cannot be ignored. Since 1958, the trend of strikes by state and local employees has risen sharply.

In 1968, public school and library employees accounted for one hundred twelve stoppages; sanitation workers for sixty-three; administration and protection workers for twenty-eight; and hospital and health service workers for twenty-one (see table III–5).

IMPASSE PROCEDURES

Sixteen states have statutes providing for settlement of disputes. The procedures in other states have been mutually established or consented to by employee groups and the city.

In some cities boards of review for settling impasses have been established by the municipality and the union. In Cincinnati the agreement between AFSCME and the city provides for the appointment of a board of review in case of impasse. The board is composed of one representative of the city, one representative of the union, and one representative appointed jointly by the city

---

* Includes stoppages lasting a full day or shift or longer and involving six workers or more.

† "Hospitals and other health services" were included in "miscellaneous services," 1958–62.

NOTE: Data on stoppages and workers involved refer to stoppages beginning in the year, man-days idle refer to all stoppages in effect during the year. Because of rounding, sums of individual items may not equal totals.

SOURCE: U.S. Bureau of Labor Statistics.

and the union. In 1967 an impasse on an increase in pay went to the board of review. The city council accepted the board's recommendation, but claimed lack of funds to implement the recommended increase. The AFSCME eventually received the money through political pressure.

In New York City a dispute panel may be formed after the failure of collective bargaining, which may or may not have included mediation. The panel may be formed at the joint request of the union and the city or on the recommendation of the chairman of the Office of Collective Bargaining. The union and the city each select a consultant to the panel, which consists of the number of impartial persons deemed appropriate for the matter at hand. The panel may mediate, hold hearings, call witnesses, collect data, and take whatever action is considered appropriate to settlement of the dispute. If the panel fails to settle the impasse, it may make recommendations, which the chairman, with the advice and guidance of the OCB, can release to the parties and the public.

Mediation is perhaps the most common impasse procedure used by government employers and employee organizations. Mediation is usually conducted by a state board representative. Although either party can usually request mediation, the union files the request in most cases.

Mediation is generally intended to bring together parties to negotiate an agreement. In some cases, a fact-finder may serve as a mediator prior to formal fact-finding. The fact-finder can sometimes mediate a dispute merely by stating to the parties his view of the issues and the facts.

National data on the success of mediation in municipal disputes are not available, but the Connecticut experience may be illustrative. Prior to passage of municipal employee legislation, the Connecticut Mediation and Arbitration Board worked informally with cities and employee organizations. As of September 1967, the board, under legislation, has functioned as mediator in thirty-one cases involving twenty-seven different municipalities. Seventeen cases were settled through mediation; fourteen were sent to fact-finding, and the fact-finder mediated a settlement in two of the fourteen cases. The major issues involved money. Checkoff provisions, grievance arbitration provisions, and seniority provisions were also mediated. The number of sessions needed for mediation varied from one to fourteen.

Fact-finding has been used increasingly to settle public employment impasses. The awards usually are advisory, but in some jurisdictions, such as Massachusetts, the unions are required to accept the fact-finder's recommendations. In these cases, unions object that the award is binding on only one of the parties. The rationale for the unilateral position seems to be that the public employer cannot be legally bound by a third-party decision.

Fact-finding sometimes is voluntarily agreed to by the union and the employer. At other times, fact-finding has been imposed on the parties by legislation. Of special interest are the attitudes of union leaders toward fact-finding as an alternative to the strike. In New York City, AFSCME is committed to fact-finding, although in New York as elsewhere, it considers the fact-finders award as equivalent to an award under compulsory arbitration.

In another city where fact-finding had been imposed by legislation, the union leadership intends to use the procedure only if it is to the union's advantage. One union leader has said:

> We use fact-finding where no other alternatives are available. We will use an effective strike before we use fact-finding. We are opposed to fact-finding as a terminal point in negotiations. We use it only when we are too weak to use anything else. When we do use it, we make it quite clear that the union considers it to be tantamount to binding arbitration. If the fact-finder's award would not be accepted, we would strike. We have run into instances where employers wanted to negotiate the fact-finder's award rather than accept it. This is ridiculous.

A Midwestern union leader feels that public response to fact-finding is related to the nature of the services performed by public employees. The public is not concerned about the employees whom he represents. "The public can get aroused in a school-teachers' strike but not sewerage. Most of the time it does not react to the disputes my union is involved in."

Another union leader explained why his organization had not used fact-finding. "Unions only use it to take the heat off the leadership. If the city has no money, the fact-finder's decision tells the union membership that the city cannot pay so the officers are not faulted by the rank and file."

If unions are reasonably assured of success, some would rather strike than go to fact-finding. It has been argued that the union should be allowed to strike if the city refuses the fact-finder's recommendation. In practice, many unions have treated the fact-finder's decision as the decision of a compulsory arbitrator, and, therefore, if the city did not accept the decision, the unions usually have called strikes.

In many cases the parties return to negotiations after the fact-finder's award is issued. Some unions have been willing to settle for less than the fact-finder's decision. For instance, the union representing West Haven, Connecticut, custodial employees agreed to accept less pay for its members than the fact-finder had recommended.

Fact-finding has also been used in noneconomic issues. In Stratford, Connecticut, negotiations were stymied over the form of the final step in the grievance procedure, and the issue was submitted to fact-finding. In East Haven, Connecticut, the issue of the check-off went to fact-finding.

Arbitration has rarely been used in agreement negotiations. On the municipal level, arbitration has been used for some disputes involving public-safety personnel, but rarely in those affecting general city employees.

Government officials have been reluctant to give a third party the authority to make a final decision. In many instances, the officials claim they do not have the legal authority to agree to arbitration of new contracts. In others, officials are confident that they can do better through collective bargaining even with the possibility of a strike or through the use of alternative impasse procedures.

Generally union leaders do not feel that compulsory fact-finding or arbitration is a substitute for the right to strike. The unions believe that government officials would welcome arbitration, because it would enable the city to blame someone else for the settlements. In other words, the attitude exists both in management and in the union that arbitration would be beneficial primarily to the other party. In this connection it is interesting to note that, under the new Canadian federal law, only five of forty-five unions initially chose the legal right to strike instead of compulsory arbitration.

Conclusion

This chapter has emphasized the tremendous variety in employment relations at the state and local levels. The variety is caused by the widely differing kinds of employees working for state and local governments as well as the range of experience and wide background of collective bargaining found there.

Negotiation statutes affecting state and local employees are being passed at an increasing rate, and employment at this level is predicted to continue its rapid rise. These two factors will undoubtedly cause even greater collective bargaining activity. Several groups of employees will probably face special problems because of the unique characteristics of their working environment. Two of these groups, teachers and protective service employees (police and fire fighters), are singled out in the next two chapters for special consideration.

Appendix: Criteria
for Unit Determination

New York State

1. The unit shall correspond to a community of interest among the employees to be included in the unit.
2. The officials of government at the level of the unit shall have the power to agree, or to make effective recommendations to other administrative authority or the legislative body with respect to the terms and conditions of employment upon which the employees desire to negotiate.
3. The unit shall be compatible with the joint responsibilities of the public employer and public employees to serve the public.

Connecticut

1. The board determines the bargaining unit to insure a clear and identifiable community of interest.
2. Fire and police shall each be in separate units.
3. Unless a majority of professionals vote for inclusion, they shall be separate units from non-professionals.

4. The board also has the duty to exclude supervision, except in police and fire departments.

Delaware

Considerations are:
1. Duties, skills and working conditions of employees.
2. The history of bargaining.
3. The extent of organization of the employees.
4. The desires of the public employees.

Massachusetts

State employees. The Director of Personnel and Standardization determines the appropriate unit based on community of interest which may include similar working conditions, common supervision and common location.

Municipal Employees. The State Labor Relations Board decides in each case whether the unit should be the municipal employer unit or any other unit. Otherwise, firemen shall be in a separate unit; and unless professionals vote for inclusion, they shall be in separate units from non-professionals.

Michigan

The state board decides the unit in order to ensure the employees the full benefits of their rights to self-organization.

Minnesota

Considerations are:
1. Efficient administration.
2. Existing position, classification and compensation plans.
3. History and extent of organization.
4. Occupational classifications.
5. Levels of authority.
6. Geographical location of employees.
7. Recommendations of the parties.

Oregon

No criteria are set out for the public employers who administer the law, but supervisory employees, employees who occupy a position of trust, and temporary employees are excluded from units under the rules of the Oregon Civil Service Commission.

Rhode Island

Municipal Employees. The unit shall be the employer unit, craft unit, plant unit or other unit as decided by the board. Supervisors are excluded.

State Employees. No criteria.

Wisconsin

Two acts covering state and municipal employees both have the same criteria, namely that the board shall decide the unit, but an opportunity shall be given to the employees to decide the unit by secret ballot. Further, employees in a craft or profession may constitute a separate unit. The state law excludes supervisors.

SOURCE: Andrew W. J. Thomson, *Unit Determination in Public Employment* (Ithaca, N.Y.: New York State School of Industrial and Labor Relations, Cornell University, 1968), pp. 8–9.

IV collective bargaining for teachers

Organization of Public Education

In terms of economic importance as a government function, education ranks second to national defense and international relations. Of $258.5 billion spent by all levels of government in 1966–1967, $74.6 billion, or 28.9 percent, was spent on national defense and $40.5 billion, or 15.7 percent, on education. In the academic year 1968–1969 a total of $34.7 billion, approximately 3.3 percent of our gross national product, was spent for public elementary and secondary education in the United States.

Responsibility for guaranteeing the establishment and the maintenance of a system of public schools in the United States is given to each of the fifty states. The actual operation of the schools is delegated locally, however, and 20,406 local school districts presently exercise this delegated responsibility.

In 1962, 93.7 percent of local school districts were administratively independent. Administratively dependent school systems are run by local units of governments—townships, municipalities, cities, counties, and states—which operate and govern schools and perform other government functions. Although only 6.3 percent of the school systems were classified as administratively dependent, 18.4 percent of the schools and 22.2 percent of the pupils enrolled fell in this category.[1]

In the administratively dependent school system, three state-dependent systems operate in Alaska, Hawaii, and Maine. All public schools in Hawaii are administered directly as part of the state government; in the other two states this arrangement applies only to certain sparsely populated areas.[2]

The number of local school districts in the United States has declined rapidly in recent years. The 20,406 reported in 1968–1969 represents a 'decrease of 53.1 percent in the previous ten-year period and a decrease of almost 84 percent from 1931–1932. This trend is mainly a result of widespread efforts toward reorganization and consolidation of school districts.[3]

Each school district has a governing board, usually called a board of education or a school board, which is given administrative powers by state statute. The local school board is legally a state agency, but it is also the instrument by which the operation of schools is locally controlled.

The United States educational system is based on lay control. Teachers and administrators employed in a school district are specifically prohibited from serving as members of that district's board of education. The board consists of local citizens usually elected by the constituency of the district. About 15 percent of the boards of education, mostly in large cities, are appointed by the mayor or by the municipal governing body. Most boards of education consist of between seven and twelve members who serve without compensation. The board is supposed to be a policy-making body; the implementation and application of its policies are delegated to the school superintendent and his administrative staff.

Most school districts have a superintendent of schools, who serves as executive officer of the board of education. In larger districts, the superintendent has a staff of administrators and specialists in areas such as curriculum, personnel, and budgets. Each school has a principal, who is almost always a full-time administrator; secondary schools usually have department chairmen, who teach part time.

Each state regulates its local school districts by constitutional provisions or by legislation. The most common state regulation of schools covers such areas as minimum length of the school terms, compulsory school attendance, required elementary and high school programs, course offerings, textbooks, teacher certification and minimum salaries, school facilities, pupil personnel services, and transportation of pupils.[4]

The source of funds for financing of public education varies among states, but most funds usually come from local sources. In 1968–1969, the state governments increased to 40.9 percent their share of financial support for public education, and the federal government, to 7.3 percent (see Table IV–1). The fiscal structure

Table IV–1
Percentage Distribution of Public School Revenues, 1957–58 to 1968–69

	Percent of school revenue derived from		
School year	FEDERAL SOURCES	STATE SOURCES	LOCAL AND OTHER SOURCES
1957–58	4.0%	39.4%	56.6%
1958–59	3.6	39.5	56.9
1959–60	4.4	39.1	56.5
1960–61	3.8	39.8	56.4
1961–62	4.3	38.7	56.9
1962–63	3.6	39.3	57.1
1963–64	4.4	39.3	56.4
1964–65	3.8	39.7	56.5
1965–66	7.9	39.1	53.0
1966–67	7.9	39.1	53.0
1967–68	8.0	39.3	52.7
1968–69	7.3	40.9	51.9

SOURCE: National Education Association, Research Division, *Estimates of School Statistics,* (Washington, D.C.: 1968–69), p. 18.

of local school districts varies. From one-half to three-fourths of all school districts in the United States are fiscally independent; that is, they have the authority to set their own tax rates within state-legislated millage limits. Depending on how close a school district is to its legislative millage limit, the school board may have a great deal of autonomy in setting tax rates. Some fiscally independent districts must obtain voter approval of their budgets, usually in a special referendum. The remaining school districts are fiscally dependent, that is, they must obtain approval of their budgets from another local government body or its representative —typically a city council, a mayor, an auditor, a budget officer, or a city clerk. These agencies vary widely in their authority to modify school budgets. Most large city school systems fall into the fiscally dependent category, so that a disproportionately large number of teachers work in such systems.

School districts vary widely in terms of grade levels. Most school districts include grades from kindergarten through the twelfth grade. Some school districts, particularly on the West Coast, include junior college grades 13 and 14; others are limited either to elementary grades (K to 8) or to secondary grades (9 to 12).

Student population also varies widely among districts. New York City has the largest school district in the United States, with over one million students; many districts throughout the country enroll fewer than 100 students. Approximately 20 percent of the school districts in the United States enroll over 75 percent of the total student population.

EMPLOYMENT IN PUBLIC EDUCATION

In 1967, 3,797,000 persons were employed in public education on a full-time-equivalent basis by federal, state, and local governments. This figure represents 32.1 percent of all public employees and 5 percent of total employment in the United States.[5]

Of the total number of persons employed in public education in 1967, 83.3 percent worked for local governments, 16.2 percent for state governments, and 0.5 percent for the federal government. The 3.2 million local government employees who worked in the field of education represented 26.7 percent of all public employees.[6]

From 1957 to 1962, total public employment in the United States increased by 1.3 million persons, or by 18.2 percent. Nearly one-half of this net rise was accounted for by an increase in employment in education—the increase amounted to 639,000, or to 30 percent. For all other public employment combined, there was a net increase of 656,000 persons, or 13 percent.

Employment in public education in relation to population

varied from 94 to 162 employees per 10,000 inhabitants. The wide variation resulted from numerous factors, including interstate differences in the age distribution of population, proportion of all pupils enrolled in public as opposed to private schools, and size of public school classes.[7]

Approximately 72 percent of all employees of local school systems are classroom teachers. Principals, consultants, librarians, guidance personnel, psychological personnel, and other nonsupervisory instructional personnel account for another 6 percent. Thus, total instructional staff accounts for about 78 percent of the employment in public education at the local level. The only other groups of any appreciable size are custodians, cafeteria workers, and transportation personnel.[8]

For 1968–1969, the total number of classroom teachers in public schools was estimated at 1,918,245, which represents a gain of 3 percent over the revised estimate of 1,863,260 for 1967–1968. From 1958–1959 to 1968–1969, the total number of classroom teachers increased by 48.4 percent. It is projected that by 1977 there will be 2,044,000 classroom teachers in public schools.[9]

Employment in public education varies widely among school districts. Large city school systems each employ over 10,000 classroom teachers, with over 50,000 teachers working in New York City. At the other end of the scale are the districts that have only one school, employ about twenty-five teachers, and have a superintendent, who serves as principal of the school and also teaches part time.

Although approximately 70 percent of all teachers are female, the percentage of male teachers has increased in recent years. Men now constitute a majority in high schools and have recently made strong inroads into the lower grades as well.[10] The average number of years spent by teachers in preparing for their profession and in improving their abilities is increasing. A large number of teachers, particularly unmarried females in their twenties and thirties are not committed to teaching as a career. Turnover rates remain high—at about 14 percent. Male teachers hold second jobs more frequently than does any other occupational group in the United States.

Male teachers frequently move into administrative positions or to other occupations, because the maximum salary of teachers is relatively low. In a 1960 study of median earnings, male teachers ranked thirty-two among forty-nine professional-technical groups.[11]

Development of Collective Bargaining in Public Education

Public education is one of the most rapidly developing sectors of public-employee collective bargaining in the United States. Prior to 1962, no board of education in the United States was required by law to negotiate with its teachers, and only a handful of boards of education had signed written collective bargaining agreements. By early 1969, however, dramatic changes had taken place. Twelve states had passed laws requiring school boards to engage in some kind of negotiations with their teachers, and over 1,500 school boards had some type of written negotiation procedure. The two national teacher organizations, the National Education Association and the American Federation of Teachers, had made important changes in their policies on collective bargaining. Even more important, citizens and educators were astonished by the rash of teacher strikes and work stoppages, including a three-week statewide strike in Florida.

LEGAL FRAMEWORK

Public school teachers, along with all other employees of federal, state, and local governments, are specifically excluded from federal labor legislation. Regulation of employment relations in public education is left to the states. The statutes regulating bargaining by teachers that have been passed vary widely.

The statutes in Wisconsin (1961), Michigan (1965), and Massachusetts (1965) follow closely the National Labor Relations Act and state labor relations statutes. All three statutes cover all public employees within the state. Exclusive representation is provided; unit determinations are made on a case-by-case basis; representation procedures including secret-ballot elections are provided; unfair labor practices are enumerated; the scope of negotiations is limited to wages, hours, and working conditions;

strikes are prohibited; and impasse procedures such as mediation and fact-finding are provided. All three statutes are administered by state labor relations boards, which also administer statutes covering private employees within their respective states.

Seven other states have passed employment relations statutes applying only to certified public school personnel—California, Connecticut, Maryland, Minnesota, Oregon, Rhode Island, and Washington. The California (1965), Oregon (1965), and Minnesota (1967) statutes provide for teacher councils based on proportional representation instead of exclusive recognition. Members on the teacher council in Oregon are elected directly by all teachers in the district; representatives in California and Minnesota are chosen by the teacher organizations in proportion to their membership strength in each school district. The scope of negotiations under the Oregon law is limited to salaries and related *economic* policies. Under the Minnesota law, good-faith bargaining is required on economic matters, but only discussion and consultation are provided for noneconomic topics. The statutes of these three states do not require good-faith bargaining on most topics, and only the Minnesota statute requires school boards to sign written collective bargaining agreements.

The Connecticut statute (1965) provides a mechanism whereby teachers and administrators can decide whether they should be in the same bargaining unit or in separate units. The Washington law (1965) does not require good-faith bargaining, but mandates a broad scope of negotiations including such topics as "proposed school policies relating to, but not limited to curriculum, textbook selection, in-service training, student teaching programs, personnel, hiring and assignment practices, leaves of absence, salaries and salary schedules, and non-institutional duties." A unique feature of the Rhode Island statute (1966) is its provision for binding arbitration of new contract disputes not involving the expenditure of money. The statute also permits the parties to choose the agency they wish to administer the impasse procedure. As of March 1968, only one case had been submitted to binding arbitration under the Rhode Island statute. In this case, the arbitrator ruled that the legislature intended the scope of bargaining to be the same as that in private employment.[12]

The New York statute, commonly known as the Taylor Act, (1967) provides collective bargaining rights for all public employees, including teachers. The statute permits flexibility, frequently allowing the parties to decide the procedure that best fits their own circumstances. The type of recognition procedure, bargaining unit, and impasse procedure are all decided by the parties. A separate agency called the Public Employee Relations Board (PERB) has been established to administer the statute. Strikes are prohibited, while penalties such as loss of checkoff, fines, and imprisonment of organization leaders are imposed against the organization leading a strike. In 1968, the statute was amended to include penalties against individual strikers. The New Jersey statute (1968) resembles the Taylor Law by establishing a Public Employment Relations Commission (PERC) to administer the law.

REASONS FOR TEACHER MILITANCY

Public elementary and secondary school teachers are "at the head of the class" in the collective bargaining movement by public employees. Why has this group of traditionally peaceful public employees recently displayed such militancy and moved so rapidly to collective bargaining? The following are some causal factors partially explaining this complex phenomenon.

CHANGES IN THE LABOR FORCE

The changing composition of the total labor force has caused union leaders to look toward white-collar and professional workers, who traditionally have been difficult to organize. As part of its attempt to organize white-collar workers, AFL-CIO has given active support to the American Federation of Teachers in its drive to unionize teachers. Public school teachers, if successfully organized, could improve the image of unions in the eyes of other white-collar workers.

Most of the labor support for organizing teachers has come from Walter Reuther, formerly head of the Industrial Union Department[13] of AFL-CIO. In 1963, Reuther revealed that two IUD organizers had been assigned to the American Federation of Teachers and three full-time organizers were being subsidized by IUD. Furthermore, financial support was being furnished to AFT for twenty-three part-time organizers.[14]

In addressing the 1964 AFT convention, Nicholas Zonarich, director of organization of IUD said:

I have not come here to dictate the policies of the AFT, nor has the Industrial Union Department ever indicated at any time that this was our aim, because it is not. All we say is this—that I have come here to tell you we are with you—and we are here to support you—and we are going to continue that support.[15]

Later in his speech, Zonarich pledged that IUD would match, dollar for dollar, any funds AFT spent for organizing.

The AFT used IUD support to initiate its "Co-Ord" plan, "a new massive cooperative organization program utilizing the resources of the national, state, and local AFT Federations along with aid from the Industrial Union Department (IUD). . . ." In 1964, James Mundy, director of organization for AFT, stated: "Within three years . . . we will be able to shoulder complete responsibility for our operations, but without the interest and the aid for the rest of the labor movement we would not be able to get started."[16]

ORGANIZATIONAL RIVALRY

The National Education Association and its affiliates have responded rapidly to the attempts of the American Federation of Teachers to gain representation rights for teachers. NEA has developed its program of professional negotiation and sanctions, and has demonstrated that it can be as militant as AFT. As a result, intense competition occurs between the two organizations in their attempts to represent teachers. The competition has been extremely fierce in representation elections for the selection of bargaining agents.

Each organization gives widespread publicity to its achievements; its rival publicizes its losses and failures. The competition spurs local and state affiliates to push for increased benefits for teachers, and raises teacher expectations and demands.[17]

LARGER SCHOOL DISTRICTS

The consolidation of school districts, noted previously in this chapter, has been identified as a further cause of the rapid development of negotiation procedures. Apparently the merging of small school districts in order to obtain economies of scale further separates the classroom teacher from the decision makers in the district. The additional levels of supervision necessitated by the increase in the size of the district tend to enhance the need and the desire of the teacher for protection by an organization specifically devoted to his interests. Furthermore, large districts are more subject to organizing activities by teacher associations and unions, because of the economies of scale in organizational activities.

CHANGES IN TEACHER ATTITUDES

The "new breed of teachers" may be a major cause of the rapid development of collective bargaining in education. The percentage of male teachers has increased, and the turnover rates for all teachers have decreased in recent years. These changes have occurred particularly in secondary and junior high schools, where teachers appear to be more militant than in elementary schools. The changes indicate the development of a greater commitment to a teaching career. As a result, more teachers desire a voice in the determination of their working conditions and of certain policy questions in education.

EXECUTIVE ORDER 10988

President Kennedy's Executive Order 10988, which granted negotiation rights to federal employees, probably had some "spill over" effects among public school teachers as well as other public employees. If federal employees could have the right to negotiate on working conditions, why not other public employees?

By the same token, once a few state legislatures pass a negotiation statute for public school teachers, it becomes much easier for other state legislatures to do so. Similarly, the obstacles faced by a school board in signing a collective bargaining agreement with teachers decrease when other school boards sign similar agreements. This snowball effect is not confined to the development of collective bargaining in education; it occurs with many social changes.[18]

Teacher Organizations

Two national organizations represent teachers in the United States: the National Education Association (NEA) and the American Federation of Teachers (AFT).

The structure of the National Education Association and its affiliates is quite different from labor unions in the United States. The NEA is a national organization which enrolls members directly from school districts and other educational agencies. State and local education associations enroll their members and collect dues separately, and these associations affiliate with NEA by paying an annual $5 fee. The national organization does not actively charter locals, as do most labor unions.

Only 67 percent of the members of state associations have joined NEA. The percentages vary widely among states: 100 percent of state association members in nine states and less than 30 percent in three states. Recently, NEA has encouraged unified membership by decreeing that a person cannot join only one of the local, state, or national organizations but must join all three. In 1968, nine states had unified membership.

The loose structure of NEA has important implications for its activities in collective bargaining. The NEA cannot exercise strong control over the activities of its state and local affiliates. It can only provide assistance when requested, and state and local affiliates can act independently, even contrary to the policy or advice, of the national organization.

The national organization has more than one million members consisting of "classroom teachers, school administrators, and specialists in schools, colleges, and educational agencies which are both public and private." Classroom teachers in public schools constitute over 85 percent of the total membership. One of the major beliefs of NEA, however, is that since education is a profession unique unto itself, membership in associations should not be limited to classroom teachers. Most state and local affiliates therefore accept both teachers and administrators as members. In fact, several state associations will not accept local affiliates unless they are open to both classroom teachers and administrators. According to the NEA *Handbook:*

> The NEA is an independent, voluntary nongovernmental organization available to all professional teachers. It believes that all educators, regardless of position, rank, or authority, are workers in

a common cause. It cooperates with all groups in American life who seek to improve education. It works for better schools and, to further that end, for the improvement of the professional status of teachers. Under such policies, the National Education Association has become the largest professional organization in the world and the only over-all professional association for teachers in the United States.[19]

The NEA has thirty-four departments (Figure 1), twenty-five commissions and committees, eighteen headquarters divisions, and a staff of over nine hundred. Its research division is staffed by twenty professional and administrative personnel and about thirty-five skilled clerical, secretarial, and statistical workers. It has a state-level affiliate in each of the fifty states and a local affiliate in over 8,000 school districts.

The thirty-four departments reflect the diversity of the activities of NEA. The largest department is that of classroom teachers, which includes approximately 800,000 teachers in elementary and secondary schools. Until 1969 school administrators were members of departments such as the American Association of School Administrators (AASA), the National Association of Secondary School Principals (NASSP), and the Department of Elementary School Principals (DESP).

In June 1969, the superintendent group and the secondary-school-principal group severed their ties as departments and became "Associate Organizations" within the NEA framework. In this category they operate as highly autonomous organizations, and neither their officers nor their members are required to become members of NEA.

The state education associations with almost 1.6 million members, representing 89 percent of the instructional staff, have had a substantial impact on education in the United States. Dayton D. McKean documented the power of the New Jersey teachers' lobby in the 1930s;[20] Virgil Blanke found that chief state school officers perceived education interest groups (the state NEAS were prominent in these groups) as having about average influence with legislators.[21] According to Campbell:

> Each legislative session in each state finds state association lob-byists working feverishly for passage of teacher welfare bills. Elaborate mechanisms for enlisting grass roots support for all kinds

Figure 1—ORGANIZATION CHART

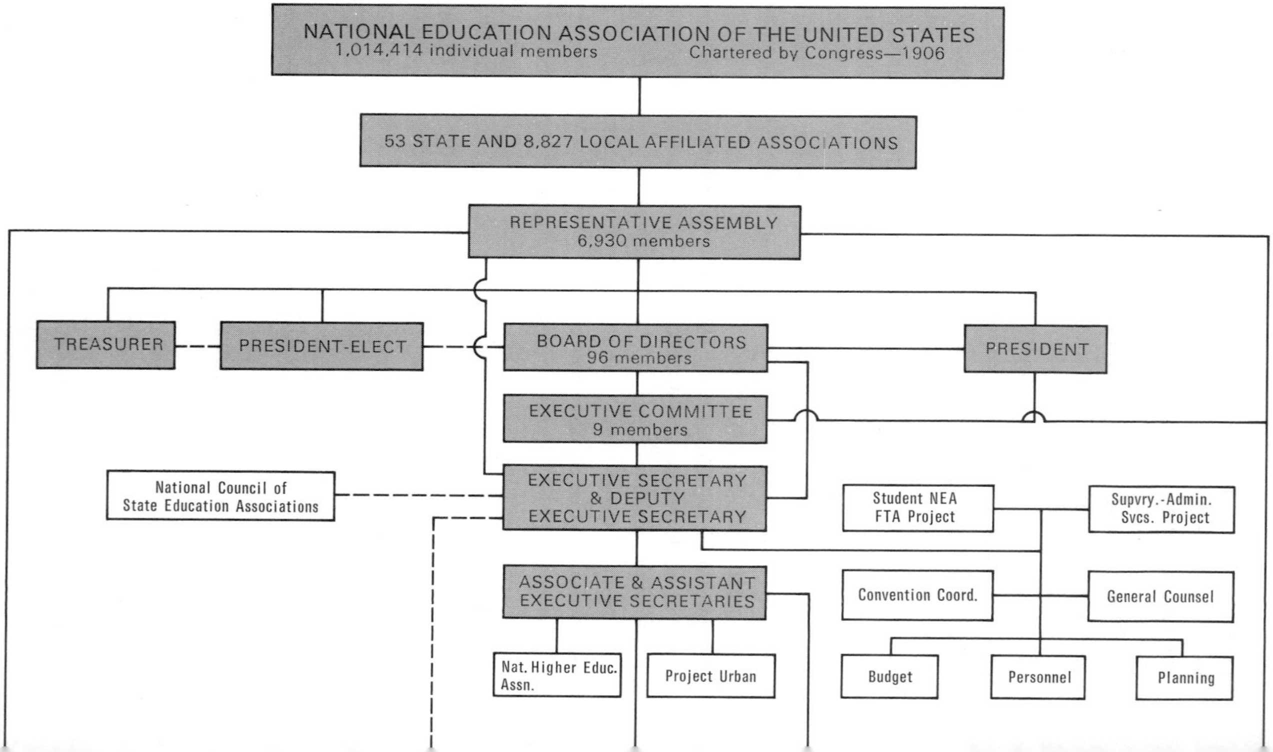

NATIONAL EDUCATION ASSOCIATION OF THE UNITED STATES
Chartered by Congress—1906
1,014,414 individual members

53 STATE AND 8,827 LOCAL AFFILIATED ASSOCIATIONS

REPRESENTATIVE ASSEMBLY
6,930 members

PRESIDENT

PRESIDENT-ELECT

TREASURER

BOARD OF DIRECTORS
96 members

EXECUTIVE COMMITTEE
9 members

EXECUTIVE SECRETARY
& DEPUTY
EXECUTIVE SECRETARY

National Council of
State Education Associations

ASSOCIATE & ASSISTANT
EXECUTIVE SECRETARIES

Nat. Higher Educ.
Assn.

Project Urban

Student NEA
FTA Project

Supvry.-Admin.
Svcs. Project

Convention Coord.

General Counsel

Budget

Personnel

Planning

GOVERNING BOARDS

DEPARTMENTS	NATIONAL AFFILIATES	ASSOCIATED ORGANIZATIONS	HEADQUARTERS DIVISIONS	COMMISSIONS, COMMITTEES & COUNCIL
Classroom Teachers*	Administrative Women	Business Education*	Accounts*	Center for Instruction*	Auditing	NEA and National Congress of Parents and Teachers
Driver Education*	Art Education*	Educational Data Systems*	Adult Education Service*	Legislation & Federal Relations Office*	Budget*	NEA and National School Boards Association
Rural Education*	Audiovisual Instruction*	Exceptional Children*	Business Service*	NEA Journal*	Bylaws and Rules	Planning & Organizational Development*
School Nurses*	Educational Secretaries*	Higher Education*	Data Processing	Organization Relations*	Citzenship*	Professional Ethics
	Elementary/Kindergarten/Nursery*	NTL Institute for Applied Behavorial Science*	DuShane Emergency Fund*	Press, Radio, and TV*	Credentials	Professional Rights and Responsibilities Commission*
	Elementary School Principals*	School Administrators*	Educational Technology*	Publications*	Educational Finance	Resolutions
	Health, Physical Education & Recreation*	School Librarians*	Educational Travel*	Records*	Educational Travel	Safety Commission*
	Home Economics*	School Public Relations*	Field Services and Regional Offices*	Research*	Elections	Special Services*
	Industrial Arts*	Science Teachers*	Human Relations Center*	Special Services*	International Relations*	Teacher Education and Professional Standards Commission*
	Journalism Education	Secondary School Principals*			Legislative Commission*	Teacher Retirement Council
	Mathematics Teachers*	Speech			NEA and American Legion	
	Music Educators*	Women Deans & Counselors*			NEA and American Library Association	
	Public School Adult Education*				NEA and American Medical Association	
	Retired Teachers Assn.				NEA and Educational Publishers	
	Social Studies*				NEA and Magazine Publishers Association	
	Student Teaching*					
	Supervision & Curriculum Development*					

* Units marked with asterisks have staffs at the NEA Headquarters.
Source: NEA HANDBOOK, 1969-70, p.16

of educational legislation have been perfected. Local associations and individual members are kept well informed on activities of legislatures and legislators. Score cards and progress charts are maintained and success is measured in terms of bills passed or defeated.[22]

On the other hand, until recently local education associations were usually weak organizations. Although the number of full-time staff members working for local associations has increased rapidly in recent years, less than one hundred local associations have paid staff. In 1960, Myron Lieberman described the local associations as typically engaging "in futile efforts to improve their conditions of employment. Other than this, they give teas for new teachers in the Spring, and perhaps listen to a few travelogues in between."[23]

AMERICAN FEDERATION OF TEACHERS

The American Federation of Teachers, affiliated with AFL-CIO, was formed in 1919. The stated objectives of AFT are:

1. To bring associations of teachers into relations of mutual assistance and cooperation.
2. To obtain for them all the rights to which they are entitled.
3. To raise the standards of the teaching profession by securing the conditions essential to the best professional service.
4. To promote such a democratization of the schools as will enable them better to equip their pupils to take places in the industrial, social, and political life of the community.
5. To promote the welfare of the childhood of the nation by providing progressively better educational opportunity for all.[24]

With approximately 450 local affiliates, AFT has approximately 140,000 members, most of whom are concentrated in large cities. The AFT permits each local to decide whether it will accept principals as members; its constitution excludes school superintendents from membership. Separate locals for administrators are now prohibited; prior to 1966 they were permitted only if the local AFT affiliate approved. The AFT constantly emphasizes that it is the only organization specifically devoted to the interests of the classroom teacher.

Although NEA and AFT have been in competition since 1919,

the struggle gained new impetus in December 1961, when the United Federation of Teachers, a local affiliate of AFT, was elected bargaining agent for 44,000 New York City public school teachers. The UFT received nearly three times as many votes as NEA's hastily formed contender, the Teachers Bargaining Organization. More important though was the fact that for the first time the labor movement gave active support, in the form of personnel and financial resources, to a local of AFT. If AFT could run a successful nationwide membership drive, the image of unions in the eyes of other white-collar and professional workers would be greatly improved.[25] For this reason UFT received more aid than any other union local had so far received in a collective bargaining election.[26] Shortly after the victory, AFT joined the Industrial Union Department of AFL-CIO, which had been the major contributor to UFT.

After its overwhelming victory, UFT immediately began negotiating with the school board. When negotiations broke down in April 1962, UFT called a strike and over 20,000 teachers refused to work. The work stoppage lasted only one day, however, and after the mayor of the city and the governor of the state became involved, a salary agreement was reached. By the end of August, the parties had negotiated a forty-page written agreement, which was surpassed in its detailed provisions only by later agreements reached between the same parties.

CHANGES IN NEA POLICY

While UFT was negotiating its written agreement in the summer of 1962, NEA was holding its annual convention in Denver. Dr. William Carr, executive secretary of NEA, entitled his address "The Turning Point," which aptly describes the dramatic changes that took place in NEA's policy toward collective negotiations at this convention.

In earlier years, NEA had occasionally discussed the necessity for group action by teachers, but it had no organized program and issued no guidelines or directives for implementation. At the 1962 convention NEA official policy on negotiations was formulated. NEA passed a resolution emphasizing the need for "professional negotiation," thus ending its search for a suitable substitute for the term "collective bargaining." In earlier years, other terms sug-

gested included "cooperative determination," "collective determination," and even "democratic persuasion."

Another 1962 convention resolution of particular significance
is resolution 19 entitled "Professional Sanctions":

> The National Education Association believes that, as a means of
> preventing unethical or arbitrary policies or practices that have a
> deleterious effect on the welfare of the schools, professional sanc-
> tions should be invoked. These sanctions would provide for appro-
> priate disciplinary action by the organized profession.
>
> The National Education Association calls upon its affiliated state
> associations to cooperate in developing guidelines which would
> define, organize, and definitely specify procedural steps for in-
> voking sanctions by the teaching profession.[27]

This resolution, which was introduced from the floor of the convention instead of by the resolution committee, marks the beginning of the official adoption of a pressure tactic by NEA.

The main significance of Carr's speech to the 1962 convention
was that it set the stage for the battle between AFT and NEA. Carr
identified unionization as a major crisis in education, and he out-
lined the policy NEA would follow to meet the challenge from
the labor movement. "This . . . is the first time in which forces of
significant scope and power are considering measures which
could destroy the Association."[28]

At the February 18, 1962, meeting of the NEA board of directors,
less than two months after the UFT victory in New York City, a
motion was passed urging each state affiliate to hold regional conferences to ". . . explain *why* professional organizations should
exist on an independent basis, with professional responsibility and
autonomy." More extensive conferences dealing with the same
topic were urged in cities with populations over 100,000. State
affiliates were also urged to secure passage of state legislation
implementing NEA policy on professional negotiations.[29]

At the convention itself, Carr explained that the urban project
would be formed to meet the needs of large city teachers and to
direct the NEA fight against unionization of teachers. The urban
project budget was set at $203,900 for fiscal year 1962–1963. In
fiscal year 1964–1965 the urban project cost $884,663, including
$437,990 which had been ". . . spent from the Reserve for Future
Emergencies as authorized by the Board of Directors."[30] By 1968,

the urban project had been elevated to the divisional level in NEA, with a budget of over $1 million out of a total NEA budget of almost $10 million.

In reality "professional negotiation" is a generic term used by NEA for a wide variety of different relationships between school boards and local teacher associations. For example, a local affiliate is considered to have a level-I professional negotiation agreement if the school board has made a written statement (which may be included in the minutes of the board meeting) that it recognizes the association as the representative of all teachers in the district or even merely as the representative of its own members. Level-II agreements consist of recognition and establishment of a negotiations procedure. If a means for settling impasses is added, the agreement is considered level III. When an impasse arises, it provides for various forms of third-party intervention, most of which consist of modified forms of mediation and fact-finding. Level-III agreements rarely provide for the utilization of state labor relations agencies or state mediation agencies, because, NEA believes disputes should always be settled through "educational channels." In extreme cases or when agreement cannot be reached, NEA will resort to sanctions, ranging from publicizing unfavorable teaching conditions in a particular school district to a mass refusal to sign contracts by all teachers employed in the district. At its 1967 convention, NEA took an even more militant stand by voting to support local affiliates who had gone on strike. Level-IV agreements include terms and conditions of employment.

Since 1962, NEA policy on professional negotiations has gradually become firmly established. The association favors exclusive recognition whereby one organization represents all staff members in the district and negotiating units which include both teachers and administrators, although decisions on negotiating units are a matter for local option. The NEA now favors written agreements that include terms and conditions of employment, a grievance procedure with binding arbitration as the terminal point, and a termination date to the agreement.

Clearly, NEA and its affiliates have changed drastically. State-wide and local sanctions and strikes have been used on numerous occasions. Local associations have called strikes or "professional holidays" when agreement on employment conditions has not been reached. At other times they have refused to lead extra curricular activities or have publicized "unprofessional" conditions in a district as a means of enforcing their demands. In brief, NEA and most of its state and local affiliates are now militant and determined organizations.

AFT POLICY ON COLLECTIVE BARGAINING

The AFT makes no effort to distinguish its approach to teacher-board relations from the collective bargaining carried on in private industry. Delegates to the 1963 national convention passed a resolution which recognized the right of locals to strike under certain circumstances and urged ". . . the AFL-CIO and affiliated international unions to support such strikes when they occur."[31] This resolution constituted a change in AFT policy; in prior years, it had no official strike policy, even though it had supported locals when they had gone on strike.

Since 1935, AFT has advocated collective bargaining for teachers; before that time the union had encouraged teachers' councils and more teacher participation in policy-making. Evidence indicates that only after the UFT victory in 1961 did AFT actively begin to encourage its locals to strive for collective bargaining rights. For example, a survey conducted in 1947 showed that none of the forty-one AFT locals, whose members constituted the majority of teachers in their district, had ever engaged in collective bargaining. In answer to the question in the same survey "What further part does the local feel it should play in administration and policy formation?" only seven of 141 respondents answered "bargaining agents."[32]

Until recently, AFT displayed no clear understanding of exactly what collective bargaining for teachers entails. In fact, the confusion over the AFT definition of collective bargaining was similar to that exhibited by NEA on professional negotiations. For example, although AFT claimed to have approximately twelve written agreements between school boards and teachers' unions in 1964, only four of them included terms and conditions of employment; the others were merely recognition agreements. Moreover, several agreements did not provide for exclusive recognition, and in two cases the school boards signed written agreements with both the NEA local and the AFT local.

The agreement negotiated by the United Federation of Teachers in New York City rapidly became the model for agreements negotiated later in other cities. By 1969, AFT locals had won representation rights for teachers in many of the large city school systems in the United States—Baltimore, Boston, Chicago, Cleveland, Philadelphia, Washington, D.C., and Wilmington. They had negotiated collective bargaining agreements covering approximately 10 percent of the classroom teachers in the United States.

The development of collective bargaining in public education has brought NEA and AFT closer together on policies and objectives. Two main differences between the organizations have decreased in importance. First, administrators are withdrawing from NEA and its affiliate as the associations bargain with teachers, often directly across the table from school administrators. Second, the withdrawal from the AFL-CIO of Walter Reuther and UAW, long the major supporter of AFT within the federation, reduces the importance of AFT affiliating with the labor movement. Little difference can now be found between affiliates of NEA and AFT when they represent their members in bargaining. As a result, a possible merger between the two organizations has become a real possibility in the early 1970s. More will be said about this development in Chapter VI.

Collective Bargaining

RECOGNITION AND UNIT DETERMINATION

By 1969, legislation providing for or permitting some form of collective bargaining between teachers and school boards had been enacted in 16 states. Nine state statutes provided for exclusive recognition whereby school boards were required to recognize a single organization chosen by the majority of teachers in the school district. Two states provided for proportional representation, and one state, Oregon, provided for teacher councils. Four states permitted but did not require school boards to recognize teacher organizations. Table IV–2 gives the breakdown of state statutes by form of recognition.

In 1967, 1,426 school districts had written negotiation procedures designating a single teacher organization as exclusive representative of all teachers in the district. Teacher organizations had dual or proportional representation in an additional 88 school districts with written procedures. Teacher councils had been established in 105 school districts with written procedures.[33]

Table IV–2
State Statutes Providing for Recognition of
Teacher Organizations, 1968

EXCLUSIVE RECOGNITION	PROPORTIONAL REPRESENTATION	TEACHER COUNCIL	PERMIT BUT DO NOT REQUIRE RECOGNITION
Connecticut	California	Oregon	Alaska
Maryland	Minnesota		Florida
Massachusetts			Nebraska
Michigan			New Hampshire
New Jersey			
New York			
Rhode Island			
Washington			
Wisconsin			

The policy of NEA on recognition has changed in recent years. Initially, it accepted teacher councils and proportional representation as alternative forms of "professional negotiation." It now strongly favors exclusive recognition, although some of its state affiliates, for example the California Teachers Association, continue to support proportional representation.

State statutes vary with regard to criteria and procedures for unit determination. For instance, the state of Washington requires bargaining units to include all teachers and administrators except superintendents of schools. In Connecticut, principals and other administrators have the option of deciding whether they wish to be represented by the organization representing the teachers. The statutes of most other states give the state labor board or the mediation board the authority to determine bargaining units on a district-by-district basis. In Massachusetts, Michigan, Rhode Island, and Wisconsin, the state labor boards have followed the criteria established by the National Labor Relations Board.

Many school boards have recognized teacher organizations even though they are not required to do so by state legislation. A large number of elections have taken place in states without negotiation statutes. Since 1964 the American Arbitration Association has conducted many representation elections in school districts including Newark, New Jersey; Rochester, New York; Philadelphia, Pennsylvania; and Washington, D.C.

Unit determination has caused some problems for the National Education Association, whose members include both classroom teachers and administrators. Most building principals and other school administrators clearly perform supervisory functions, such as making decisions or recommendations on hiring, promotion, assignment, transfer, tenure, and discharge. The NEA and its affiliates have attempted to de-emphasize the conflict of interest between teachers and administrators, and stress that they are all working for the common goal of educating the children. Most of the legislation proposed by state affiliates of NEA provides for all-inclusive bargaining units. The NEA recognizes, however, that some classroom teachers prefer to confine membership in their organization to classroom teachers only. Sometimes administrators also prefer to be represented by a separate organization. The policy of NEA is to emphasize the advantages of all-inclusive bargaining units, but to permit its members to decide the composition of the bargaining unit on a local basis.

Interesting deviations from the national policy of NEA and AFT on unit determination have occurred in local school districts. For example, a local of AFT in Wisconsin attempted to establish a separate bargaining unit for secondary school teachers, probably because it enrolled very few elementary teachers as members. In Philadelphia, the NEA affiliate attempted to exclude department chairmen from the bargaining unit on the grounds that they were supervisors. The AFT affiliate in Philadelphia favored including department chairmen in the bargaining unit, probably because the president of the Philadelphia Federation of Teachers was a department chairman. The decision was submitted to a neutral moderator, who ruled in favor of AFT. An important lesson to be learned from experience is that local affiliates of both organizations will often attempt to establish a bargaining unit coterminous with their greatest strength.

Another important development in collective bargaining in

public education has occurred among employees excluded from the basic teacher bargaining unit. Nonprofessional employees, particularly cafeteria workers, secretaries, bus drivers, and maintenance workers, have pressed for bargaining rights once the board of education started negotiating with a teacher organization. Principals and other administrators excluded from teacher bargaining units have also attempted to bargain with the school board, even though they perform supervisory functions. The principals in Michigan schools have lobbied to amend the Michigan negotiations statute to include their group, but so far no changes have been made in the statute. In many cases the efforts of these groups to obtain bargaining rights have been successful.

SCOPE OF BARGAINING AND WRITTEN AGREEMENTS

The decentralized education system in the United States places ultimate responsibility for public education in the fifty states, which in turn in almost all instances, delegate this power to local boards of education. Nevertheless, state legislation, state education department rulings, and state constitutions establish requirements that must be adhered to by local districts. The following section describes some of the state-level provisions affecting local collective bargaining.

DECISION MAKING ON STATE LEVEL

Examples of state legislation that have affected salaries and working conditions of teachers are numerous. Thirty-one states have minimum-salary laws for teachers, and in most cases these laws also establish a minimum salary for teachers at the upper levels of the salary schedule. For example, if the minimum for a starting teacher with a bachelor's degree is $4,500, school districts will be required to pay teachers with ten years' experience a minimum salary of $6,500. All states currently have legislated pension and retirement programs for public school teachers.[34]

In some states, legislation has been passed providing each teacher with a duty-free lunch period. These laws have been called "right to eat" laws. Where such legislation does not exist, teachers often must supervise students during their lunch hours.

Another subject of bargaining occasionally affected by legislation is the grievance procedure. For example, in Pennsylvania and New York, legislation requires each school district to establish a grievance procedure according to certain standards enunciated in the statutes.

Each state has a law requiring districts to keep schools open a certain number of days and a certain number of hours each day in order to qualify for state funds for the operation of the schools. Laws sometimes regulate the maximum size of classes in both secondary and elementary schools.

Thirty-seven states have passed laws giving tenure of employment to teachers after they serve a probationary period—usually three years. Once tenure is received, a teacher can be dismissed only for causes that are usually stated in the tenure law. While the grounds justifying termination of employment vary widely among states, the most usual causes written into the laws, in order of frequency, are immorality or immoral conduct; incompetence; insubordination; inefficiency; persistent violation of, or refusal to obey, school board rules; and neglect of duty. Moreover, most tenure laws provide for dismissal because of contingencies such as reduction in pupil enrollment, abolition of position, or reduction of teaching staff. Some laws outline a seniority procedure under which reductions in force and reemployment will occur.[35]

Sometimes state departments of education issue rulings that affect the working conditions of teachers. For example, under some state laws, school districts must offer specific courses in both secondary and elementary schools—for example, a course in the history of that particular state. Some state laws mandate that teachers use certain textbooks in specific courses; however, courses and selection of textbooks are more commonly determined by the state department of education.

Provisions in state constitutions frequently affect the working conditions of teachers. Minimum school terms are provided in the state constitutions of Arizona, California, Colorado, Kansas, Michigan, Mississippi, Montana, Nevada, New Mexico, North Carolina, and Virginia. The California state constitution specifies a minimum salary for public school teachers.

Constitutional amendments in some states also affect the curriculum and the adoption of textbooks. The Louisiana constitution provides for control of the entire elementary school curriculum; the North Dakota constitution provides for "teaching truth, temperance, purity, public spirit, and respect for honest labor"; the Utah constitution provides for instruction in the metric system; the Oklahoma constitution provides for courses in agriculture; and the Arizona, Michigan, Nebraska, New Mexico, and Oklahoma constitutions require instruction in the English language. The Colorado and Utah state constitutions specifically prohibit the adoption of textbooks by the legislature or the state board of education.The Wyoming constitution prohibits adoption of textbooks by the state superintendent or the legislature. On the other hand, constitutions in California, New Mexico, and North Carolina provide for uniform state textbook adoption.[36]

The preceding description of subjects decided by state legislatures, state education departments, or constitutions does not mean that local school districts have little decision-making power. Actually, they have much autonomy within the overall requirements set at the state level.

The state level decisions, however, have significant implications for teachers and their organizations. For this reason, state teacher organizations have traditionally concentrated their efforts on improvements in working conditions in lobbying activities at the state level. Lobbying has been successful in some cases, but it is a highly unpredictable method and subject to the vagaries of the legislative process. As a result, teachers are resorting to statewide strikes and sanctions to enforce their demands.

Teachers are now also increasing their efforts at the local level, where they can become more intimately involved in decision-making. Ultimate responsibility at the local level lies with the local board of education, a much smaller legislative body than the state legislature. Even more important, because the board of education and its administrative staff is the employer of the teachers, the parties are able to agree on specific working conditions for the teachers in a given community. This arrangement is more satisfactory than regulation by general statewide rules, which naturally must apply to many highly diverse school districts.

SCOPE OF BARGAINING

Teacher organizations are increasingly adopting local-level collective bargaining as a method of obtaining a share in decision-making in public education. The kind of collective bargaining taking place parallels collective bargaining in private employment, but it is modified to account for the unique environment of public education. An increasing number of boards of education and local teacher organizations are signing formal collective bargaining agreements that detail specifically the salaries and the working conditions of the teachers employed in the district. In 1967, 1,531, or 25 percent, of all school districts in the United States had some type of written negotiations agreement with its teachers. Over 41 percent of the teaching staff in the United States was employed in these districts. In contrast, in 1965 only about 1 percent of all school districts had written negotiations procedures, and in 1963 only one-tenth of 1 percent had such procedures.[37]

Agreements signed in different school districts are frequently similar. Several state associations have formulated model agreements, which are distributed to local affiliates and often adopted with little change by local boards of education. Agreements negotiated by both AFT and NEA affiliates are printed and distributed to other affiliates for organizational purposes. NEA has fed over 1,500 agreements into its computer to categorize them according to specific clauses. Furthermore, the Urban Service Division of NEA employs a highly experienced labor law firm to assist its affiliates in negotiations. The firm tends to use a common format for all its agreements, making changes to accommodate local conditions.

Most collective bargaining agreements in public education are patterned after agreements in private employment. These agreements tend to be highly legalistic, and are often more than fifty pages long.

The first provision in the agreement is usually a recognition clause stating that the board of education recognizes the teacher organization as the exclusive bargaining representative of all teachers in the school district.

The Board hereby recognized the LSEA as the exclusive bargaining representative, as defined in Section II of Act 379, Public Acts of 1965, for professional personnel, including personnel on tenure, probation and per diem appointments, classroom teachers, guidance counselors, librarians, school psychologists and social workers, remedial reading teachers, advanced instruction teachers, helping teachers, teachers of home-bound or hospitalized, attendance or truant officers, school nurses, tenure teachers holding a letter of assignment to federal or state programs administered by the Board, employed by the Board, but excluding supervisory and executive personnel.

Another clause found in most collective agreements in public education reaffirms the authority vested by statute in the board of education.

There is reserved exclusively to the Board all responsibilities, powers, rights, and authority expressly or inherently vested in it by the laws and Constitutions of Michigan and the United States, excepting where expressly and in specific terms limited by the provisions of this Agreement. It is agreed that the Board retains the right to establish and enforce in accordance with this Agreement and its authority under law reasonable rules and personnel policies relating to the duties and responsibilities of teachers and their working conditions including, but without limiting the generality of, the foregoing to: the management and control of school properties, facilities, grades and courses of instruction, materials used for instruction, and the selection, direction, transfer, promotion or demotion, discipline or dismissal of all personnel.

A clause or series of clauses lists and explains the rights of the teacher organization. The teacher negotiators almost always attempt to obtain released time, without loss of pay, for conducting contract negotiations and organization activities. Boards of education almost always give the organization the right to hold meetings in school buildings. For a small service charge they agree to deduct organizational dues from the teachers' salaries, thereby guaranteeing a steady income to the organization.

After spelling out recognition and organizational rights, typical agreements consist mainly of clauses detailing working conditions for the teachers in the district. Salary schedules and supplemental pay—severance pay, health and medical insurance, summer school pay, and tuition reimbursement—are included either as appendixes or as clauses in the agreement. Working conditions usually covered include the school calendar, length of the school day, length and frequency of faculty meetings, relief from non-teaching duties, alleviation of overcrowded conditions, teacher lounges, and parking spaces for teachers' cars. Also usually included are clauses covering promotion, reassignment, and transfer of teachers. Teachers are frequently guaranteed the right to see their personnel file.

Most agreements are in effect for one or two years, after which time they are extended or renegotiated. During the term of the agreement, questions frequently arise relating to the interpretation of some clause in the agreement. The grievance procedure, found in most comprehensive collective negotiation agreements, details a procedure for interpreting the agreement.

Grievance procedures consist of four or five steps for resolving complaints submitted by teachers concerning the interpretation of the agreement. The complaint first goes to the principal or immediate supervisor of the teachers. If the complaint is not resolved, the teacher may appeal to an associate superintendent or to the superintendent of schools. If the teacher is still dissatisfied, he may then appeal to the board of education.

Prior to 1965, the final step in the grievance procedure almost always was review by the board of education. In grievance procedures established in the absence of collective bargaining, appeal to the board of education usually remains as the final step. Since 1965, however, an increasing number of collective negotiation agreements use binding arbitration as the terminal point of the grievance procedure. In 1968, the Michigan Labor Mediation Board ruled that grievance arbitration was a mandatory subject of collective bargaining in education. Under grievance arbitration, the parties agree in advance to accept as binding the decision of a neutral person they select to serve as arbitrator. The arbitrator rules on the grievance, using as his criterion the collective agreement negotiated by the parties. In 1966–1967, 24 percent of all written agreements contained grievance procedures, 85 percent of which provided for final appeal to an agency outside the school district. Of the negotiated arbitration procedures, 41.4 percent provide for binding arbitration and 58.6 percent provide for advisory arbitration.[38]

EDUCATIONAL POLICY AND WORKING CONDITIONS

Many provisions in collective bargaining agreements in education, such as class size clauses, involve matters of educational policy as well as working conditions. A large class affects a teacher's working conditions since he must grade additional papers and supervise more students. Class size also affects the quality of education, the design of school buildings, and the methods of instruction—all matters of educational policy.

Most comprehensive collection agreements contain clauses establishing committees to discuss various topics. The most common kinds of groups are professional study, consultation, or liaison committees, which discuss broad educational policies. Approximately 30 percent of all committees focus on personnel policies, and about 20 percent discuss instructional programs.[39]

Another provision of teacher collective bargaining agreements that involves both working conditions and educational policy relates to teacher transfers. Many school districts have recently attempted to integrate their faculty and students as a result of court decisions and government agency orders. Citizens and civil rights groups have applied pressure to boards of education for more rapid integration. In their attempts at integrating school faculties, boards of education have met with opposition from teacher organizations, which suggest that choice of assignment and transfer of teachers be based on length of service. Teacher organizations claim that teacher transfer policies affect working conditions because the distance a teacher must travel to his job affects his satisfaction with it. On the other hand, if length of service is used as the criterion for teacher transfer, experienced teachers will be concentrated in upper-middle-class neighborhoods because many teachers prefer not to teach in the slums. As a result, inexperienced teachers will gravitate to schools in slum areas which, other things being equal, presumably will result in poorer educational opportunities in those areas.

In addition to affecting educational policy, voluntary teacher transfer policies also affect public policy when they result in segregated school faculties. Segregated faculties may result because teachers prefer to teach students of their own race. On the other hand, segregated housing and the natural tendency of teachers to work close to their homes may be a further cause of segregated faculties. In any case, teacher transfer provisions are clearly matters of educational policy, public policy, and working conditions.

Handling children difficult to discipline has recently become a subject of great concern to citizens in large cities. Any regulation on the removal of children from a classroom is a matter of educational policy, public policy, and working conditions. School administrators almost always have the power to isolate disruptive children into separate classes or schools, and they sometimes believe it is educationally desirable to do so. Teachers claim that, in addition to their task being easier and more pleasant, their productivity increases when they do not have to spend time handling disciplinary cases. In some cases, teachers charge that principals are reluctant to remove unruly children from classes because the principals are afraid that such removal is a reflection on their ability to run their schools. Moreover, some citizen groups are increasingly concerned about what becomes of the students who are isolated into separate classes or schools; they believe that isolation may make it more difficult for such students to become productive members of society.

The essential point of this discussion of the interrelationship of educational policy, public policy, and teacher working conditions is to show that bargaining on certain working conditions may decide policy matters. As the scope of bargaining increases to these interrelated topics, teachers assume a voice in policy matters, a step that has implications far beyond problems associated with the scope of bargaining in private employment. Teachers may claim that increasing the scope of bargaining to policy areas is another step toward their becoming "true professionals," but valid objections can be raised to giving such power to tenured employees instead of to a legislative body.

ORGANIZATION SECURITY

Organization security promises to be an important topic of teacher negotiations in future years. Historically, a significant number of NEA affiliates relied upon school administrators to recruit members from teacher associations. In 1958–1959, an NEA study reported that 6.3 percent of local associations depended upon principals and superintendents to recruit members, 14.5 percent depended on them to recruit state association members, and 12.3 percent depended on them to recruit NEA members. The study also reported that, on the average, the small local associations tended to rely more heavily on administrators for recruitment than did the larger associations.[40] In a 1964 survey of teachers from three different sections of Pennsylvania, 48 percent of the respondents reported that administrative pressure was placed upon them to join a teacher association.[41]

The AFT asserts that NEA still relies upon administrators to recruit most of its members and that the organization is dominated by the administrators. In recent years, however, an important change seems to have taken place in NEA and most of its affiliates. Administrator recruitment of association members appears to have been reduced substantially. Superintendents and school-building principals in Michigan have withdrawn from the Michigan Education Association. In 1965, the NEA representative assembly voted to ". . . raise classroom teacher representation as rapidly as practicable to majority status on all committees, commissions, or appointed boards."[42]

The decreased reliance upon school administrators as recruiting agents for local associations places added pressure on associations to work for organization security provisions. The Michigan Education Association and the Wisconsin Education Association adopted resolutions favoring the agency shop for local associations whereby a teacher would be required to pay a service fee to the association as a condition of employment, but the teacher would not be required to join the organization. An increasing number of local associations had negotiated agency shop clauses by the end of 1969.

The AFT and its affiliates inadvertently placed themselves in an awkard position regarding organization security. In line with their constant criticism of NEA for administrator domination and recruitment, AFT has emphasized that any teacher should be free to join or refrain from joining the American Federation of Teachers. Any attempt to negotiate agency shop or union shop clauses would open the door to criticism from NEA. Thus AFT has not encouraged organization security clauses other than dues deduction and union representation in grievances. In late 1968, no AFT locals had negotiated agency shop or union shop clauses. One AFT local, the United Federation of Teachers in New York City, negotiated an alternative means of organizational security. In its 1965 negotiations, the New York City Board of Education agreed to give the union $140 per teacher per year to be used for a union-administered welfare fund. The fund—"UFT Welfare Fund"—was intended to cover every teacher in New York City regardless of whether he was a member of UFT. Many teachers apparently thought they had to be members of the union in order to gain welfare fund benefits. Within three years after the welfare fund had been negotiated, membership in UFT increased from approximately 30,000 to 52,000.

CONDUCT OF NEGOTIATIONS

The manner in which negotiations are conducted has varied widely among school districts. School superintendents rarely have experience or training in labor relations. In large systems, an administrator is usually designated "associate superintendent for personnel" or "personnel director," but these persons are accustomed to dealing with individual employees and not with employee organizations. Traditionally, the superintendent of schools has been described as the executive officer of the school board and the educational leader of the school district. In this dual capacity, he has been responsible for both administering the school district and being familiar with educational policies such as curriculum, selection of faculty members, and methods of instruction. In this latter capacity, some superintendents have considered themselves leaders of the teaching staff and have attempted to play leadership roles in local teacher organizations.

Recently, critics of the superintendent's traditional role have claimed that it is unreasonable to expect a school superintendent to perform both functions, because of the inherent conflict of interest and of the enormity of the job. On the other hand, the American Association of School Administrators, a professional association for school superintendents, favors maintaining the dual function of the superintendent and his playing a neutral role in collective bargaining.

The development of collective bargaining will probably help clarify the role of the superintendent. More and more, school boards are directing superintendents to represent their interests in negotiations. At the same time, classroom teachers are increasingly choosing local, state, and national organizations to represent them in collective bargaining.

School boards have followed three different patterns in conducting collective bargaining. (1) The entire school board or a committee of the board has negotiated directly with the leaders of the teacher organization. Usually under this approach, superintendents either have served as a resource person and fact supplier for both parties, or have been members of the school board negotiating team. In some cases they have not participated in negotiation sessions.

(2) The school board has delegated negotiating authority to the superintendent and his staff. This pattern has been particularly prevalent in large city school systems because much time is required for negotiations. An increasing number of school boards who originally served as negotiators have been delegating this responsibility to the superintendent.

(3) The school board has appointed an attorney or an experienced negotiator to represent it in negotiations. Under this approach, the superintendent appoints a negotiating committee to assist the attorney or the experienced negotiator, who typically reports directly to the school board.

Negotiating sessions are almost always private meetings. Some citizens have objected to the closed sessions on the ground that boards of education are public agencies and their activities should be open to scrutiny by their constituents. In California, the government code provides that all meetings of the school boards, except four, shall be open to the public. In 1968, California boards were not permitted to prepare for negotiations by themselves nor to negotiate privately with the teacher representatives. On the other hand, in 1967 the Massachusetts Attorney General ruled that negotiating sessions were not subject to the state's Open Meeting Law.[43] The Massachusetts law permits school boards to hold executive sessions; such sessions are not permitted in California.

Most large school systems have hired or assigned persons to process grievances and to administer the collective bargaining agreements. Ida Klaus, who is thoroughly conversant with private and public collective bargaining, serves on the New York City school board as director of staff relations. Some of the other large school systems have also hired persons experienced in collective bargaining, but most assign this responsibility to the previously established personnel department.

A number of mediators and arbitrators have reported that individuals acting as school board members behave differently in negotiations than they would as managers in private industry. Because board members volunteer their time for school board matters, they often expect teachers to make special concessions in negotiations. Some board members take a stronger stand in school negotiations than they do when they negotiate for their own private companies. Of course school board members without experience in labor relations are often poor negotiators.

On the other hand, local teacher organizations are hiring full-time executive secretaries whose primary function is to bargain and to process grievances. Some local teacher organizations hire attorneys or consultants; in most cases, however, the national and state organizations assign staff members or attorneys to assist the locals. In general, teacher organizations appear to be developing expertise in labor relations more rapidly than are school boards and school administrators. A group of attorneys and specialists in accounting, insurance, public relations, and teaching—the Public Employees Negotiating and Consultation Service—offers teacher organizations a special-package approach to labor negotiations. For a fee of one dollar per teacher, the group handles all aspects of collective bargaining, including negotiations, press releases, fringe benefit proposals, rallies, and even a newsletter. In its first year of operation, the service handled negotiations for teachers in nine Long Island school districts.

A school district's fiscal structure may also affect the conduct of negotiations. Three alternative negotiating procedures have occurred in fiscally dependent districts. First, some fiscally dependent school boards formulate their own budgets unilaterally and submit them to the reviewing agencies for approval. When they are returned with the guarantee of a definite sum of money, negotiations between the school board and the teacher organization commence. In this procedure, there is no "shadowboxing" in negotiations, because the exact amount of available money is known. The disadvantages of this system are that the teachers have no say in the initial request, and that the actual allocation of funds may be so small as to negate any meaningful bargaining on monetary items.

Second, some school boards conduct negotiations before their budget is submitted to the reviewing agency. If the budget is reduced by the agency, allocations within the budget may be cut according to a prearranged formula. A more common variation of this approach is "before and after bargaining." Under this system, the school board and the teacher organization negotiate, reach an agreement, and then incorporate this agreement in the budget, which is submitted to the reviewing agency. If any changes are made in the budget, a second round of bargaining takes place in order to distribute the modified allocation. Under this plan, the initial bargaining does not actually result in a binding agreement but rather in a joint recommendation to another governmental body.

Third, three-way bargaining takes place among the teacher organization, the school board, and the reviewing agency. Variations of this system range from a formal three-way bargaining session to informal contact with the reviewing agency while the school board and the teacher organization bargain bilaterally. When all three parties are represented at a common meeting, the sessions often develop into a two-way bargaining session, with the reviewing agency on one side of the table and the school board together with the teacher organization on the other side. In this case, instead of making joint recommendations to the reviewing agency, the other two parties have engaged in collective bargaining with the agency.

STATE-WIDE NEGOTIATIONS

Because the largest share of funds for public education comes from state revenues, many teacher organizations will probably concentrate their efforts to increase allocations to education at the state level. It is possible that state-level bargaining will occur on some issues. For example, many states have laws establishing minimum salaries for public school teachers. Instead of amending these laws by legislative action each time increases are required, the legislature could delegate responsibility for setting minimums to a state administrator, whose actions would be limited by legislative guidelines. A state teacher organization could negotiate these minimum salaries as well as other minimum working conditions.

Recent events indicate that state-level bargaining may develop more rapidly in some states. State education associations have called statewide teacher strikes or invoked sanctions in Utah (1964), Oklahoma (1966), and Florida (1968). In 1968 statewide action was threatened in New Mexico, Colorado, South Dakota, and Oklahoma. In the same year, the Pennsylvania State Education Association, not usually known for its militant actions, organized a march on the state capital in an attempt to persuade the governor and the legislature to increase the state-legislated minimum salary. Interestingly, most school boards in Pennsylvania closed their schools on the day of the teachers' march so that teachers would not be considered strikers.

The three-week shutdown in Florida in 1968 was the first time a state teacher association continued a work stoppage until agreement had been reached with the state authorities. Previous statewide work stoppages lasted for a specific period. It is difficult to determine whether the Florida teachers were successful, but they clearly experienced difficulty in persuading the governor and the legislature to act.

Teacher organizations will probably find that they have less bargaining power at the state level, because of the great difficulty in organizing teachers, spread across an entire state, to act in unity. Furthermore, it is probably easier for a governor or a state legislature to shift responsibility for impasses to each other and to local school boards than it is for a local school board to pass the responsibility to anyone else.

STRIKES AND SANCTIONS

Teacher strikes have increased greatly in recent years (see Table IV-3). The peak of strike activity thus far was reached in 1968, when 146,000 teachers were on strike in 94 different school districts. Although teacher strikes are clearly illegal, affiliates of both NEA and AFT seem to turn more and more to the strike or some variation of it. Four teacher organization leaders received jail sentences in 1967 for violating court orders enjoining teacher strikes.

Sanctions have been developed by NEA as a different approach to applying pressure on school boards. The NEA defines sanctions as follows:

Sanctions within the context of this statement are defined as a means to prevent the violation of a right or responsibility. A community should support its schools; school boards should discharge their functions with integrity and impartiality; administrators should use the procedures essential for democratic administration of good schools; teachers should make every effort to provide the best possible learning experiences for students. Against those who fail by such standards, organizations of the educational profession may impose sanctions.

As used by a professional education organization, sanctions mean censure, suspension or expulsion of a member; severance of relationship with an affiliated association or other agency controlling the welfare of the schools; bringing into play forces that will enable the community to help the board or agency to realize its responsibility; or the application of one or more steps in the withholding of services. Sanctions are used only to improve educational opportunities through the elimination of conditions detrimental to effective education. The most severe types of sanctions should be invoked only as a last resort where conditions are such that it is impossible for educators to give effective professional service.[44]

Actually, sanctions include a wide variety of different pressure tactics used by NEA affiliates. Examples include:

Censure through public notice including release of investigation report; articles in national and state journals; reports through various mass media of communication.

Notification to state departments of education of findings concerning unsatisfactory conditions.

Notification to certification and placement services of unsatisfactory conditions of employment for educators.

Warning to members that acceptance of employment as a new teacher in a school district would be considered as unethical conduct and could lead to discharge from and future refusal of membership in the national professional association. Advice to members presently employed that, if their private arrangements permit, they should seek employment elsewhere.[45]

There are many other forms of sanctions and pressure tactics. One NEA tactic is the "professional holiday." The NEA attempts to distinguish the professional holiday from the strike by stating that the "professional holiday" is for a specified period only and that teachers intend to return after this period has elapsed, whether it be one or two days.[46] In 1964, this technique was used in a two-day work stoppage by all teachers in Utah. Later that year the Oklahoma Education Association instituted professional holidays in Tulsa.[47]

Another form of work stoppage used by teachers is to withhold services when students are not in school. This technique was used in Illinois by the Morton Council of the West Suburban Teachers Union, Local 571, AFT, in 1964. The Maywood Council of the West Suburban Teachers' Union called a similar strike at 1:00 P.M. on June 4, 1964, when school was closed for the children but open for the teachers.

> On a bright sunny day surrounded by newsmen and television cameras the elementary teachers of Maywood walked the picket line. 140 (more than 70 percent of the teachers) participated. The teachers obviously enjoyed themselves; small children drove their bicycles and tricycles past the picketters and commented simply but admiringly "They want more money."[48]

Teachers have refused to participate in extracurricular activities. The Morton Council of the West Suburban Teachers' Union, AFT, initiated the following program in successive steps: (1) withdrawal from substitute assignments, (2) withdrawal from non-student committee work, (3) withdrawal from student clubs.[49]

Skokie, Illinois, teachers have utilized the "work to rule" device to pressure the school board.[50] The device has been used frequently in Great Britain. Duties are carried out strictly according to the rules, and the effect is identical with that of a slowdown.

Picketing is used frequently by public school teachers. The UFT emphasizes that picketing not only applies pressure to the school board but also unifies the teachers behind the union leaders and gives them a stake in the union program. Sometimes modifications of picketing are used—for example, teachers form a motorcade and circle the board of education building or city hall to attract attention and to win support for their cause.[51]

A common practice of teacher organizations is to "pack a public meeting of the board of education." The purpose, of course, is both to apply pressure directly to the school board and to attract public attention to the needs of the schools and the teachers. Public support of the teachers' cause may enable the school board to increase taxes without a great deal of opposition.[52]

Table IV-3
Work Stoppages Involving Teachers, 1940–68

Year	All Schools			Public schools			Other schools		
	NUMBER OF STOPPAGES	WORKERS INVOLVED*	MAN-DAYS IDLE	NUMBER OF STOPPAGES	WORKERS INVOLVED*	MAN-DAYS IDLE	NUMBER OF STOPPAGES	WORKERS INVOLVED*	MAN-DAYS IDLE
1940	2	100	900	2	100	900	—	—	—
1941	1	120	120	1	120	120	—	—	—
1942	2	170	2,090	2	170	2,090	—	—	—
1943	2	100	330	2	100	330	—	—	—
1944	4	1,710	7,960	4	1,710	7,960	—	—	—
1945	1	20	160	—	—	—	1	20	160
1946	16	3,060	37,100	14	3,030	36,400	2	30	730
1947	20	4,720	21,100	20	4,720	21,100	—	—	—
1948	12	4,210	60,300	10	4,140	59,800	2	80	490
1949	9	440	920	5	350	490	4	90	430
1950	4	90	860	—	—	—	4	90	860
1951	10	4,510	67,000	6	4,310	65,200	4	200	1,830
1952	7	1,570	7,540	7	1,570	7,540	—	—	—
1953	1	170	510	1	170	510	—	—	—

Year									
1954	2	600	1,910	2	600	1,910	—	—	—
1955	1	220	14,900	1	220	14,900	—	—	—
1956	5	640	1,500	5	640	1,500 ·	—	—	—
1957	2	870	4,730	2	870	4,730	—	—	—
1958	1	50	110	—	—	—	1	50	110
1959	2	210	670	2	210	670	—	—	—
1960	3	5,490	5,490	3	5,490	5,490	—	—	—
1961	1	20	20	1	20	20	—	—	—
1962	2	20,000	20,100	1	20,000	20,000	1	20	120
1963	3	2,210	2,630	2	2,200	2,590	1	10	40
1964	9	14,400	30,600	9	14,400	30,600	—	—	—
1965	7	1,310	8,280	5	1,220	7,880	2	90	400
1966	33	37,400	68,000	30	37,300	58,500	3	100	9,490
1967	81	93,000	973,000	76	92,300	969,000	5	670	3,450
1968	94	146,000	2,190,000	88	145,000	2,180,000	6	500	5,170

* "Workers involved" includes all workers made idle for one day or longer in school systems directly involved in a stoppage. These figures represent the number idle on the day of peak or maximum idleness. In those instances in which idleness fluctuates during the strikes the actual number of workers idle on varying dates is used in computing the man-days of idleness.

NOTE: Because of rounding, sums of individual items may not equal totals.

SOURCE: U.S. Bureau of Labor Statistics.

In conjunction with the application of local sanctions, NEA has appointed an investigatory committee to study the school system.[53] This type of study attracts public attention, and is always made before NEA will invoke national sanctions on a school district. National sanctions include recommendations that no teacher sign a new contract with the school system, notification to teacher employment agencies across the country of the financial inadequacies of the schools, or, possibly, recommendation that teachers within the system may sign new contracts but that no new teachers enter the system.

A technique used with reasonable success by public school teachers has been impugning the integrity of either the school administrator or the school board members. The administrator does not have tenure and his employment is subject to the desires of the school board. Thus, any type of criticism, including criticism from teachers, can cause him serious hardship.

School board members are often in a position similar to that of a school administrator. If they are elected, criticism from the teachers can hinder the board members' chances of reelection because teachers often campaign in school board elections. If a school board member is appointed, any criticism against him is shifted to the person who made the appointment. In this case teachers campaign for the election of the city official who ultimately has control over appointments to the school board.

Newspaper advertisements have also been frequently used by teachers. Sometimes they have been used in campaigns to elect school board officials; more often, however, they have been used to inform the public of certain adverse conditions in the public schools or of the low level of teacher salaries in comparison with other school districts.

Another tactic resorted to by public school teachers is the "strategic alliance."[54] In cases where a group of teachers has little bargaining power, it allies itself with other groups who do have power or who, when united with the teachers, form a powerful force. Locals of AFT have often received aid from the City Labor Councils or from locals of other unions. The aid in money and personnel which AFT receives from IUD is a form of "strategic alliance." Strikes have also been run jointly by AFT and NEA locals in Jersey City, New Jersey; Anderson, Indiana; Pocatello, Idaho; and Kansas City, Missouri.

There have been many experiments in developing procedures to resolve impasses over new contract terms in public education. As part of its original formulation of "professional negotiation" in 1962, NEA encouraged its local affiliate to negotiate procedures for resolving impasses in written agreements with the school boards. In 1968, about one-third of all written agreements in public education included an impasse procedure. Most impasse procedures provided for mediation and fact-finding; only a few provided for compulsory arbitration of new contract terms. School boards in several communities—Newark, New Jersey, and Rochester, New York for example—have agreed to submit unresolved disputes to binding arbitration after impasses have been reached in contract negotiations.

All the statutes proposed by state affiliates of NEA provided for mediation and fact-finding under the auspices of the state department of education. By 1968 little use had been made of such impasse procedures. The Rhode Island provision for binding arbitration of nonmonetary terms in new contracts had been used only once. The impasse procedures in Michigan, New Jersey, and New York that apply to all public employees were used extensively by school boards and teacher organizations. During the Public Employment Relations Commission's first year of existence about one hundred mediators and fact-finders were appointed in New Jersey school districts.

Conclusion

This chapter has focused entirely on public school teachers. Because of the characteristics of the teaching profession, collective bargaining has developed faster among teachers than among any other group of public employees. Furthermore, the evidence indicates that collective bargaining will continue to spread rapidly among teachers in future years.

There is another reason, perhaps equally important, for singling out teachers for special consideration. The development of collective bargaining among teachers has important implications for other professional employees such as nurses, social workers, engineers, scientists, physicians, and lawyers. Many of the problems that have occurred when teachers bargain with boards of education undoubtedly will develop when bargaining spreads to other salaried professional employees. For example, all professional groups espousing collective bargaining must eventually face up to the problem of formulating policies on strikes and other pressure tactics. This involves considerable soul-searching by individual practitioners as well as by leaders of professional organizations.

Of course, many problems associated with teacher bargaining are still unresolved. Increased community involvement in education is just beginning to have its impact on bargaining between school boards and teacher organizations. As discussed earlier, teacher bargaining eventually includes public educational policy. Professional autonomy, then, is pitted against citizen involvement. This type of problem, particularly important in the health and welfare fields, will be analyzed in more detail in Chapter VIII.

V collective bargaining for police and fire fighters

Policemen and fire fighters are a distinctive group in public employment. The nature of their work, their place of work, and their traditions set them apart from other public employees. Police and fire fighters are the most highly organized municipal employees, and their organizations are among the oldest in public employment.[1] The general public, too, regards policemen and fire fighters as a special breed. Their services affect each citizen and are probably considered the most essential of all public services. It is therefore not surprising that labor relations for policemen and fire fighters often have unique aspects in public employee collective bargaining.

Organization of Public Safety Services

EMPLOYMENT

In 1968 about 745,000 paid employees provided police and fire protection in the United States (see Table V–1). Almost two-thirds were engaged in police activities. Not included in the number of public safety employees were more than one million

Table V-1
Number of Paid Employees (full time and part time)
in Police and Fire Protection, October 1968

LEVEL OF GOVERNMENT	POLICE	FIRE FIGHTERS
Federal	26,000	°
States	52,000	—
Counties	72,742	8,392
Municipalities	314,101	202,010
Townships	24,902	25,965
Special districts	9	19,080
Total	489,754	255,447

° Although exact figures are unavailable, several thousand fire fighters are employed by the federal government. The U.S. Civil Service Commission reported that, as of November 1968, 2,400 employees were in exclusive bargaining units represented by the International Association of Fire Fighters.

SOURCE: U.S. Bureau of the Census, *Public Employment in 1968,* Tables 1, 3, and 4.

volunteer, unpaid fire fighters found largely in rural areas and smaller communities. In some departments both volunteer and paid fire fighters serve together. A survey of 1,287 fire departments showed that 232 were composed of volunteer members; only 47 consisted of paid and unpaid employees; 176 paid all members on call for alarms and drills; and 832 had only salaried full-time employees.[2]

Employment in police and fire protection is primarily a local matter. Federal and state governments employ only one-sixth of all police personnel and an even smaller percentage of fire fighters. The size of local departments varies from one-man municipal and county police forces to Los Angeles County's 5,515-man police department and New York City's 27,671-man police department. A similar spread is found among fire departments, from one fire fighter paid on call to New York City's 13,781-member force.

Employment in both police and fire-fighting agencies has been growing. The average annual increase in police employment between 1955 and 1968 was almost 4 percent; the increase in fire-fighting employment was less than 2 percent. Proportionately, state police departments are growing most rapidly, because of heavy highway traffic and additional responsibilities in assisting local police in communications, technical services, and training.

Despite recent personnel increases, public safety departments are beset with labor shortages. Over 60 percent of all cities have vacancies on their police force; more than 90 percent of the departments in the larger cities with population over 10,000 report vacancies.[3] The situation is basically the same in fire departments, except that the problem is more recent, the vacancy rates are lower, and the undermanning is especially noticeable in smaller communities.[4]

Police and fire officials have recently been pressured by the public to increase the proportion of minority-group members in their departments. The proportion of Negroes in the police and fire departments is generally smaller than that of Negroes in municipal employment; the proportion is always smaller than that of Negroes in the city's population (see Table V–2). The problem results

Table V–2

Selected Data on Proportion of Negroes in Population, in City Employment, in Police Force, and in Fire Department (1966)

CITY	POPULATION	CITY EMPLOYEES	POLICE	FIRE FIGHTERS
New York	14.0%	23.0%	4.9%	4.1%
Chicago	29.0	10.0	20.0	4.6
Philadelphia	29.0	40.0	24.3	10.0
Detroit	31.0	39.0	5.0	2.5
Cleveland	34.5	10.0	9.0	4.0
Milwaukee	12.0	6.1	2.0	.06
Pittsburgh	19.3	18.0	9.5	3.0
Atlanta	44.0	34.0	14.0	15.0
Newark	50.0–55.0	8.0–10.0	17.8	3.0

SOURCE: U.S. Equal Employment Opportunity Commission, *Negro Employment Statistics in Nine Major Cities* (Washington, D.C.: August 1967).

from discrimination against hiring members of minority groups, hostility of minority groups toward public safety departments, and inability of minority groups to meet various entrance standards. In 1966, less than 50 percent of the police departments in any population category and 13 percent of all police departments, reported any special efforts to recruit minority-group applicants.[5]

The proportion of nonuniformed employees in public safety departments is small but is growing. The proportion in police departments increased from less than 8 percent in 1960 to 10 percent in 1965.[6] Some department administrators believe that use of nonuniformed personnel is detrimental to the flexibility and the morale of the force. Current manpower shortages are causing administrators to reevaluate such positions. The Los Angeles Police Department is using college students majoring in police science as part-time desk workers and is training civilian traffic officers.[7] The New York City Police Department employs nonuniformed school-crossing guards, stenographers, radio dispatchers, and fingerprint technicians. Continued manning difficulties most likely increase the proportion of nonuniformed personnel in public safety departments.

NATURE OF POLICE AND FIRE FIGHTING WORK

Police and fire fighting work involves physical effort as well as judgment, out-of-doors assignments around the clock, and many kinds of hazards. A recent work-accident study calculated sixty-nine deaths per 100,000 fire fighters and forty-four deaths per 100,000 policemen.[8] Both police and fire fighting jobs require ability to handle people, as well as equipment, in emergencies. In the job of the fire fighter greater emphasis is placed upon equipment, physical techniques, and knowledge of material reactions; the policeman's concern is more with human reactions.

Despite the glamour and the strain attributed to both policemen and fire fighters, much of their working time is spent in routine activities. For instance, 25 percent of police time is devoted to traffic functions. Most police time is spent on patrol duty, which is likely to require attention to minor disturbances, domestic situations, and the like.[9] Much of the formal investigation in identifying criminals is performed by detectives, who represent about 10 percent of the total police force, and by laboratory specialists.

Fire fighters respond to fire alarms and calls and investigate causes of disasters, but they do not patrol, as police do. A study of over 500 fire departments showed that a typical twenty-four-hour shift included three hours of housekeeping, two hours of drills, two and one-half hours of recreation, and one hour of calisthenics.[10] Fifty percent of the departments reported that fire fighters perform building maintenance, such as painting and carpentry, and 2 percent reported that fire fighters serve as school-crossing guards.

The nature of the work of police and fire fighters requires a different form of work organization for each. Although fire fighters may do individual fire prevention work, answering alarms and fighting fires is a supervised group effort. Policemen may also work in teams, but the trend has been to gain better utilization of manpower by individualizing and mobilizing patrols. This practice reduces the opportunity for constant direct supervision.

For many years fire fighters have enjoyed a more favorable public image than have policemen, an image that may affect recruitment and work satisfaction. But the difference in reputation appears to be disappearing in major urban areas. In the summer of 1967, fire fighters in New York City were the targets of nine shootings and seventy incidents in which they were the objects of bricks, stones, and bottles.[11]

To upgrade the image and the job content of public safety employment, police and fire fighting organizations are stressing "professionalism." The International Association of Fire Chiefs and the International Association of Chiefs of Police are active in promoting professional education. Fact-finders have invoked professionalism to justify higher wages.[12] The ultimate sanction has been given by institutions of higher learning. Between 1962 and 1967, the number of colleges offering degrees in criminology and police science increased to 186—more than a threefold increase.[13]

DEPARTMENT STRUCTURE

INTERNAL STRUCTURE

Both police and fire departments are pyramid-shaped, paramilitary, authoritarian organizations. The number of rank levels in each department depends upon the size of the department, the number of men per shift, and the number of physical facilities. Departments in medium-sized communities have the full gamut of superior officers, including deputy chiefs, district or battalion commanders, captains, lieutenants, and sergeants (in the case of police). Uniformed personnel of all ranks may be referred to as officers. Less than 30 percent of uniformed personnel in fire departments are superior officers; the percentage in police departments is frequently smaller.

A strict hierarchy of control exists in police and fire departments, with final authority in the hands of the chief or the commissioner. Individual police precinct stations or firehouses are under the command of a captain; each shift is under the command of a lieutenant. Deputy chiefs may be in charge of particular functions, for example traffic operations or fire prevention. The chief exercises centralized authority and delegates fewer powers than his counterparts in private industry or in other areas of public employment. In the disciplinary process, the chief receives recommendations from subordinate officers, conducts disciplinary hearings, and imposes punishment. He also has authority for placing and scheduling his forces.

Employment in the police and fire departments always begins at the lowest level, regardless of a candidate's skills. Advancement within either service is usually slow. The only exception is the top administrator(s) of the departments, who may be appointed by the appropriate authority in the community for a specified number of years or at the authority's pleasure. In the case of volunteer fire departments with paid personnel, the chief may be elected annually by the membership or may be appointed by the executive board. Larger cities sometimes attract top public safety executives from other departments, especially police chiefs or commissioners. In general, however, top administrators are selected from within the department.

EXTERNAL RELATIONSHIPS

Police and fire departments are usually part of regular political units of government, and operate as other agencies of the political units. The head of the department reports to the chief political authority, he prepares budgets which are processed with operating requests of other agencies, and vies with the heads of other agencies for funds from general tax revenues.

There are exceptions to the above setup. Fire fighting services are organized in some areas along special geographic lines rather than on the basis of political boundaries; in this respect, fire districts are similar to school districts. Under the Lakewood Plan, individual municipalities contract with the county for police and fire protection services. In some instances, fire departments are private corporations chartered by the state, as in Maryland, and are operated outside the traditional political framework. The departments receive funds by establishing a fire district property tax, which is collected and disbursed by the counties. In such cases the fire departments are responsible to no one but themselves.

The number and kinds of jobs available in police and fire departments for a long time made them subject to political patronage—and in some departments they still are.[14] Political interference affects appointments, promotions, work assignments, and discipline. In many municipalities this factor has led to the extension of civil service restriction of appointed positions in police and fire departments. Pittsburgh did not formally rid itself of a "spoils" system in its protective services until 1963.

Isolating department operations from political interference may extend beyond the personnel aspects covered in a civil service system to the exclusion of any outside intervention. The matter was clear to the police commissioner in New York City during Robert F. Wagner's term as mayor: "These things are none of the Mayor's business. The department is a military organization that must be run by the commissioner alone."[15]

Police and fire departments work together in individual emergency situations, but they do not generally maintain close relationships. Each is jealous of its jurisdiction and conscious of its traditions, and any attempt to consolidate functions is vigorously opposed by both groups. In some communities there may be hostility between the two groups, but the more general tone is one of rivalry or of apathy; the result is further isolation of each department and its personnel.

PERSONNEL ADMINISTRATION

Neither the management of a public safety department nor the political authority of the community may control departmental wages, hours, insurance, pensions, holidays, residence requirements, and work regulations. Many state legislatures have preempted authority in these matters. In Wisconsin, for instance, a fire fighter cannot be scheduled to work more than seventy-two hours a week. The Illinois state legislature, for example, sets the minimum salaries of police and fire fighters in cities over 5,000. States have also developed pension plans for the protective services or have mandated pension eligibility requirements and levels of payments. New York State is an example of the latter, though funding is left to the city. On the other hand, some states —Maryland, for example—have virtually no state provisions affecting the compensation or working conditions of local policemen and fire fighters.

Two other types of organizations outside the police and fire departments may affect personnel administration. Many cities and some states have civil service commissions for policemen and fire fighters. These commissions give examinations for appointment and promotion and may also review the major disciplinary cases of the departments. Civilian review boards have also been established in six cities to hear citizens' complaints against policemen and, in some cases, to recommend discipline. A number of these boards have been disbanded.[16]

Employee Organizations

Within their separate groups, policemen and fire fighters have a reputation for being close knit. In the early history of many departments, this cohesiveness led to the formation of employee social and benefit organizations. Some continue to function according to their original purpose and structure; others have changed over the years.

FIRE FIGHTERS

In 1918 fire fighters formed the International Association of Fire Fighters (IAFF) as an affiliate of the American Federation of Labor. This group is by far the largest and most influential organization of fire fighters, having as members about one-half of all paid fire fighters. The jurisdiction of the organization includes all professional fire fighters except those working in shipyard fire departments; nonuniformed employees of fire departments are also ineligible for membership. In recent years, IAFF has conducted seminars to promote collective bargaining concepts in its local affiliates. From 1930 to 1968, however, its constitution contained a no-strike clause. As a member of the National Fire Protection Association, the union also encourages the use of improved fire-fighting methods and equipment and provides various types of insurance. In some cases, locals reportedly are little more today than the social groups they were originally.

In 1968, IAFF claimed to represent over 132,000 members, almost 90 percent of whom lived in the United States. Although the union has members in every state, one-fourth of the members reside in New York State and California and another 30 percent is concentrated in six states (Massachusetts, Ohio, Illinois, Pennsylvania, Texas, and Michigan). A correlation exists between the size of a municipality and the probability of union organization of fire departments; all cities with populations over 500,000 reported employee membership in IAFF in 1966 compared to 31 percent of cities with population betwen 10,000 and 25,000.[17] Forty-eight percent of all cities with over 10,000 inhabitants reported that fire fighters were members of national labor unions. Where IAFF has organized, its members include virtually every member of the fire department.

The activities of the union at the national level are circumscribed. In 1968 the international staff consisted of sixteen persons, all located in Washington. At its 1968 convention the union raised its per capita dues to $1 a month, thus retaining its claim to the lowest dues for any AFL-CIO union in the United States. Fifteen vice-presidents, each in charge of a geographic area, are fire department employees and can therefore devote only part of their time to organizing, representing the union in state legislatures, and performing other duties of an executive board member. As a result, locals have considerable autonomy in policy and operating decisions.

The IAFF locals are organized by geographic area and employer jurisdiction; a local of municipal fire fighters and one of federal fire fighters may be found in the same community. In New York City and Baltimore, supervisors are organized into separate locals. In thirty-nine states, locals are affiliated at the state level in an IAFF state body; they may also be affiliated with the state AFL-CIO. The formal organization of each local parallels the organization of the fire department. To take care of grievances a union steward is assigned to each fire company or to each shift. Superior officers of the fire department are commonly officers of the local union.

Because fire fighters have been affiliated with organized labor for fifty years, their jurisdiction has been widely accepted, and no other national union has made any serious attempt to organize fire fighters. Many local independent fire fighting employee organizations, however, continue to operate. In a study of council-manager cities one-sixth reported that fire department employees were members of such organizations. Independent organizations were most common in medium-sized cities (population 50,000–250,000) and in the West.[18]

POLICE

The development and current status of employee organizations of policemen differ from those of fire fighters. Following the 1919 Boston police strike, widespread efforts to form police organizations were delayed by the labor movement's initial wariness toward policemen and by public suspicion of police employee organizations. Nevertheless, policemen did not abandon their attempts to organize.

The main difference between police and fire-fighter employee organizations has been that police groups have been more likely to fragment on a rank basis, with separate organizations for patrolmen, detectives, and various officer groups.

The Fraternal Order of Police (FOP) was founded in 1915 but did not significantly add to its membership until the 1930s. Today it is the largest national police employee organization, claiming 90,000 members in forty-two states, with major concentrations of members in Pennsylvania, Ohio, Rhode Island, and Virginia. The FOP represents police in 22.6 percent of council-manager cities.[19] It affiliates local organizations, called lodges, assists in the formation of state lodges and convenes biennially. Policemen of all ranks are eligible for membership in FOP, and associate memberships are available to the general public. The FOP's original purposes were directed toward securing civil service protection and bolstering pension systems through lobbying.[20] In time, local FOP lodges expanded their interests to all police financial matters and working conditions; FOP also stresses recreational facilities and activities. The only full-time member of the national staff is the president. The FOP does not consider itself a labor union, because it is not affiliated with AFL-CIO. It ensures autonomy for local lodges and maintains a substantially lower dues structure than AFL-CIO affiliated unions.

Another national organization, the National Conference of Police Associations, was established as a coordinating agency for autonomous local police organizations and speaks for 275,000 members. Its annual survey of police wages and working conditions parallels the efforts of FOP.

While police were organizing themselves in independent employee organizations, national labor unions have also become active in recruiting police as members. In 1945 policemen in forty-five cities were organized in AFL locals; twelve years later, only twelve of these cities reported the existence of an active union.[21] The American Federation of State, County, and Municipal Employees (AFSCME) has approximately 10,000 police members, with principal strength in Connecticut and Illinois; the largest city department represented by AFSCME is the Baltimore police department. The union typically organizes policemen in separate locals, but some locals include police with other employees. The AFSCME program consists of a full range of union activities. However, policemen are considered a special group of employees; the union charter for police locals includes a provision to the effect that the charter will be revoked if policemen "strike or refuse in concert to perform their duties."

Other unions have also organized policemen because of the interest shown in public employee collective bargaining in the 1960s, because of no clear union jurisdiction over policemen, as over fire fighters, and because police were not identified with any single organization. The Service Employees' International Union, the International Association of Machinists, the International Brotherhood of Teamsters, Chauffeurs, Warehousemen and Helpers of America all have active locals of uniformed policemen. The last has police members in more than one dozen locals, including those in Minnesota, Washington, Connecticut, Wisconsin, and Michigan. In February 1969, the executive council of AFL-CIO approved the formation of a national police union.

The confusion in identifying police employee organizations extends beyond the variety of organizations. Local organizations sometimes change affiliations; the Toledo, Ohio, lodge withdrew from FOP in 1966 and became an independent organization, the Patrolmen's Benevolent Association of Ohio. Moreover, dual membership in organizations is not uncommon for policemen. Officers rising through the ranks become eligible for membership in new employee groups, but they do not want to lose insurance benefits paid for in employee organizations to which they have belonged. Since the original employee organization desires to maintain the dues and the friendship of this group, a modus vivendi is often found. In New York City, patrolmen who are promoted may retain membership, but are not permitted to vote in the Patrolmen's Benevolent Association. Still another case arises when several associations exist in the same department, ostensibly for different reasons; many policemen simply join them all.

The variety and changing nature of police employee organizations make it difficult to compile accurate membership data. A 1966 survey showed that 30.6 percent of U.S. cities with over 10,000 population reported police membership in national unions or associations; the percentage was higher in larger cities and in the East Central and Middle Atlantic states.[22] Altogether, the previously cited organizations account for 375,000 memberships. Cities with less than 50,000 population most likely have no police organization. Where there is an organization, policemen are likely to join in very high proportions, as are fire fighters.

REACTION OF ADMINISTRATORS

Chiefs and commissioners of police and fire departments have often been outspoken in their views on employee organizations in their departments. Police chiefs have been decidedly more vociferous than fire chiefs in attacking such organizations, probably because many fire chiefs have been or still are members of IAFF. In fact, the professional organization of fire chiefs, the International Association of Fire Chiefs, has formally endorsed the concept of collective bargaining for fire fighters.

Police chiefs frequently make a distinction between a "union" and a "police employee organization," although some view with suspicion any national organization. A representative attitude is contained in the 1967 remarks of the Police Commissioner of Baltimore:

> It is the opinion of professional police administrators that a police union is not compatible with police responsibilities. . . . While I do not feel that an affiliated union is necessary or proper for members of law enforcement agencies, I do recognize the need for a professional association made up and governed by police officers which can both serve a social purpose and as a means of bringing grievances and other pertinent matters to the attention of management.[23]

This statement appears to approve of FOP, and is a far cry from the order issued by the Detroit Police Commissioner in 1944 which banned memberships in all national organizations and made no distinctions between FOP and CIO unions.

There are three principal reasons for administrative opposition to employee organizations: (1) An employee of a protective service who joins a union will have "two masters" and can no longer impartially serve the public. (2) The presence of an employee organization may thwart the authority of the police chief and interfere in the operation of the department. (3) The appearance of an employee organization is an indictment on the ability of management of the department.

Collective Bargaining

The existence and the role of employee organizations among policemen and fire fighters are affected by the conditions under which they must operate. Statutes, court decisions, department rules, and attitudes of department officials help determine the presence and the nature of such organizations.

LEGAL FRAMEWORK

As public employees, policemen and fire fighters are exempt from the federal statutes and machinery that protect the organizing rights of most workers in the private sector of the economy. State legislation affecting organizing and bargaining rights of public employees has, however, increased rapidly in recent years. A summary of states enacting such legislation by early 1969 is presented below.

A. States with legislation giving all municipal employees the right to organize and to bargain collectively:

Connecticut	New York
Delaware	Oregon
Massachusetts	Rhode Island
Michigan	Vermont
Minnesota	Washington

B. State with legislation giving police and fire fighters the right to organize and to bargain collectively:

     Pennsylvania

C. States with legislation giving fire fighters only the right to organize and/or to bargain collectively:

Alabama	Iowa
California	Maine
Florida (county)	Nebraska
Illinois	Wyoming

D. States with legislation giving right to organize and bargain to all municipal employees except law enforcement personnel:

Missouri	Wisconsin

E. State with legislation giving state employees except law enforcement personnel right to organize and bargain:

     Rhode Island

F. States with legislation prohibiting union membership by:

Fire fighters—	Police—Georgia
North Carolina	North Carolina

G. States with legislation prohibiting bargaining with public employee unions:

Texas	Virginia

Almost all the legislation was passed since 1958, and most statutes guaranteeing the right to organize and/or bargain were enacted since 1963. Organization and representation of employees by unions sometimes preceded legislation; clearly, however, legislative activity has eased the way for employee organizations to deal with employers.

Some states have chosen to single out the labor relations activities of policemen and fire fighters. Ten states exclude all policemen from the rights to organize and bargain, but grant these rights to fire fighters. The favored position of fire fighters must be attributed either to their superior lobbying power or to the unfavorable image evoked by police in bargaining organizations. Nevertheless, very few states prohibit members of the protective service from joining organizations that engage in collective bargaining—two states prohibit policemen and one state prohibits fire fighters.

In February 1969 the North Carolina statute barring police and fire fighters from membership in unions was declared unconstitutional by a federal district court. The decision, based on the right of free association, permits unions to organize but not to negotiate with public employers.

Policemen and fire fighters may be prohibited from engaging in organized activities by means other than legislative enactment. In 1945 the Attorney General of Alabama upheld municipal authority to prohibit police membership in a union. Sometimes local ordinances and rules of municipal and state police departments also forbid such membership. At the insistence of the police commissioner, police were excluded from the original 1955 order issued by the mayor of New York that provided a program of labor relations for city employees. In 1966, one of every seven cities in the United States prohibited policemen from belonging to a national union or association; only one of every eighteen cities prohibited fire fighters from joining a national union.[24] Presumably the court decision noted above invalidates these membership prohibitions.

Permissive bargaining laws, municipal ordinances, and department rules may also encourage organization of public safety workers. Alaska, North Dakota, and New Hampshire are examples of states with permissive legislation. The city of Hartford (Connecticut) passed an ordinance in 1944 that reversed the board of police commissioners' refusal to recognize a police union.[25] At the insistence of the Fire Fighters' Union, the Seattle (Washington) City Council passed an ordinance authorizing collective bargaining, in accordance with the newly enacted state law.[26]

RECOGNITION AND UNIT DETERMINATION

The term "recognition" means anything from recognition by a department administration that an employee organization exists to formal relationships between the organization and the department. Even the latter definition can vary from permitting the organization to present requests or to function on department property or during working hours to authorizing the organization to represent employees in grievances and negotiations.

For all these reasons, figures about recognition must be treated skeptically; in fact, few figures are available. A 1960 study showed that only 24 percent of police departments extended formal recognition to employee organizations, even though organizations existed in 86 percent of the departments.[27] One-half the recognitions were accorded to unions. If a similar study were made today, the total number of recognitions, however defined, would be substantially higher.

UNIT DETERMINATION

With the increasing number of states that have granted police and fire fighters the right to organize and to bargain have come the attendant problems of what is the appropriate unit and which organizations are appropriate to be employee organizations. Unit determination for police and fire-fighting employees involves three issues: (1) the distinction between protection service department employees and other public employees, (2) the distinction between uniformed employees and other employees within the departments, and (3) the distinction of supervisory personnel in such departments.

The problem of separating public safety employees from others is generally not a serious one. Where state legislation specifically includes the subject, as in Connecticut, separate units are required for police and fire departments. When the law is silent, it has been determined that the special nature and community of interests of protection service personnel warrant separate recognition. Such findings also follow the desires of department administrators and employee organizations.

Although uniformed personnel dominate police and fire departments, these departments include other employees as well. The question of representing the interests of the latter is particularly acute when membership in an employee organization is restricted to certain groups. The Wisconsin Employment Relations Board decided that nonuniformed members of the Milwaukee fire department should be in the same unit with uniformed department personnel; the nonuniformed members are formally represented by IAFF but cannot be members of the union. In a case before the Connecticut State Board of Labor Relations, the issue was whether school-crossing guards, clerks, mechanics, and equipment maintenance employees should be in the same unit with

uniformed policemen. The municipality and an employee association favored a comprehensive unit; a union representing the
police did not. The board ruled in favor of two separate units
and, in a subsequent case involving a separate unit for school-
crossing guards, upheld its decision.[28]

The most frequently encountered problem relating to recognition of employee organization in police and fire departments is
the definition of supervisory personnel. For the most part organizations of uniformed employees have sought as inclusive a unit
as possible. The question hinges on the duties and the authority
of ranking members of police and fire departments rather than
on the community of interest between officers and rank-and-file
employees. In a summary finding, the Connecticut State Board of
Labor Relations concluded:

> It has appeared that all ultimate disciplinary authority has resided
> in the chief or the chief and police commissioners; that all officers
> below the chief have come up through the ranks . . . ; that officers
> often work with patrolmen, do the same tasks, and incur the same
> dangers; that the supervisory functions of officers are sometimes
> performed by men of lower rank when occasion arises. . . .

> The pattern of organization of the firemen's and policemen's
> union . . . has traditionally represented officers and men as a unit.
> . . . In many municipalities agreements made by the parties under
> the Act have included officers within the unit; indeed, this has been
> the rule rather than the exception.

> The Legislature contemplated the possibility of different treatment
> of supervisors in the police and fire departments from that of other
> supervisors. . . .[29]

The IAFF has been highly successful in gaining representation
rights for officers as well as rank-and-file fire fighters. All ranks
up to assistant chiefs are likely to be included in the bargaining
unit; in Philadelphia the assistant chief is included as well. The
Michigan statute limits the definition of supervisor in fire departments to "a fire commission, fire commissioner, safety director, or
other similar administrative agency or administrator. . . ."[30] Several state labor relations boards have ruled that all positions up to

chief or deputy chief in the fire department are to be considered a single bargaining unit. The city of Medford, Massachusetts, has unsuccessfully appealed to the courts such a decision by the Massachusetts Labor Relations Commission. In Seattle (Washington), however, the bargaining unit was limited to employees below the rank of battalion chief.[31] In an unusual case, the Wisconsin Employment Relations Board drew the supervisory line between captains and lieutenants in the Milwaukee fire department, although IAFF had wanted to include both categories in the unit and the city had wanted to exclude both categories.

Although the problem of defining supervisory personnel is much the same in police departments, the results have been somewhat different. In the first place, the employee organizations themselves may have limited membership and hence interests. In New York City and Detroit, for instance, several organizations represent uniformed policemen of different ranks. In the second place, state labor relations boards have been loath to insist that all police below the level of chief should be in one unit. The Wisconsin board has ruled that lieutenants in the Milwaukee Police Department are supervisors and therefore are excluded from the bargaining unit. The Connecticut board reached an opposite conclusion in a case involving the Windsor police department. The Massachusetts State Labor Relations Commission has also held that captains and lieutenants are not executives.

A popular solution, derived from the "Globe election doctrine" developed by the National Labor Relations Board, has been to permit the employees in question to determine whether they wish to be part of a bargaining unit with patrolmen. In unit determination cases in Boston (Massachusetts) and in Bridgeport and Stratford (Connecticut) self-determination was invoked for the ranks of sergeant, lieutenant, and captain. In Bridgeport, a subsidiary issue was whether all three ranks should vote together; the board decided that captains should vote as one group and sergeants and lieutenants as another group. At first, the three ranks voted to remain outside the collective bargaining unit; later they reversed the decision, presumably because the pay differential between officers and patrolmen was not maintained in negotiations. A more complex situation arose in the Boston case, because one of the two concerned organizations wanted to represent patrolmen only. The sergeants, lieutenants, and captains voted to be part of a single bargaining unit; however, the patrolmen's organization won the overall representation election. Thereupon the Massachusetts Labor Relations Commission was forced to revise its original unit determination decision to meet the factual realities. The New York State Public Employment Relations Board originally decided on three units for the state police: a unit of troopers through the rank of lieutenant; a unit of captains and majors, on grounds that they were middle-management representatives; and a unit of criminal investigators, on grounds that their work was distinct and at times constituted a conflict of interest with that of the other two groups.[32] Subsequently the units were redefined by shifting lieutenants into the same unit as captains and majors.[33]

QUALIFICATIONS OF ORGANIZATIONS

Sometimes the qualifications of an employee organization to represent members is questioned. This is likely to occur if more than one organization seeks to gain recognition and if organizations themselves are in a period of changing functions and aspirations. The Boston police case was complicated because one of the petitioners represented a federation of four organizations: a police charity association, a police legislative lobbying agency, a social club of police executives, and an organization assisting in the defense of policemen charged with brutality. The trend is to permit employees themselves to decide on the qualifications of organizations rather than to have an administrative agency decide the issue.

The qualifications of an organization may also be questioned if the organization includes workers outside of protective service departments. Some state laws follow the Taft-Hartley doctrine of separating guards from other workers and therefore require policemen to be represented by separate organizations. The Massachusetts Labor Relations Commission decided, however, that police could be represented by a union that also represents other workers.[34] The Wisconsin Supreme Court upheld a decision by the Wisconsin Employment Relations Board that police may be represented by a nationally affiliated union even though they legally may not be members of such a union. The problem of organizational qualifications is not major because employees and the traditions of most employee organizations in the field concur with administrators in this regard. Police officials, however, may consider union affiliation a violation of the concept.

SCOPE OF BARGAINING

The variety of subjects negotiated in collective bargaining agreements of fire and police departments is presented below.

A. Economic matters
   1. Wages: base rates, shift differentials, longevity pay, overtime pay, callback pay, pay for temporary service out of rank, pay for jury duty
   2. Time off: vacations, holidays, sick leave, leave to attend a funeral
   3. Insurance: medical/surgical, life
   4. Other: pensions, uniform allowance, uniform cleaning, tuition reimbursement, severance pay
B. Hours
C. Employee organization matters
   1. Union security
   2. Dues deduction
   3. Time off for union business
   4. Use of department facilities
   5. Basis of steward representation
D. Management rights
E. Seniority
   1. Filling of vacancies
   2. Choice of vacation time
   3. Layoff and recall in case of reduction in force
F. Grievance procedure
G. Right to substitute work assignments
H. No-strike provision

The list is neither exhaustive nor representative; no one agreement includes all these subjects. Some negotiations are concerned only with economic matters; others go much further in regulating working conditions.

As long as the governing authorities provide sufficient financial resources, the results of economic bargaining are perhaps of less concern to department officials than are other parts of the negotiations. In fact, department officials may support wage increases as a means of improving morale and aiding recruiting efforts.

Items such as overtime pay, callback pay, and pay for temporary service out of rank, however, may affect department operations as well as department budgets.

Other negotiated items may affect department operations more directly and are therefore of greater concern to department officials. Bidding systems for promotions, role of seniority, and substitution of work assignments have been negotiated in some instances. Many police and fire department officials object to the inclusion of such items in negotiations.

The role and rights of the employee organization are usually also considered negotiable subjects, although some department officials are concerned about the effects of such rights on department authority and operations. The principal bones of contention are the role of the organization in grievances (to be discussed later) and union security. All forms of union security have been negotiated. For example, union-shop agreements are found in Connecticut and Rhode Island police departments; an agency shop exists in the Rochester (New York) police and fire departments; and a maintenance-of-membership provision has been negotiated in the Detroit police department. Checkoff of organization dues is also common. Time for organization business, including conventions, negotiations, and grievance processing, may also be discussed. The use of department facilities includes bulletin boards, official department publications, and physical space.[35]

Management has held that a number of topics are nonnegotiable—size of the work force, number of men in a squad, manning of work stations including patrol cars, selection of assignment, maintenance of residential requirement for employment, and moonlighting. Management's basis for excluding these subjects from negotiations has been that they concern department efficiency and management responsibility and are therefore wholly within the discretion of management. It should be noted that selection of work assignment has been included, if rarely, in the negotiable list.

Arbitrators have distinguished between nonnegotiable subjects and the negotiable impact of management decisions in such areas. For instance, determining the size of the force is a management prerogative, but should management decide to reduce the force, the manner of effecting the reduction may be held negotiable.

Municipal negotiators have found that employee organizations do not always agree that a subject is nonnegotiable, and will sometimes seek their demands through other channels. When the practice of moonlighting was declared nonnegotiable in New York City, the patrolmen successfully lobbied in the state legislature for permission to moonlight. The Milwaukee Fire Fighters Union has asked the Wisconsin Attorney General to decide whether protective service department rules are "working conditions" and are thus subject to collective bargaining under the state act. In rare instances, to force negotiations on particular subjects, employee organizations have filed charges of unfair labor practices with state commissions, but none has been processed. For the most part, however, public safety employee organizations have not resisted management's refusal to bargain on particular issues.

The scope of bargaining seems to be increasing, especially where the parties have gone beyond bargaining baptism. Court decisions tend to support mutually determined agreements. The New Hampshire Supreme Court overruled objection by the Berlin police chief to an agreement between a union and the city's police commissioners containing provisions for a union shop, seniority, and arbitration of grievances.[36] Once employee organizations have dealt with economic matters, they are likely to seek negotiation of other matters. Such topics as transfers and allocation of overtime are possible subjects for discussion in the immediate future.

AGREEMENTS

The number of agreements between local governments and policemen and fire fighters is small compared to the number of employee organizations that engage in collective bargaining. In 1966, 314 of 607 cities with IAFF locals reported bargaining activity. Only 152 of these municipalities had signed contracts with IAFF locals out of the 314 that were bargaining.[37] The International Office of AFSCME claims about one dozen locals, or one-fifth of all police locals have signed agreements.

The above statistics should not be given too much importance. As in other areas of the public sector, bargaining involving police or fire fighters may result in agreement without a signed contract. Because many issues must be processed by various third-party boards and commissions, before being implemented, the conclusion of bargaining becomes a matter of mutual intent instead of becoming immediately binding. In some states a signed agreement is illegal, and the results of bargaining must be incorporated into ordinances, regulations, or other instruments.

The question whether a signed agreement or a voter referendum authorizing different benefits has priority has been raised. A 1967 contract between a mayor and the fire fighters required a reduction of working hours by 1970; a subsequent voter referendum approved the same reduction immediately; the town lawyer ruled that the contract was binding.[38]

CONDUCT OF BARGAINING

BARGAINING REPRESENTATIVES

In negotiating agreements, the employee organization bargaining committee usually consists of the local executive board, which has drawn up bargaining demands and submitted them to the membership for approval and amendment. Negotiations are usually conducted by a select team. The organization may also choose to have a union staff member on the negotiating team, though few employee organizations are able to afford a professional staff. More common is the addition of a lawyer who is not part of the organization's staff. In some cases employee organizations have included lawyers only after having first dealt with the municipal corporate counsel. The organization's lawyer may be assigned various roles, from advising the organization bargaining team to conducting the entire bargaining himself.

The municipality's bargaining team most frequently consists of several city administrative officials in charge of such activities as labor relations, personnel, and finance. Sometimes a labor relations specialist may negotiate by himself, but only larger cities have hired specialists. Less frequently the team consists of elected officials, such as the mayor or council members; rarely will it include the chiefs or other officials of the police and fire departments. As one employee organization official put it, "The city is our employer. The department is merely the administrative agency."

There may be another reason for excluding department officials from the municipality's bargaining team. Department chiefs who have risen through the ranks identify closely with the rank and file; they may even be members of the same bargaining unit. Prior to the initiation of collective bargaining, some chiefs present the salary demands of their men to the budgetary officials, and support the men in these requests. In an effort to neutralize the role of top department officials in the bargaining process, city negotiators seem consciously to exclude such officials from their bargaining team.

Protective service department officials usually have neither a role nor a voice in the bargaining process. Few municipalities bother to keep department administrators informed about negotiations. If administrators are involved at all, they provide factual information requested by city negotiators. The exclusion of administrators may adversely affect department operations which in turn may lead to dissatisfaction with bargaining. Many subjects have operational implications—for example, work assignments. Even economic benefits, such as time off, affect schedule as well as budget. A passive or nonexistent bargaining role precludes police and fire departments from initiating management proposals. The International Association of Fire Chiefs has therefore endorsed a resolution requiring that the fire chief be part of the bargaining team. At least one municipal negotiator meets with the fire chief to determine the impact of the union demands.

RELATIONS OF POLICE AND FIRE EMPLOYEE ORGANIZATIONS

Considering the similarity between problems and benefits of policemen and those of fire fighters discussed earlier in this chapter, it would seem logical that organizations representing the two groups work closely together during negotiations; they rarely do. More commonly, the rivalry between the groups hampers collective bargaining. In one city, the policemen's organization purposefully protracted negotiations to obtain a long-term agreement that appeared to offer higher wages than had been given to fire fighters.

In a few instances police and fire fighters have bargained jointly. A notable example occurred in New York City in 1966 when the Uniformed Firemen's Association and the Patrolmen's Benevolent Association jointly presented their demands to the city and insisted on joint negotiations until agreement was reached. The two organizations worked together, even though the negotiations went to fact-finding and eventually to the mayor—when the fire fighters threatened to strike.

Even organizations representing different ranks in the police department in the same community will tend not to formulate joint demands nor to request joint sessions.

In May 1969, Indianapolis fire fighters and police announced that they would present uniform demands for parity in wages, and that they would work together with the city in 1969 negotiations. The action was surprising in view of the $500 advantage in starting salary enjoyed by the police in 1968. Most bargaining alliances are temporary, however, and even then they are tenuous.

If policemen and fire fighters do not bargain jointly, the one group pays close attention to the results of the other's bargaining. Traditionally, police and fire fighters of a community have enjoyed the same compensation. Increasingly police organizations claim that parity is no longer valid, because of differences in job duties and responsibilities. Some erosion of wage parity has resulted, much to the distress of fire fighters. In Lansing, Michigan, fire fighters rejected a 1968 city offer, because it was less than the amount granted to police.[39] A common practice in protective service agreements is to insert a "savings" clause requiring the political authority to grant the same wages and economic benefits to the unit as those negotiated with other units of the protective service departments during the same fiscal year.

ATMOSPHERE FOR BARGAINING

Economic gains negotiated for police and fire fighters require several steps after bargaining before they are fully implemented. The negotiators must have sufficient time beforehand to complete bargaining, particularly when changes in wages and fringe benefits must be included in a budget submitted to a municipal council or to a referendum. Some negotiators have agreed to an elaborate timetable for subsequent negotiations. Even such schedules have not eliminated the practice of negotiators bargaining past the expiration date of the existing agreement, with the settlement made retroactive to the expiration date.

The results of collective bargaining with public safety employees directly affect the public. Some cities have therefore held that negotiating sessions must be open to the public. Such practice does not generally promote the give-and-take required for effective collective bargaining. In one case, both municipal and organization representatives have agreed to skirt the problems by conducting two public sessions for the exchange of demands and then to retire to private sessions, during which bargaining actually takes place.

REFUSAL TO BARGAIN

Where bargaining is a right given by law to certified representatives of public employees, both the employee organization and the governing authority have a duty to bargain in good faith. There have been few tests of what constitutes "good faith" among police and fire fighters. The Connecticut State Board of Labor Relations ruled that a unilateral introduction of a personnel practices plan during negotiations with employees of a fire department constituted an unfair labor practice. A bizarre situation occurred in Cranston, Rhode Island. The mayor of the city had negotiated on nonmonetary issues with police and firefighter representatives. Wages were subsequently negotiated in a meeting of the employee representatives, the mayor, and the city council. Later the mayor unilaterally reduced the wages previously agreed to, sent administrative assistants to meet with the employee representatives, and mailed to the organizations an ultimatum to sign a contract including changes in nonmonetary items as well as the lower wages. The Labor Relations Board held that the mayor was not guilty of bargaining on wages in bad faith, because economic issues were in the province of city council; it did, however, charge the mayor with unilateral changes in nonmonetary items that were solely in his control and ordered him to bargain in good faith on these items.

GRIEVANCES

Many public safety departments have some kind of formal grievance procedures. A typical procedure in fire departments consists of four steps. The first step is filing of the grievance with the captain of the company. The second, third, and fourth steps are appeals to: (1) the battalion chief, (2) the deputy chief, and (3) the chief of the department. The chief may delegate his authority to, or receive advice from, a trial board consisting of other uniformed department personnel and/or outside members. In some places, even the final decision can be appealed to political authorities. Certain personnel issues may be outside the jurisdiction of the department and may be the responsibility of other agencies, such as civil service commissions and retirement boards.

There are no necessary relations between grievance systems and collective bargaining. Of cities with IAFF locals in 1966, 314 reported bargaining and 451 reported grievance procedures.[40] Similarly an employee organization and a grievance procedure are not necessarily bedfellows in public safety departments; one may be present without the other. A survey of police departments revealed grievance procedures in about three-fourths of the departments, including those with no employee organizations of any kind.[41]

The presence of an employee organization may affect the grievance procedure, regardless of the procedures origin. Of primary importance is the organization's role in representing employees in grievance matters. Then, too, the organization may seek changes in the grievance procedure that can affect utilization of the procedure. Employee organizations generally seek to have as the terminal step in the grievance procedure a neutral arbitrator selected by the parties.

In general, public safety administrators are wary about yielding final authority, including final determination of grievances. In 1967, nine years after all other city employees were given the right to appeal grievances outside their department, New York City police were given access to impartial binding arbitrations in exchange for union support of the city's Office of Collective Bargaining.

Grievance arbitration clearly is becoming more common than it has been. Binding arbitration is included in the bargaining agreements of police in Detroit, New Haven (Conn.), and Rochester (N.Y.), and for fire fighters in Cranston (R.I.) and Rochester (N.Y.). In Boston, however, the fire fighters may appeal only to advisory arbitration.

The establishment of grievance procedures may appear almost

unwarranted in some departments, considering their lack of usage. In many cities, only a few grievances are processed formally each year. A fire-fighter union official in a major city boasted that his organization had not introduced a written grievance in three years. Grievances reaching the final step are rare. Only one grievance has ever gone to the police commissioner of New York City.

The absence of formal grievances does not necessarily indicate an absence of grievances. Other reasons for lack of usage of procedures could be that grievances are not submitted or that employee organizations and departments have generally resorted to other, more satisfactory channels. Outside the formal procedure there are two levels at which employee organizations have found it possible to resolve grievances and some times to exert pressure. Before a grievance becomes a matter of record, it may be taken up with the superior officer in charge of the platoon or the company. Top organization representatives deal directly and informally with such an officer, who in many cases may be a member of the employee organization. Group social pressures or veiled threats of embarrassing the officer with his superiors have been employed to settle grievances.

Many grievances have been referred directly to top officers of employee organizations. This step is the result of the cohesiveness of employee organizations and the reluctance of shop stewards to press grievances with their immediate superiors. Employee organization officials see department administrators, including the chief, in periodic meetings with employee organization representatives, official department ceremonies, and social functions. Grievances are often raised and settled informally on these occasions.

The subject matter of grievances in public safety departments is different from that in other organized work groups. Discipline is sometimes exempted from the grievance procedure. So is the chief's authority to issue rules affecting working conditions. Both areas affect the control deemed necessary for a paramilitary organization. What is left then are application and interpretation of regulations, procedures, and terms of the agreement, if any. These could include matters of pay, eligibility for supplementary compensation, and assignments of duties outside of regular occupational classification.

STRIKES AND PRESSURE TACTICS

Recent militancy by public safety employee organizations may be reminiscent of the first quarter of the twentieth century, when at least three strikes by policemen and twenty-nine by fire fighters occurred in the United States.[42] From the end of the Great Depression until the mid-nineteen-sixties, however, strikes by policemen and fire fighters were practically unknown. The leading employee organizations have not changed, but the atmosphere in which the organizations operate and the temper of the members have. Consequently, strikes are once again a part of labor relations for policemen and fire fighters.

Since 1967, strikes lasting five hours to five days have occurred in the fire departments of Atlanta (Georgia), Kansas City (Missouri), Danville (Illinois), Saginaw (Michigan), Madison (Wisconsin), Des Moines (Iowa), and Kalamazoo (Michigan); in the police departments of Joliet (Illinois), Indiana (Pennsylvania), and Pontiac (Michigan); and simultaneously in the fire and police departments in Youngstown (Ohio) and Carbondale (Illinois). The technical forms of the work stoppage were mass resignation, calling in sick ("blue flu"), continuous professional meetings, or simply a walkout. Most of these forms were attempts to circumvent antistrike statutes. The employee organizations involved were independent associations and affiliates of IAFF and FOP. The issue in almost all cases was economic. Several strikes have also been threatened, including one by New York City fire fighters, which was supported by the Central Labor Council.

Some forms of work stoppage previously mentioned are also used in slowdowns that fall short of complete stoppages but that harass department administration and affect operations. Others in this category are epidemics requiring a large number of emergency leaves to take care of family; concerted refusal to work voluntary overtime; slowdown in "nonessential" work (maintenance and hydrant and building inspection by fire fighters; traffic ticketing and summonses issuing by policemen); and conversely, literal enforcement of rules and regulations (reporting holes in the street). In addition to these forms of pressure tactics, different forms of publicizing disputes have been employed: picketing municipal offices and/or station houses during off-duty hours, advertising, and placing in public media stories embarrassing to the department. Publicity affects reputations rather than operations, but the purpose of publicity may differ only slightly from that of work stoppages. Generally the purpose of slowdowns and strikes is to attract the attention of the public rather than to hurt the public safety department financially— the object of most strikes in the private sector.

In several situations, employers have responded strongly to pressure tactics. The strike of an independent employee organization led by two captains against the Atlanta Fire Department in 1966 resulted in suspension and dismissal of over one-half the force. Some of those discharged were later rehired as new employees, together with many new recruits. Over two-thirds of the Kalamazoo (Michigan) Fire Department was discharged for striking in 1969. In the Detroit Police Department, suspensions were also meted out to participants in a 1967 slowdown of ticket writing and to abusers of sick-leave privileges. Saginaw (Michigan) authorities docked the pay of fire fighters who used sick leave to stage a walkout in 1967; this action precipitated a 5-hour strike by the entire fire-fighting force. In most cases, however, no retaliatory measures seem to have been taken against those who used pressure tactics. State laws, such as Ohio's Ferguson Act, have not been invoked. When departments are already understaffed and many members participate in pressure tactics, the repercussions of severe discipline may hurt the department as much as the individuals being disciplined. Moreover, some forms of pressure tactics may be difficult to prove, or may be legal and therefore unpunishable.

National employee organizations have for the most part not publicly reacted to the locals' pressure tactics that could be considered work stoppages. Only AFSCME has expelled one of its police locals—Joliet, Illinois—for violating its charter by engaging in a one-day walkout. Neither FOP nor IAFF has officially condemned its affiliates. The response of IAFF, on the contrary, was to establish a commission to study the future course of the union's no-strike rule. The commission recommended that strikes be authorized by the union president only after all other means of ending the dispute had been exhausted.[43] The 1968 convention of IAFF rejected the recommendation and repealed the no-strike provision in the constitution.[44] This change in a long-established policy indicates the different mood and self-image of fire fighters and reflects the attitude of all public safety employees.

Impasses in public safety employee negotiations are particularly critical, because pressure tactics are considered inimical to public interest. The complete withdrawal of pressure tactics, however, may give employers little incentive to bargain. To end the impasse and to hasten settlement, several states and some municipalities make provision for mediation, fact-finding, and arbitration.

Impasses seem to occur more frequently in negotiations with police and fire fighters than with other public employees. In Connecticut, for instance, about two-thirds of mediation cases in the first eight months of 1967 involved policemen and fire fighters. Of the first twelve fact-finding cases in the state, five concerned police; three, fire fighters; two, public works employees; and two, other public employees.

States with experience in fact-finding for local police and fire fighters include Connecticut, Michigan, New York, Rhode Island, and Wisconsin.

Fact-finding may be an expensive procedure for both employee organization and employer. It has been estimated that the two New York City public safety rank-and-file organizations spent over $100,000 to present their case in the 1966 negotiations. In their last fact-finding session, the Milwaukee policemen spent about $60,000.

Invariably wages are the primary issue at dispute in fact-finding, but other issues may be raised. In one situation a municipality and an organization had already agreed to all issues except wages and supplementary benefits; the organization's lawyer talked the bargaining committee into submitting all issues to fact-finding, whereupon the organization lost ground on some items previously settled.

Fact-finding is an advisory procedure, and the impartiality of the fact-finder and public support of his conclusions hopefully influence the parties to accept the fact-finder's recommendations. Authorities may use a recommendation as a screen to give employees what they would be unwilling to defend publicly; or, employee leaders may use it as an excuse to accept an offer previously considered unpalatable to the membership. In several cases, however, the fact-finder's suggestion has been rejected. In Rhode Island, the mayors of Providence and Cranston have not accepted fact-finding regarding salaries of public safety employees. In 1967 negotiations between Bridgeport (Connecticut) and its police, the final agreement was a compromise between the fact-finder's decision and the city's "final" offer. In the 1966 negotiations New York City fire fighters rejected the fact-finding award and threatened to strike. In 1969 the Des Moines fire fighters rejected the advisory award and went on strike.

The availability and the rejection of fact-finding have raised questions about the effect of the fact-finding process on collective bargaining for public safety employees. Employer officials fear that fact-finding may reduce the union's willingness to bargain. Everyone is concerned with locating well-informed fact-finders, but the cost of fact-finding may deter the small, financially weak parties who are least able to bargain for themselves. The time involved in the fact-finding process may encourage longer-term agreements. In the final analysis, the attitude toward fact-finding, and its use in the future, is clearly colored by experience. In the same city, a police employee organization has obtained substantial increases through fact-finding and feels that the city bargains in bad faith, while the fire-fighter organization has had dissatisfying experiences with fact-finding and prefers to deal directly with the city.

One step beyond fact-finding is binding arbitration of disputed wages and working conditions of police and fire fighters. Voluntary arbitration has been used in specific negotiation impasses, for example, in a wage dispute in 1967 between New York City and police and fire-fighting officers. Compulsory binding arbitration, however, has generally been resisted on the grounds that it would force a settlement on parties who had not consented to either the settlement or the process of reaching a settlement, that it would destroy the parties' willingness to bargain collectively, and that it would enable a nonelected person to impose his will on a political jurisdiction. Despite these reservations, four states have legislated compulsory arbitration, but only for disputes involving public safety employees: Rhode Island, Pennsylvania and Michigan for police and fire-fighter impasses, and Wyoming for fire-fighter disputes only. The overriding concerns in each state were to insure continuous work performance by public safety employees and to provide a terminal point of contract negotiations.

Until 1968 a Rhode Island law provided for compulsory binding arbitration of nonmonetary issues in disputes between fire fighters and municipalities; the law offered only advisory arbitration for police deadlocks. In 1968 the law was amended so that all matters, including finances, in dispute between municipalities and public safety employees would be subject to compulsory binding arbitration. The amended provisions were unsuccessfully challenged in the state court on constitutional grounds in the first application, involving the city of Warwick and the fire fighters.

Compulsory binding arbitration of negotiation impasses involving police and fire fighters was approved in Pennsylvania by popular referendum in 1967 and was enacted by the state legislature in 1968. All public safety employee organizations as well as other organized labor groups in Pennsylvania supported the measure. In the first year under the new act, more than 60 cases were taken to compulsory arbitration and an award rendered. Three separate test cases were submitted to the state and federal courts, but the constitutionality of the act was upheld.[45]

The Wyoming Supreme Court has upheld the constitutionality of the state's Fire Department Collective Bargaining Act, which provides for compulsory arbitration of contract disputes between communities and fire fighters.

LOBBYING

The emergence of collective bargaining for policemen and fire fighters has not ended their efforts at lobbying for improved benefits and working conditions. These groups employ political pressure more frequently and more effectively than does any other group of local public employees. The amount of lobbying depends on legislative history, response of elected officials to lobbying efforts, resources of the organizations, and effectiveness of other means for achieving objectives. Although the amount of lobbying activity varies, there is little question that it is widespread and that it affects collective bargaining.

The interest of public safety employees in lobbying is the result of a number of factors. Police and fire departments and their employees have been politically involved longer than have other public employees. Policemen and fire fighters are tightly organized and highly visible, and have gained much sympathy from the public and the legislature. Personnel policies and programs for public safety employees have been subject to legislation more than have those for other public employees, largely because public safety employee organizations have been dissatisfied with and distrusted unilateral local actions. Consequently, long before the advent of collective bargaining, public safety employee organizations established close ties with local and state legislators and with political parties.[46] Their success in achieving their desired objectives has encouraged them to continue the practice of lobbying.

Police and fire fighter organizations develop separate lobbying programs covering many issues at the state level. Most of the issues pertain only to the organizations' respective constituents: hours, holidays, rates of pensions and medical insurance, reduction of residence requirements, credit for military service in determining promotions and retirement, shift differentials, work assignments, and reduction in chief's authority by requirement that all suspensions be reviewed by independent commissions. Other issues may affect all workers, such as increases in workmen's compensation. Still other lobbying efforts may be directed to matters directly or indirectly affecting collective bargaining— for example, compulsory arbitration and extension of home-rule charters. On particular issues, police and fire-fighter employee organizations may join forces in lobbying.

Department administrators also lobby at the state level. The New York City Police Department, for instance, had long tried to persuade the state legislature to approve a fourth shift to overlap evening hours when need and demands for police protection are particularly heavy. Until 1969, the attempts were defeated, largely because of the opposition of the Patrolmen's Benevolent Association. Once the bill was passed, PBA turned its attention from legislative lobbying to promoting a claim that collectively bargained provisions limited the department's ability to implement the statute.

Lobbying at the local level in the context of collective bargaining usually means seeking political pressure to circumvent bargaining, either during negotiations or on conclusion of an unsatisfactory agreement. All items subject to bargaining may be involved. Lobbying may also occur indirectly, as exemplified in the following incident. A fire department had consolidated its operations, thus reducing the total number of positions. The matter was not bargained, because staffing is regarded as a management prerogative. The employee organization "worked through" aldermen to restore part of the staff cuts, basing its request on inadequate fire protection. It is now following the same method to add more positions for the department.

Organizations follow one or more lines of attack to persuade politicians to adopt their views. In addition to using lobbyists of state associations, large-city organizations often employ their own lobbyists at sessions of state legislatures; organizations may offer money and manpower to state and local election campaigns; dues checkoff provides organizations with more financial resources than were previously available. One fire-fighter official noted that his organization could demonstrate lobbying strength by having men on duty write letters to legislators. Using the mass media may also indirectly affect political thinking.

Where matters are brought to popular referendum, the organizational lobbying efforts are directed to public relations. Again, the mass media becomes a prime vehicle for projecting a favorable image. In Pennsylvania the campaign for compulsory arbitration was conducted under the slogan, "Support your policemen and fire fighters." Other efforts to gain support include speaking to groups and financing of films, perhaps under the guise of fire prevention or police protection.

The problem faced by public employers is how to control lobbying efforts. One issue is that of the budget. In New York State, pensions and eligibility requirements are set at the state level, but funding is left entirely to the municipalities. The mayors' lobby has attempted to obtain legislation that would require the state to supply funds for benefits imposed on the cities by the legislature. Another issue involves control of local elected officials who undercut bargaining limits and established budget plans by yielding to demands of employee organizations, especially those representing the uniformed forces. A third issue relates to the problem of dealing with the organizations themselves. Some cities have considered the negotiating of a provision prohibiting lobbying on specific issues, but the effectiveness of such a provision is questionable, considering the organizations' methods. This problem will be discussed in more detail in Chapter VIII.

Conclusion

Collective bargaining in police and fire departments is beginning at a time when change is prevalent in these departments. Change may bring opportunity for some public safety employees, uncertainty for more, and unrest for all. Joining employee organizations and participating in their activities provide greater security for many employees.

External forces place new pressures on public safety employees. The public demand for law and order puts department efficiency at a premium. At the same time, policemen and fire fighters have seldom encountered more violent resistance in their work.

Changes within departments also affect public safety employees. A large segment of the uniformed forces is changing as new types of recruits, such as professionally trained personnel and minority-group members, are being added. The retirement of men who joined public safety departments during the Great Depression for good pay and security leaves the departments with a younger group who have less incentive to remain on the job and are less willing to accept the status quo. Moreover, the introduction of more nonuniformed employees may alter the character of the department as well as the nature of the uniformed employees' job.

These changes affect employee organizations and collective bargaining in public safety departments. New types of employees may challenge established interests and may cause strains within employee organizations, which in turn can be transmitted to relations between organizations and employers. For instance, the increasing number of Negroes on urban police and fire-fighting forces may affect not only the composition of employee organizations but also the existing relationships within the organizations. Changing concepts of professionalism may also increase tensions among present employees and lead to new employee demands.

Collective bargaining is only beginning to have a real impact on police and fire departments. As labor relations for public employees lag behind those for the private sector, so employer-employee relations in police and fire departments seem to be at a slightly earlier stage of development than those of other public employees. Public employers and employee organizations generally lack sophistication in collective bargaining. Yet the pressures to accelerate the development of collective bargaining are many. If recent history is an indication of the future, collective bargaining will soon have a much greater impact on police and fire departments, regardless of whether the parties are ready to cope with it.

VI participants in collective bargaining

Each situation discussed in the preceeding chapters has unique aspects. Yet a review of the total picture reveals the similarities and the differences of collective bargaining within the public sector and permits a comparison of labor relations experience between the public and the private sectors. This chapter will analyze the participants in public employment in the larger context of labor relations in the United States.

To understand collective bargaining is to appreciate those who participate in such bargaining. These participants, called actors in an industrial relations system, include management and their representatives; workers and their organizations; and other individuals and groups, often government agencies, who assist the other two parties at various times in their relationship.[1] In this chapter, first each participant will be described; then the implications of his role in collective bargaining and of the impact of collective bargaining on the participant will be analyzed.

Management

Management constitutes the first group of participants in collective bargaining. Management in the public sector differs greatly from management in the private sector, although in some cases the differences appear more sharply in theory than in practice. These differences are sufficiently important, however, to affect the conduct of labor relations.

POLITICAL NATURE OF PUBLIC MANAGEMENT

Management in the public sector is highly visible. At most levels of government the person(s) ultimately responsible for labor relations in the public sector is an elected official or a group. In cities, this person is the mayor; in school districts, the group is the school board. In the federal government on the other hand, an appointed agency head has authority for labor relations; he, too, is generally well known to the public. Furthermore, the actions of public managers are widely known, thanks to coverage by communications media and to public interest. Access to public management is relatively easier than it is to private management. Finally, the plans and operations of public managers are likely to be open to inspection; budget hearings provide an opportunity for those affected to review the budget and to offer opinions. While much government activity proceeds unnoticed, significant portions are a proverbial open book to anyone who cares to inquire; the political nature of government demands that actions of public managers be open to inspection.

The political character of public management is also reflected in the kinds of pressures to which the public employer responds. While the private employer is not immune to political pressure in decision making, there is little other effective pressure to account for many decisions in the public sector. Some of these pressures may operate at cross-purposes; nonetheless they are political in origin and intent. For instance, civil rights groups may insist on employment of more members of minority groups at the same time that taxpayer representatives propose slashes in the budget.

The effectiveness of pressure groups varies widely, depending partly on their numerical and financial strength, organization, and "knowing the right people." Their effectiveness may also vary on the basis of political jurisdiction. For instance, school teachers may receive less support in retirement areas such as Florida, where a sizeable proportion of the population does not use their services and therefore may be less interested in their problems.

In one sense, an employee organization may be considered another pressure group, as public employees vote in local, state, and national elections. At the same time, employees can affect the inclinations of others in the community, who may form their own pressure groups and state their own political preferences.

Although responsibility for labor relations is sometimes delegated to management personnel who are not elected, the basically political character of management does not change. The person who delegates the responsibility to subordinates remains susceptible to political pressure, and his subordinates, whether political appointees or civil service appointees, are generally well aware of this fact. If the administrator responsible for labor relations is a political appointee, his job depends on recognition of the political elements in the environment. Moreover, pressures may actually force the collective bargaining process out of the hands of those to whom the responsibility has been delegated and back to the elected officials. Such a situation occurred in the 1967 negotiations between New York City and its fire fighters and policemen.

The involvement of elected officials in negotiations outside the established framework is often recognition of the political nature of the officials' positions. More than one mayor has intervened at the minute before—or after—a strike deadline, to announce settlement of a dispute involving critical employees. This last minute effort is given wide publicity, and the mayor emerges as a hero to his constituents. The extent of the mayor's role in negotiating the settlement, the timing of his involvement, and the cost of the settlement are often unknown or not of immediate concern to the public. The public has only the impression that catastrophe has been averted by an official devoted to the public interest. The collective bargaining process has helped the official retain public favor.

Still another facet of the political nature of government is the upward flow of authority. Public managers must be responsive to the public. In smaller jurisdictions, actions of public managers may be submitted in the form of budgets and appropriation requests to popular referendum. In larger jurisdictions, indirect approval is expressed through periodic elections. In both cases, authority flows from the people to elected officials or their representatives. Compare this situation with that of the manager in the private sector, in which management is responsible to the owners or the board of directors. The flow of authority is distinctly downward from the top. In the public sector the owners are also the consumers, so the system is circular.

SOVEREIGNTY

The upward flow of authority represents the concept of sovereignty in the United States, for sovereignty belongs to the people. By definition, no one can challenge sovereignty. This orthodox version of sovereignty was invoked by public employers to thwart collective bargaining by public employees, even while they encouraged employee organizations to challenge managers in the private sector.

The logic of sovereignty demands that the sovereign can do whatever he pleases—a logic long recognized in practice. In labor relations, sovereign jurisdictions have bargained with employee representatives without awaiting enabling legislation or other approval.

A modified form of the sovereignty concept grants a sovereign the right to permit collective bargaining as long as it does not interfere with government operations. This form of the doctrine maintains the right of the public employer to change terms and conditions of employment. The sovereign reserves final authority by subordinating agreements to administrative regulations, requiring agreements to be terminated at the discretion of the public employer and prohibiting binding arbitration. Executive Order 10988 contained these limitations and leaves the final determination of collective bargaining decisions to federal agency heads.

The modified sovereignty doctrine does not render collective bargaining useless. Agreements are unenforceable but are not illegal. Of course, if the public employer repeatedly and indiscriminately invokes the termination clause or disregards advisory arbitration decisions, the value of collective bargaining will be destroyed. In this situation the effectiveness of collective bargaining depends on the good faith of the signatories, with a special burden falling on the public employer.

Even the modified form of the sovereignty concept may be in transition. Almost all those involved in labor relations in the federal government agreed that the initial system of collective bargaining was inadequate. In the choice between sovereignty theory and more effective labor relations, pragmatism dictated that the former give way as demonstrated in Executive Order 11491.

The concept of sovereignty is used less and less as an argument in collective bargaining in the public sector. First, public employers have reduced the validity of the concept by granting employees the right to bargain collectively. Second, other currently more convincing arguments have been raised to differentiate labor relations in the private and the public sectors. For instance, the meaning of the withholding of services by employees in a noneconomic environment poses problems for the participants and the public. The diminishing use and logic of sovereignty do not necessarily mean that employers in the public and the private sectors are in the same position. It does lessen the importance of one distinction that had long been considered paramount.

DISTRIBUTION OF POWER

A continuing difference between private and public employers is the structure and distribution of power. The diffusion of power in all political jurisdictions is the result of two concepts: the theory of federal and state sovereignty and the theory of checks and balances within a government system. This diffusion reduces the authority of the public employer in relation to that of the private employer. The result affects the scope and the process of collective bargaining in the public sector.

The diffusion of authority in the public sector is related to the scope of bargaining, which will be discussed in the next chapter. The responsible authority may differ depending on employee demands. A department or an agency head may have authority to negotiate only certain issues. On a specific issue, therefore, the official will refuse to make concessions because the decision is not in his hands. Such action is obviously frustrating to the employee organization. A union leader once remarked, "The only way to accomplish anything in this city is through an eyeball-to-eyeball crisis confrontation." In this case a crisis had to arise before the problem of divided authority could be resolved.

The executive officer may be able to bargain with employee representatives but may not have final authority to accept labor's proposals. Instead, he may have to present the results of negotiations to a legislature or a council for ratification. If the union's demands concern the civil service system, another level of authority is drawn into the decision-making process. If final proposals require a change in existing law of the political unit, the entire electorate may be part of the ratification system.

A significant part of the separation of powers in the public sector is the absence of fiscal control by the employer. Invariably, monetary matters are crucial in collective bargaining. The private employer has authority on monetary matters; the public employer can usually only recommend monetary settlements. The budget decisions are rarely in the public official's hands entirely. The public employer and employees may work together to alter the budget constraint. When a group of employees is confronted with a limitation on the employer's ability to pay, it may combine with the employer to seek additional appropriations from the council, legislature, or electorate.

The employer has little voice in determining some monetary items—for example, salaries at the federal level or pensions in many municipalities. The effects of dual-payer systems on employee organizations are frustration and opportunity—frustration in not being able to deal with one employer for all demands, and opportunity in being able to place pressure at several points in an attempt to enhance the economic position of the members.

The separation of power may actually make it difficult to identify the nominal employer. In attempting to establish a collective bargaining relationship in Michigan in 1968, Wayne County employees found themselves in the middle of a dispute between the Road Commission and the Civil Service Commission as to who was the employer. The decision in such an instance clearly affects the collective bargaining relationship that will be established.

WHO IS THE PUBLIC EMPLOYER?

Public employers are often thought to be alike. Such a generalization is useful for comparing public and private employers, but it oversimplifies the variety and the nature of the public employer. This section will compare various types of public employers.

There are a large number of political units in the United States. Even a single government jurisdiction contains a startling number of different employers. At the federal level, each of the more than fifty agencies is a separate employer for purposes of collective bargaining. Likewise at the local level, the designated employer may be distinguished by function.

The splintering of "employers" between and within political jurisdictions has implications for collective bargaining. Inevitably certain bargaining situations and settlements will be regarded as key and a pattern for other jurisdictions. Where numerous employers exist within a single political jurisdiction, employee representatives are presented with a natural opportunity for whipsawing, or playing one employer against another in an attempt to escalate gains.

Some public employers consist of groups of persons with authority to make decisions. School boards, special districts headed by commissions, and townships and counties run by a group of commissioners are all multiperson employers. If an employer composed of a number of individuals engages in collective bargaining directly, it does not always speak with one voice. Employer's bargaining team may be undisciplined rather than unified like the usual single-authority employer team. Such a situation invites communications problems among members of the employer group as well as between employer and employee representatives. It also makes it easier for the employee organization to put pressure on the employer and to exploit any weaknesses within the employer group; as more than one person has authority, there is greater likelihood for different interests and views. Finally, the multiple-person employer complicates delegation of labor relations by the employer to a subordinate, because the person to whom the authority is delegated will have several masters.

Public employers are both elected and appointed. Appointed public employers, except for local heads of federal agencies, generally obtain their job through patronage. Presumably the employer appointed by patronage has primary loyalty to the appointing official; the elected employer, to the electorate. The elected official may be more sensitive (and therefore more subject) to pressures of the electorate than will the appointed employer. The latter, however, will think in similar political terms if he is organizationally and geographically close to the elected official who appointed him. The distance between elected and appointed officials is far shorter in local government than in federal government, so the difference in reactions of elected and appointed officials to pressures is likely to be minimal. The local electorate identifies actions of appointed officials with local public administration more directly than with higher levels of government.

Job tenure of the public employer is often relatively short. The length of office of the elected official depends on the term of office as well as his ability to gain reelection or to seek another office. His successor may have different political affiliations as well as different views of government's role and operations. The term of the official appointed by patronage is often more a function of alignment with successful political candidates than of performance, though in exceptional cases appointed officials may rise above political associations. In jobs not subject to political appointment, the duration of the job may also be limited. For example, planned job rotation assures military officers a limited stay in each assignment. In each case there is reason for short terms: the electorate must have reasonable opportunity to be heard; the elected official must have the loyalty and support of his subordinates to implement policies; the military officer must be flexible and unattached to a particular job and location.

In contrast to the high turnover among public employers, the employee organization, once recognized, often maintains its position indefinitely. In the developing employer-employee relationship, the employee representative gains experience, whereas the employer starts relatively afresh with changes in officeholders. High turnover among public employers disrupts continuity and stability in labor relations in the public sector. This is especially the case when a change involves persons of different political leanings, because public officials may be more concerned with personal and party success than with that of the political unit. The relative imbalance created by differing tenures of public employers and employee representatives gives these representatives an unusual advantage. It may also force public employers to find other means, such as staff personnel, to provide the necessary continuity.

Civil service systems are an established part of public employment in many government sectors. In challenging the public employer, employee organizations frequently challenge civil service rules and interpretations. Civil service has thus come to be identified with the employer, even though its original purpose was to protect employees from the employer. Public employers must sometimes reconcile employee organization objectives with the civil service system. The two may appear incompatible, as when employee organizations urge seniority as a criterion for promotion. Nevertheless, civil service concepts have been modified for political reasons—for example, veteran's preference for employment —and may be further modified in the future. Strong employee organizations may feel little need or desire for extension of civil service systems. Whether existing systems will prove to be an aid or a hindrance to public employers in dealing with employee organizations remains to be seen.

MANAGEMENT REACTION TO COLLECTIVE BARGAINING

Legislation or administrative procedures requiring public employers to bargain with employee representatives have been readily accepted by public employers. Thirty years' experience with widespread bargaining by employers in the private sector has undoubtedly made the prospects of bargaining with employees more acceptable to public employers. Prior to 1960 the isolated experiments with collective bargaining in the public sector reinforced the notion that collective bargaining could work in public employment. Moreover, public employers recognized that legislation requiring them to bargain was an expression of the public will. Open resistance to such expression would now have quite different repercussions than employer opposition to the Wagner Act in the 1930s. Defiance of legislation by public employers, would invite political attacks and would be virtual political suicide.

Some public employers have been willing to recognize employee organizations and to accept collective bargaining even though not required to do so by legislation. In some cases recognition and acceptance of it was first accorded in areas having strong unions in the private sector—for example, New York City, Philadelphia, Detroit. The political power of employee organizations, both public and private, is recognized by public employers and candidates for public office. Even in the absence of organization of private employees in the same region, public employees' organizations may wield political power. Strike action, or the threat of it, has been another reason for public employer acceptance of the employee organization and collective bargaining. School boards have often acceded to such threats. In a few cases—the Tennessee Valley Authority, for example—management has unilaterally decided to grant recognition and bargaining rights without facing political power or strike action by employee organizations.

Public employers have tempered their endorsement of collective bargaining by rejecting parts of the process common in the private sector and demanded by public employees. The most striking examples are the uses of pressure tactics and of procedures for resolving impasses. Many issues that may be regarded as working conditions, and thus subject to collective bargaining in the private sector, have also been reserved to public management's sole discretion.

The employer may desire to limit collective bargaining for one or a combination of the following reasons. (1) Civil service systems fulfill some goals usually set for collective bargaining and present obstacles to other goals. (2) The patronage system provides many public employers with a power base they wish to retain. At the same time it serves to weaken the employee organization by dividing employee loyalties between the employer and the organization. (3) The lingering sovereignty principle raises questions about the extent to which the employer should legally surrender authority. (4) Public employers, like their private counterparts, are loath to let others share in decision making for fear of losing control and reducing operating efficiency. (5) Experience in the private sector has made public employers wary of some aspects of collective bargaining. Although collective bargaining is generally accepted in the private sector, the practice is criticized by persons who point to strikes, inflationary pressures escalated by collective bargaining, and the image of some unions.

IMPACT OF COLLECTIVE BARGAINING ON MANAGEMENT

Recognition of employee organizations and collective bargaining in the public sector have resulted in many different repercussions, depending on the environment and the scope of bargaining. Collective bargaining has had less impact on management in the federal government than on local employers in states, because of the limited areas for bargaining and the restrictions on the use of outside personnel, such as arbitrators. Nevertheless, all public employers have experienced certain repercussions.

Collective bargaining has introduced a new force into the decision-making process. In those areas, however limited, where decision-making is bilateral, management has had to defend its position and to be prepared for challenges. The role of the employee organization in decision making has also formalized the employer-employee relationship and weakened the traditionally paternalistic attitude of public employers toward employees.

Collective bargaining has also forced the public employer to reevaluate itself and its organization. Perhaps the first question to be raised is: Who is management? Some person(s) must have authority to represent the employer in negotiations or to make final decisions for management in grievances. Yet the answer is often not clear for public employers, because of the diffusion of authority among and within departments of government. Collective bargaining forces an answer to this question and thereby clarifies the lines of management authority.

Besides clarifying lines of authority between departments and units of government, collective bargaining also forces a clearer distinction between management and rank-and-file within departments. In part, this distinction is a result of unit determination; defining supervisory personnel establishes the limits of the bargaining unit. Another part of the distinction, however, goes beyond formal unit boundaries. Employees with supervisory responsibilities identify more closely with management in the negotiations and administration of the bargaining agreement. Although many supervisors in the public sector may be similarly affected, the change in identification may be most evident in the school superintendent, the police chief, and the fire chief. The superintendent and the chiefs have traditionally had dual loyalties, that is, they identified professionally and personally with their subordinates while they implemented the policies of their political superiors. Indeed they often presented and defended requests of their subordinates to their superiors. Collective bargaining has taken away their representative role, has given them new responsibilities in administering procedures and working conditions, and has generally brought them to the side of management.

Another question is: What should management's role be toward its employees? A haphazard or inequitable approach to personnel administration proves unsatisfactory under the pressures of collective bargaining.

The absence of expertise in collective bargaining is common among public employers and is sometimes not recognized until the employer-employee relationship founders in a crisis. The presence of an experienced employee organization facing an inexperienced employer drives the point home sooner. To overcome this weakness, some large public employers have added to their staffs permanent full-time personnel to handle labor relations.

A more common remedy has been to employ part-time specialists, particularly to represent the public employer in contract negotiations. The latter practice highlights the importance of negotiations but may not recognize the significance of continuity in the employer-employee relationship. The part-time and full-time specialists hired by the public employer are usually persons with labor relations experience in the private sector; few persons have primary labor relations experience in the public sector. Invariably such persons bring with them their attitudes toward and practices of labor relations in the private sector, and these factors affect labor relations in the public sector. A true measure of the development of collective bargaining in the public sector is the formation of several labor relations consultant services to public employers. At least one consultant is officially endorsed by the National League of Cities and the National Association of Counties. Another has conducted seminars and consulted with state school board associations.

Collective bargaining has also increased the importance to management of the industrial relations function. The development of authority for labor relations decisions permits uniform interpretation of provisions and prevents whipsawing. The addition of labor relations specialists shifts some authority from line personnel to the labor relations staff. In some principal cities personnel staffs conduct all negotiations, a task previously performed by line managers. In New York City for instance, the responsibility for negotiations was shifted to a municipal labor relations office created in 1966.

Regardless of the addition of specialists, however, the increasing importance of labor relations in the job of *all* managers is now recognized. At the same time, most managers have little understanding of labor relations because of its novelty in public employment. Some moves have been made to provide labor relations training for managers. At the federal level, for example, the Navy Department trains line managers who negotiate local contracts. In late 1967, New York City trained the personnel staffs of line departments responsible for supervising the administration of labor agreements. Several school districts have held in-service labor relations training programs for principals and upper echelon administrators.

The increase in labor relations activity in the public sector has also led to consultation by managers within government units to coordinate efforts and to ensure uniform application of rules. The U.S. Civil Service Commission sponsors an interagency group who meet formally each month for discussion of employee relations developments. The office of the Wisconsin governor also provides coordinating services. The informal contacts resulting from such efforts are countless.

Employee Organizations

The second group of participants, employee organizations, has also been affected by the large-scale introduction of collective bargaining in public employment in the last decade.

MEMBERSHIP

The most apparent and measurable change has been the growth of the membership in and the number of employee organizations active in the public sector. Between 1960 and 1968, membership of government workers in national unions increased 100 percent, from 1,070,000 to 2,153,000.[2] Significantly, the number of unions reporting government employees as members increased between 1960 and 1966 from forty-one to fifty-eight. The growth of some individual unions active in recruiting government workers was particularly noticeable. The American Federation of Government Employees (AFGE) reported 59,000 members in 1958 and over 300,000 in 1969. The American Federation of State, County and Municipal Employees (AFSCME) added more than 50 percent to its 1964 membership of 235,000 in the next four years. Growth was not confined to unions composed solely of government workers. The Laborers International Union of North America claimed to have doubled in six years the number of government workers who are members of the union, to a total of 75,000 members in early 1968. The International Association of Machinists reported an increase of 35 percent in government employee membership in the dozen years since 1956.[3]

Prior to 1962, AFSCME and the National Association of Letter Carriers were the only public employee unions on the list of national unions with 100,000 or more members. Since then, additions to the list primarily have been organizations of public employees: in 1962, fire fighters, postal clerks, and government employees (AFGE) and in 1964, teachers.[4]

Government employees also constitute an increasing proportion of organized labor. In 1956, government workers represented 5.1 percent of 18 million members in national and international unions. In 1968 they accounted for 9.4 percent of approximately 20 million union members.

In certain classifications of organized labor, government workers have made more rapid strides than the movement as a whole. In 1960, only 18.7 percent of organized white-collar members were public employees; by 1966, 28.8 percent were public employees. Almost two-thirds of the 552,000-member gain among white-collar workers in that period was made in the public sector.

It is more difficult to estimate the proportion of government workers who are members of employee organizations. Large numbers of public employees are in national professional associations and unaffiliated employee organizations that may serve many of the same purposes as national unions. The fallacy of distinguishing employee organizations on the basis of union affiliation is apparent in comparing the behavior of and results for municipal fire fighters, who commonly are members of an international union, and policemen, who usually belong to independent local organizations. The numbers left out of the previous figures on national union membership are significant. The better known national nonunion employee organizations include the National Education Association, with more than 1 million members; the American Nurses Association, with 170,000 members, many of whom work for federal, state, or local government; and the Fraternal Order of Police, with 90,000 members. There are, in addition, national coordinating groups, such as the National Conference of Police Associations with 275,000 members, and state organizations, such as civil service employee associations.

Yet a closer investigation of union membership among government employees is warranted. Table VI–1 gives some indication

Table VI–1
Organization of Government Employees—Federal, State, and Local

Year	TOTAL CIVILIAN GOVERNMENT EMPLOYMENT, *a*	MEMBERSHIP OF GOVERNMENT WORKERS IN NATIONAL UNIONS, *b*	PERCENT, *b/a*
1956	7,277,000	915,000	12.6%
1958	7,839,000	1,035,000	12.8
1960	8,353,000	1,070,000	12.0
1962	8,890,000	1,225,000	13.8
1964	10,871,000	1,453,309	15.2
1966	10,871,000	1,717,000	15.8
1968	12,202,000	2,153,000	17.6

SOURCES: Bureau of Labor Statistics, *Handbook of Labor Statistics, 1969* Bulletin No. 1630 (Washington, D.C.), tables 36 and 136, and *Directory of National and International Labor Unions in the United States, 1967,* Bulletin No. 1596 (Washington, D.C.), Table 7.

of the absolute growth of membership of government employees in organizations representing their interests and of the relative degree of organization within the fast-growing area of public employment. The composite figures for employment and membership disguise differences in the extent of organization by levels of government and within levels of government. In 1968, over 49 percent of all federal workers were members of national unions, while less than 9 percent of state and local employees were affiliated. The primary strength of nonunion and local independent employee organizations, however, is at the state and local levels. Whatever set of figures is used, employee organizations in toto are organizing a larger proportion of public employees, despite increases in public employment. At the same time, many areas of public employment, particularly in the state and local sectors, have scarcely been touched by employee organizations interested in collective bargaining.

EXTERNAL CAUSES OF MEMBERSHIP GROWTH AND INCREASED ACTIVITY IN EMPLOYEE ORGANIZATIONS

The increase in membership in employee organizations among government employees and the developing interest in collective bargaining by employee organizations are products of several coinciding factors.

The passage of legislation and quasi legislation signaled to employee organizations a new era in public employment labor relations. The most important signal was issuance of Executive Order 10988, which covered nearly all federal employees. This executive order was followed by legislation in many states, which granted representation and bargaining rights to employee organizations. These administrative and legislative acts gave notice to public employees that support of and activity in employee organizations are appropriate.

Labor unions with experience primarily in the private sector were eager to seize upon the new organizing possibilities. Declining union membership and prospects of lower employment in traditional strongholds because of automation threatened to weaken these unions economically and politically. Public employees, largely unorganized, provided a new opportunity. Moreover, government was a "growth" industry with a high proportion of white-collar employees. Organizing success in the public area could affect organizing in other industries, a prospect that attracted the efforts of a number of unions with no experience in representing public employees and with no clear jurisdictional claim to them.

The nature of the public employee himself has been changing. Traditionally the public employee was viewed as a "bureaucrat," connoting a passive person who accepts authority and is interested only in job tenure. Perhaps the system and the conditions of government employment gave some credence to this view during the period when union membership was expanding most rapidly in the private sector. Persons employed by government during the depression years of the 1930s may have felt fortunate in having a job and may therefore have been particularly kindly disposed toward government employment and the public employer. This attitude would be reinforced by the general security of employment and by a fringe benefit package which for a long time was more generous than that offered workers in the private sector. Over time, as new employees have entered government employment and older ones have left, the character of the labor force has changed. The new personnel not only have lowered the average age of the public employee but also have introduced new views about public employment. Each employee is a product of his time. If "depression mentality" characterized the government employee of the 1930s and 1940s (along with everyone else in the labor force during those years), a spirit of unrest and involvement may be more characteristic of the government employee of the 1960s—qualities that provide fertile ground for organizing efforts.

An increasingly larger proportion of government workers are members of minority groups. This fact has not been lost on some employee organizations which have sought to combine their organizing efforts with the civil rights struggle. A notable example was the AFSCME organization of Negro sanitation workers in Memphis in the spring of 1968. About one-third of AFSCME members are Negro, a factor that reinforces the union's interest in civil rights and attracts additional members of minority groups.

Related to the changing character of the government worker are changing labor market conditions. A long period of economic expansion and employment alternatives makes the government worker more secure and more ready to challenge management. At the same time the public employer cannot afford to lose personnel if he has difficulty in replacing workers. This situation provides workers with a psychological and tactical advantage.

REPERCUSSONS ON EMPLOYEE ORGANIZATIONS

Employee organizations have had to adjust policies and structure to accommodate to the developments just described. These internal changes contribute to the changing scene in public employment labor relations.

Employee organizations change their policy and direction to take advantage of new laws permitting bargaining. Prior to the advent of collective bargaining, employee organizations are usually structured and conditioned to lobbying; in some cases, they may be suspicious of bargaining. Once collective bargaining has been authorized, the employee organization partly reorganizes its staff and programs to bargain with the employer, lest another organization should do so.

Change may be due to pressures by the membership. As a result of membership unrest the International Association of Fire Fighters was forced to review its constitutional prohibition of strikes and to remove the total ban on them. Similarly membership pressure has been instrumental in AFSCME's becoming more militant.

Once an employee organization is willing to adapt its policies to a changing situation, it may find it necessary to make further changes. NEA, which not long ago had little interest in collective bargaining, now advocates withdrawal of teacher services under certain circumstances and argues that such withdrawals are not illegal. AFSCME now opposes the civil service system as restrictive to collective bargaining. Some organizations endorse compulsory arbitration.

Policy changes by one organization are likely to pressure rival organizations to adapt to the new situation. Adjustment may consist of adopting identical policies, but it is not necessary to follow suit exactly. The increasing militancy of the American Federation of Teachers (AFT), espoused to pressure school boards, has challenged NEA to find ways of expressing militancy in professionally acceptable terms. Similarly, as a result of organizing pressure from AFSCME, some state employee associations now favor collective bargaining.

The effects of growth in membership and collective bargaining have been more pronounced for employee organizations composed entirely of government workers than for unions involved also in the private sector. Although the latter have had to learn the peculiarities of government labor relations, to devise methods suitable to the public sector, and to devote resources to organizing workers and servicing members, they have had the advantage of bargaining experience. The policies and staffs of unions operating in the private sector have been attuned to collective bargaining. Moreover, the greater part of their membership and activity has remained outside the public sector, so changes have had relatively less dramatic impact on them than on those dealing exclusively in government labor relations.

Membership changes and developments in public sector labor relations have caused leadership shifts in public employee organizations. Dissatisfaction with the response of national leadership to organizing and bargaining opportunities led to the defeat in the early 1960s of the presidents of AFT and AFSCME.

To carry out new functions, organizations have had to enlarge their staffs. The variety of problems encountered in collective bargaining has forced organizations to develop expertise in these problem areas. Many organizations hired their first research personnel to provide data for collective bargaining and expanded their publications staffs to keep members better informed of labor relations developments. Moreover, national organizations added to their organizing staffs to promote membership.

Employee organizations have frequently encountered the same problems as public employers in developing expertise and in finding suitable personnel. Some have resorted to temporary assistance, especially for initial guidance in collective bargaining; for instance, NEA used a well-known New York City law firm. Most organizations have tried to develop internal staffs to the best of their resources and to availability of personnel. A prime but unpredictable opportunity for one organization to hire personnel familiar with the public sector results from internal political disputes in another organization. The staff of the AFSCME administration defeated in 1964 is now scattered among a number of other, usually rival organizations.

The costs of organizing, bargaining, and improving services necessary to maintain the image of a progressive employee organization have caused several organizations—AFT, AFGE, and AFSCME, for instance—to raise their dues in recent years. Such increases may widen the gap in the level of dues between national unions and local independent organizations. The latter frequently make the level of dues a principal issue when facing national unions in representation elections.

The opportunity for obtaining new members has stimulated some organizations to expand on-going recruiting efforts and other organizations to enter new membership territory. At times the result has been intense jurisdictional rivalry. One measure of competition has been utilization of AFL-CIO's internal machinery for settlement of jurisdictional disputes. In recent years a number of cases has involved either AFSCME or AFGE.

A recent development in the labor movement has been consolidation of organizations by mergers. Rivalries are sometimes costly and damaging to those involved. AFT has succeeded in spurring the much larger NEA to accept collective bargaining, but the race between these two organizations for members and for gaining superior monetary settlements may end on a treadmill. A merger memorandum has been agreed upon by AFSCME and the New Jersey Civil Service Employees Association.

Some consolidations are the outcome of cooperative efforts rather than rivalry. The postal unions have talked merger to strengthen lobbying and collective bargaining. This move may be attributed to the joint bargaining experience of the seven postal unions recognized as exclusive representatives at the national level. In 1968 one postal union, the mail handlers, agreed to merge with the Laborers International Union of North America, on grounds of improved bargaining skill and services to members at least cost. The Laborers more than doubled its representation of federal workers as a result of the merger. This is one way for an organization desiring entry into or expansion of public employee membership to attain its objective quickly.

Aside from some of the few groups considering merger, there is little formal coordination among employee organizations, a fact particularly surprising for organizations dealing with the same employer. Apparently feelings of rivalry in negotiating for economic gains outweigh possible advantages of coordinated efforts. The assumption inherent in these feelings is that the size of the economic pie is fixed. On noneconomic issues there is generally an absence of common interest.

With growing membership and experience in bargaining, employee organizations have learned that they are often a political force in the community. As a whole, public labor unions have also become a force in organized labor as evidenced by the election of the presidents of two public employee unions to the AFL-CIO Executive Council in 1969.

Third-Party Participants

A collective bargaining relationship is one in which employer and employee representative determine issues affecting employees. Occasionally, the two parties voluntarily seek or are legally required to use the services of others in developing the collective bargaining relationship. These third-party participants include government agencies and private individuals, which may provide administrative help or professional expertise in establishing the relationship and in resolving impasses. Their participation affects collective bargaining in the public sector.

The variation among governments in kinds of third-party participants results from the exclusion of public employees from federal legislation of labor-management relations. Public employees have never been able to use the National Labor Relations Board to seek recognition or to compel their employers to bargain. The exclusion has been purposeful. The orginal reason for exclusion reflected the belief that in sovereignty public employees should not be given the right to organize and bargain. Even now, when such rights have been granted in one form or another to a large number of public employees, two legal issues need to be settled before Congress extends labor relations legislation to cover public employees: would federal jurisdiction of all government employees be an invasion of state sovereignty, and should public employees have the same rights as workers in the private sector.

A recent United States Supreme Court decision may be an important precedent for future cases regarding federal jurisdiction over state and municipal employees. In 1967, amendments to the Fair Labor Standards Act (FLSA) expanded coverage of minimum wage requirements to include employees of states, municipalities, and school districts. A group of twenty-seven state attorneys general appealed the amendments, but the Supreme Court upheld the right of the federal government to regulate local and state government employees.[5]

The jurisdiction of FLSA and all legislation governing private sector employment relations is based on the commerce clause of the United States Constitution, which gives the federal government the power to regulate interstate commerce. Presumably, the Supreme Court would also uphold federal regulation of employment relations of state and local employees.

In general, the third-party participants at the state and local level are the same for labor relations in the public sector as they are for those in the private sector. State labor relations boards have been authorized to determine units and to conduct representation elections. In some cases, prior to statutory authorization, the boards have assumed jurisdiction on request of the parties. State mediation and conciliation services also participate in the public sector in many states, though not in all, where labor relations boards operate. State legislatures tend to provide more alternative methods for settling impasses than for establishing collective bargaining relationships. The Federal Mediation and Conciliation Service has assisted in disputes at the federal level before formally being assigned the task by Executive Order 11491.

Private individuals invited to participate in labor relations in the public sector are also likely to be carryovers from the private sector. The passage of legislation confirms the informal practice. The names of arbitrators appointed by the Secretary of Labor to advise in representation disputes in federal government are familiar to students of labor relations in private industry. The neutrals named to the education panel of the American Arbitration Association have experience mainly in education circles, but those appointed by the parties generally have experience in private employment labor relations. The government administrative agencies responsible for naming third-party neutrals as well as the two principals themselves have preferred persons with experience in labor relations to those with no experience.

Some important exceptions to the use of identical agencies in private and public labor relations can be cited. New York State has established a Public Employment Relations Board (PERB) to handle representation questions and to institute impasse procedures; in the event of a strike, the board determines whether to revoke recognition of the employee organization. Some counties in New York State have established their own boards (called mini-PERBS), to handle these questions. The New York City Office of Collective Bargaining serves the same purpose. At the federal level Executive Order 10988 provided extraordinary channels for handling labor relations problems. In representation disputes, the Secretary of Labor decided whether advisory arbitration of the dispute was warranted and, if so, named the arbitrator. Executive Order 11491 created a special agency to resolve negotiations impasses.

Teachers have also been singled out for special attention. In Connecticut, Maryland, and Washington, impasse procedures and sometimes representation issues involving teachers are referred to state education departments for settlement. The New York State Education Department also has a special bureau to undertake a third-party role in relationships between school boards and teacher organizations.

REPERCUSSIONS OF THIRD-PARTY PARTICIPANTS

Third-party participants contribute to the transfer of procedures and concepts from the private sector to the public sector. Administrative agencies accustomed to determining units have found it appropriate to apply to public unit questions the criteria employed in private industry. Experienced mediators have often employed methods tested in the private sector to settle disputes in public employment. Third-party participants have generally not distinguished between situations occurring in the private sector and those occurring in the public sector. Perhaps the result would have been similar if inexperienced third-party participants had been invited to answer questions. Yet use of groups and individuals schooled in labor relations in the private sector has helped to ensure that this would be the case.

The use of traditional agencies and persons in public employer-employee relationships has substantially increased their work load. Existing resources were often stretched tightly before collective bargaining for government employees became widespread, yet few new staff members have been appointed to handle the new problems. State agencies have found that more and more of their time has been devoted to labor relations for public employees. Arbitrators have received an increasing number of requests from the public sector. Unless the problems decrease, which is unlikely, or unless the number of third-party participants increases, the resulting pressure on existing resources may prove to be intolerable to all concerned.

A few traditional third-party participants have begun to specialize in public employee problems. State agencies sometimes allocate their resources to provide attention and services to the public sector. In Connecticut and Michigan, personnel of state mediation agencies, trained in private sector problems, devote full time to problems in the public sector. Such specialization has been the result of increasing work loads of third-party participants and a desire for efficiency rather than any presumed uniqueness of labor relations in government employment. It is possible, however, that continued specialization within traditional third-party agencies may cause those who gained their initial experience in the private sector to think in different terms. Persons without previous labor relations experience who are hired to deal with the increasing work load may feel less restricted in applying different concepts. Similarly among private individuals, some specialization is likely to occur. Identification of private individuals with certain industries has long been common, and there is reason to expect specialization in government problems.

One difficulty usually skirted in considering third-party participants in public employer-employee relations is the potential conflict of interest of any public agency or representative. The issue is often avoided, because the public third-party participant is at a different level of government from the employer. For example, no potential conflict of interest occurs when a state labor relations or mediation board intervenes in a local dispute. On the other hand, some state agencies have helped to decide representation questions for state employees without legal challenge.

The issue has been raised at the federal level. Executive Order 10988 required the Secretary of Labor and the Civil Service Commission to issue general procedures and codes of conduct, the individual agencies to set their own regulations, and the Secretary of Labor to determine arbitrable questions in representation disputes. Employee organizations representing federal employees had charged that the establishment and regulation of labor relations was entirely in the hands of the public employer. The organizations had requested that a "neutral" agency, such as the National Labor Relations Board or a separate but similar agency, handle labor relations problems between federal employers and employee organizations. The Federal Labor Relations Council established by Executive Order 11491 is such an agency, though its members are presidential appointees who are involved in collective bargaining. The dilemma has been resolved on a pragmatic basis rather than on legal grounds.

VII recognition and the scope of negotiations

Before collective bargaining can begin, the employer must recognize, either formally or informally, an employee organization as representing a specific group of workers who compose the bargaining unit. Before and during collective bargaining, both parties must decide upon the structure of bargaining and the negotiable topics. These items—recognition, unit determination, bargaining structure, and scope of bargaining—are the major subjects of this chapter.

Recognition

Clearly the trend in public employment labor relations is toward granting exclusive recognition, which provides that the employee organization selected by a majority of the collective bargaining unit represents all workers in the unit. Statutory provisions and formal procedures covering collective bargaining in the public sector have generally followed the practice of exclusive recognition established in collective bargaining in the private sector. Public employee organizations have favored the concept of exclusive recognition because it increases their overall strength.

231

In spite of the trend toward exclusive recognition, some groups interested in public sector labor relations question or oppose the principle. The distinguished panel responsible for the Taylor Report in New York State felt unsure enough of the desirability of exclusive representation to recommend further study of the question by the Public Employment Relations Board.[1] Some scholars have advocated experimentation in types of recognition, such as recognition of employee organizations representing a minority of employees in the bargaining unit.

Experiments with recognition other than exclusive have been relatively rare. Executive Order 10988 provided for formal and informal recognition for organizations not representing a majority of workers in a bargaining unit. The objective of such minority recognition was to avoid disrupting existing forms of recognition and to give all organizations an opportunity to be recognized by the public employer. The effect was to encourage organization and to allow organizations just beginning to recruit members to get "a foot in the door." In this light, a system of multiple types of recognition is useful primarily as a transitional step in the introduction of collective bargaining. In the first formal review of Executive Order 10988 in 1967, federal agencies agreed with employee organizations that the time had arrived to reduce the types of recognition allowed in the federal government. Executive Order 11491 made provision for reduction in types to exclusive recognition.

Proportional representation, which permits the organization to represent only those employees who are members of the organization, has been developed primarily among teachers. Such a plan has been legislated in two states: California and Minnesota. In California support has come from the California Teachers Association, an NEA affiliate, which apparently thought the plan would preserve its role in collective bargaining.

In the absence of statutes governing recognition, public employers sometimes grant recognition informally. The relationships stemming from such informal recognition are sometimes also informal, lacking grievance procedures or written agreements. In other cases, however, informal recognition does not deter both parties from following all the details of collective bargaining.

The widespread use of exclusive recognition has not dispelled the problem of what rights, if any, should be accorded to minority organizations. The government remains open to all its citizens. Because some citizens are also employees and have united in collective bargaining does not change the government's basic role. Yet exclusive recognition gives the representative of the majority of employees the right to participate in decision-making. Unless other meaningful forms of recognition are provided for representatives of the minority of employees, exclusive recognition deprives the minority from a voice in those government decisions arrived at in collective bargaining. The dilemma of reconciling these concepts underscores a difference between the role of the employer in the private sector and that of the employer in the public sector.

Unit Determination

A variety of bargaining units has been established in public employment—single units covering all employees of an employer, departmental units, functional units, and occupational units, basically the same types of units encountered in collective bargaining in private industry.

The criteria for determining units have been included in the laws of some states, have been established by administrative agencies, or have been devised by the employer. The criterion stated most frequently is "community of interest of employees." In some cases, the laws single out special groups for consideration; for example policemen and fire fighters are placed in separate units, whereas unit determination for other employees is left to administrative interpretation of announced general criteria. Administrative agencies with private industry experience freely adapt to the public sector policies and practices in the private sector. For example, they have adapted the principle that professional employees should determine whether they want to be included in larger units.

The size of the collective bargaining unit may be based on the definition of the public employer and by the scope of negotiations. Executive Order 10988 designated agencies as separate employers thereby immediately limiting the size of any unit in the federal government. Within a federal agency, moreover, the lowest level of employer may be in a particular geographic location, thus further restricting the size of the unit. Limitations on subjects for negotiations also weaken the logic of including employees and curb their desire to be in a given unit. If an employer can deal with topics affecting only one group of employees, little purpose is served in including other employees in a unit.

In most cases, the public employer and the employee organization agree on the unit determination, even though each may initially prefer a unit of different scope. To avoid whipsawing, the employer generally favors a single unit for all employees. With a single unit the employee organization is required to mediate among its members and to set its own priorities for negotiations. Such a unit also simplifies administration of labor relations and forces employees to decide on a majority representative. In some cases, employers may argue for a single unit, knowing that no employee organization could win an election of such a unit.

Employee organizations prone to let pragmatic considerations govern the size of unit requests, ask for as large a unit as they believe they can win. Particularly in the early stages of labor relations, the size of this unit will tend to be far smaller than that supported by the employer. The self-image of the employee organization may also govern unit requests. Organizations with a professional image, such as nurses and fire fighters, will restrict unit requests to their professions.

A collective bargaining system must provide recourse for resolution of unit determinations if the parties cannot agree on the appropriate size of the unit; otherwise there can be no determination of a representative and no collective bargaining. Executive Order 10988 provided advisory arbitration as a guide to federal agency heads in making their final decisions. The system preserved executive authority, but it did not prove satisfactory. The decisions of ad hoc arbitrators were not necessarily consistent; nor were they binding. The system came under sharp attack in the 1967 hearings reviewing the Executive Order and was altered in Executive Order 11491.

At the state and local levels of government, unit determination disputes are generally resolved by the same administrative agencies as those in private industry. The decisions of these state labor relations boards, are final and binding. There are exceptions to the general practice. In school districts third-party neutrals selected and paid by the parties have been authorized to determine collective bargaining units, and in many cases, these decisions have been binding. In New Jersey and New York, public employee agencies are charged with making decisions about unit questions.

Supervisors present the unit question most frequently encountered in public employment—and the thorniest. Job titles and grade classifications often mask recognition of supervisory authority. In police and fire-fighting departments, for instance, only the chief has the authority to discipline or to assign personnel. Even if a supervisor can be acceptably defined, problems of recognition and appropriate units for supervisors remain. In private industry, the protection of the Labor-Managemant Relations Act is denied to supervisors. In public employment no clear public policy has been espoused. Exclusive recognition of supervisors in the federal government had raised many questions. For example, does such recognition create a conflict of interest for supervisors, and what should be the relationship within management between a supervisors' unit and a subordinates' unit. The lack of clear answers to these questions had caused federal agencies to slow down recognition of and bargaining with supervisors. The self-image of professional associations demands, however, that all employees be included in unit requests, regardless of authority. Both the National Education Association and the American Nurses Association often seek to represent supervisors, along with rank-and-file employees, in one collective bargaining unit.

The size of the unit has implications not only for collective bargaining but also for the political power of the organization representing employees in the unit. Political power may determine unit size, especially when, in the absence of legislation, the unit is determined bilaterally. The public employer is sometimes caught in the dilemma of favoring large units for efficiency in labor relations, at the same time recognizing the potential political implications of large units. Generally the larger the size of the unit, the greater the power of the employee representatives to influence decisions outside as well as within negotiations. The determination of unit size is critical for the entire collective bargaining process.

BARGAINING STRUCTURE

To understand the structure of collective bargaining, an analytic distinction should be made among three groups: (1) the group of employees eligible to vote in a representation election—the election district; (2) the group of employees covered by a negotiated agreement—the negotiation unit; and (3) the group of employees and employers affected by a particular bargaining agreement—the unit of direct impact.[2]

The administrative agency frequently plays an important role in determining the election district in the public sector. The composition of the negotiation unit, on the other hand, is decided largely by the employer and the employee organization. With few exceptions, negotiation units in the public sector have consisted of a single employing agency and a single employee organization. The structure of the negotiation unit may be modified in several ways.

One possible modification is the development of coalition bargaining, whereby two or more unions representing persons working for the same employer join together to bargain simultaneously. Coalition bargaining has become increasingly popular with unions in the private sector. The only case of coalition bargaining in the public sector has occurred among unions of postal employees at the national level. Here the unions have joined together to negotiate one agreement with the Postmaster General, although many supplementary agreements have been negotiated with local postmasters.

A second possible change in bargaining structure would result from joint bargaining. Joint bargaining may be considered the employer equivalent of coalition bargaining, because separate agencies at a single level of government join together to bargain with one or more employee organizations. Some joint bargaining has occurred in large municipalities to avoid union whipsawing. The establishment of a single agency or negotiator responsible for bargaining with all unions of city employees is a major step toward joint bargaining. In some cases, joint bargaining will not be formalized, but the effect is similar if the city's single negotiator considers negotiations with individual unions in the total context of the city's relationship with all of its unions.

Joint bargaining occurred in the 1968 negotiations between New York City and its uniformed employees. In prior years, the city agencies had negotiated separately with fire fighters, police, and sanitation employees, but agreements negotiated with one group immediately set a pattern for settlements with the other two groups. In fact, retroactive increases were sometimes granted to a group of employees who had already reached agreement because of subsequent wage settlements with one of the other groups of employees. In 1968, however, the three agencies and the city's director of labor relations negotiated jointly with the three unions.

A third possibility in altering the existing bargaining structure lies in association bargaining, whereby different employers join to negotiate a single agreement with employee representatives. Association bargaining, common in private sector industries with many small employers, has not occurred among public employees. Association bargaining in the public sector would require employers of different governmental jurisdictions to join together for bargaining. For example, a group of school districts could bargain jointly with an organization or organizations representing employees in all of the districts.

Some boards of education have shown considerable interest in association bargaining to save the time spent in separate negotiations. In 1968, a state education department commissioned a feasibility study of association bargaining for a group of school boards, which generally favored some type of association bargaining. The state teachers association, which had local affiliates in all of the school districts involved, opposed the idea and insisted that wages and most working conditions be determined locally. The objections of the teacher organization to association bargaining were based on the different tax levels in the school districts, the problems of transition from the divergent salary schedules and working conditions to a unified package, and the political problem of local organization presidents losing prestige if they could no longer take credit for settlements.

Another problem inherent in association bargaining is ratification of agreements by local public employers. Possibly, present state statutes prohibit individual employers from delegating agreement-making authority to an association. Although informal delegation would probably still be legal, the risk of an employer or the electorate rejecting the settlement remains. Furthermore, if an impasse is declared, a fact-finder probably would issue separate and possibly different awards for each jurisdiction.

Rather than becoming formally involved in coalition, joint, or association bargaining, the parties in many public sector jurisdictions bargain separately but with a close eye on settlements reached elsewhere. The pattern setter sometimes is the largest comparable jurisdiction or the most prestigious jurisdiction. In other cases, the *first* agency or jurisdiction to settle establishes the pattern. Word of settlements travels quickly because union representatives often negotiate in several jurisdictions simultaneously and because management negotiators maintain contact with their counterparts in comparable jurisdictions. Observers are continually surprised to see how quickly a specific dollar amount or percentage increase becomes a pattern for a group of geographically separate jurisdictions.

Clearly, the police were the pattern setters among municipal employees in 1968, possibly because of concern with "law and order" and urban riots. Parity formulas and the need for acceptable wage structures guarantee that wage increases for police are passed on to fire fighters and other city employees. If other employees do not receive wage adjustments, they show resentment and make more difficult the maintenance of peaceful employment relations. These problems are particularly acute when most policemen are white and the city employees not receiving comparable wage increases are largely black.

Pattern bargaining on nonmonetary issues has been especially prevalent in public education. Both AFT and the national and state education associations have reproduced sample agreements that they recommend to their local affiliates. Class size, leave policies, length of school year, and many other topics irrelevant to the particular school district are frequently negotiated.

The structure of bargaining in the public sector is changing and will continue to change in future years, subject to the wishes of the parties and their relative bargaining power. Most likely, the structure will vary according to the subjects being negotiated. For example, city agencies bargaining separately with employee organizations may start to bargain jointly on wages and possibly a small number of fringe benefits, such as holidays and vacations. Separate school districts or municipalities in the same labor market may follow a similar practice. Different negotiation units for different topics of negotiations are common in the private sector and may become more so in the public sector. After all, precedent for separate determination of issues has already been established in the public sector, with the legislature at higher government levels determining a large number of working conditions. The history of collective bargaining in the public sector has demonstrated repeatedly that legal, political, and other obstacles can be overcome if the parties wish.

Scope of Bargaining

The scope of bargaining, the range of subjects negotiated in collective bargaining, is an extremely important aspect of the bargaining relationship. A very narrow scope reduces the significance of collective bargaining. Effective collective bargaining requires a "reasonably wide range of negotiable issues." Too broad a scope of negotiations can also be detrimental to collective bargaining. Negotiating too many subjects may weaken management's operating power, thus making it difficult, if not impossible, for management to operate the organization.

In order to analyze the scope of bargaining, one must look at both the number of issues included in negotiations as well as the degree of union influence on particular issues. Frequently, the parties implicitly reach agreement on a trade-off between the breadth of negotiations and the depth or degree of influence on particular issues. Some evidence exists that the public sector manager presently opts for breadth rather than depth. "Management appears willing to place no limit on the number of 'negotiable issues' so long as the actual power of the union is severely limited."[3] One reason for this acceptance by management of a wide scope of negotiations probably relates to the fact that management is accustomed to public testimony on a wide variety of issues.

It is difficult to analyze and gather data on the scope of bargaining because the real scope of the issues jointly determined frequently differs from the formal scope of bargaining on the clauses in the contract. Quite frequently, topics are negotiated but not included in the collective bargaining agreement. Either or both parties may not want their consultation on an issue to be public knowledge. On the other hand, the parties often repeat statutory provisions in their contracts although the statute already guarantees the fringe benefit or working condition. Employee organizations frequently "fatten up" their collective bargaining agreements most likely because they believe that thicker contracts are more appealing to their members.

The National Labor Relations Act, as amended, deals very briefly with the subject matter of collective bargaining in private employment. The preface includes the phrase ". . . negotiating the terms and conditions of their employment or other mutual aid or protection," and Section 9(A) mentions "collective bargaining in respect to rates of pay, wages, hours of employment, or other conditions of employment."[4] On the basis of these phrases, the scope of collective bargaining is assumed to be "wages, hours, and working conditions." Under this classification, the subjects usually discussed by labor and management in private employment include wage rates, hours of employment, overtime, and work requirements; procedures and policies relating to discharge, suspension, layoff, recall, seniority, discipline, promotion, demotion, transfer, and assignment within the bargaining unit; conditions, procedures, and practices governing safety, sanitation, and protection of health in the place of employment; vacations, holidays, leaves of absence, and sick leaves; union security; discharge actions and reinstatement of strikers; and grievances.[5]

The scope of bargaining in private employment differs among and within industries. Similarly, considerable variation exists in public employment. Broad generalizations comparing the scope of bargaining in public employment with that in private employment are thus subject to question in specific cases. The following sections analyze the topics bargained in public employment and some issues that have arisen.

WAGES AND OTHER ECONOMIC MATTERS

Wages and other economic matters are typically the most important topics discussed in collective bargaining in private employment. In public employment, wages are sometimes excluded from the scope of bargaining.

The salaries of most federal employees are set by Congress, and therefore these employees cannot bargain on wages. However, the distribution of overtime and some other employee matters related to pay are subject to negotiation. Moreover, wage-board employees participate in the process of determining their pay rates.

State employees in Wisconsin are also prohibited from bargaining on wages. Because state employee collective bargaining has not been in effect long, it is too early to ascertain whether the Wisconsin practice will be followed by other states. For teachers and many other local government employees, wages and salaries are the primary topic of collective bargaining.

If not negotiable, wages are determined unilaterally by legislative bodies or by government administrators. Employee organizations then use lobbying and similar pressure tactics to influence legislators in their determination of wages. Even when wages are bargainable, pensions, longevity pay, and other economic matters, are sometimes not subject to collective bargaining; they are decided instead by legislative bodies. In such cases, employee organizations must divide their efforts between collective bargaining for wages and lobbying for matters excluded from bargaining. Although employee unions in the private sector also devote efforts to lobbying, lobbying is clearly more important to employee unions in the public sector, because more economic and working conditions are determined by legislative bodies.

HOURS OF EMPLOYMENT

Hours of employment, as well as vacations, holidays, and leaves of absence, are also important topics in private employment. Generally public employees are more restricted in bargaining on hours than their counterparts in private employment. Federal employees cannot bargain on hours of employment, but they are permitted to bargain on the allocation of hours. For example, bargaining can be conducted on the procedure for choosing vacation times or on the starting time of shifts. The laws of some states limit hours of employment for local government employees. In order to receive state aid, local public schools must hold sessions a minimum number of days; teachers must therefore work a minimum number of days per year. State legislation may also guarantee teachers a "duty-free lunch period." Maximum hours per week are sometimes set for fire fighters by state law.

CONDITIONS OF EMPLOYMENT

Assignments, transfers, promotions, and layoffs are often of much concern to all employees. In private employment, criteria for making decisions on these matters are frequently negotiated. Employers generally desire flexibility in making these decisions; employees desire protection from arbitrary or capricious decisions. Both parties often reach a compromise, basing their decision on the length of service and the qualifications of a given employee.

Bargaining on the criteria for movement of personnel has occurred in some areas of public employment, particularly in teaching and other local divisions. In the federal service determination of criteria is generally considered a managerial prerogative; the system for applying the criteria, however, has been negotiated. Civil service regulations frequently list criteria and procedures applying to personnel movements, including layoffs. Because personnel assignment and promotion had long been an area of political favor, public employee organizations have generally welcomed the development of criteria, procedures, and examinations established by civil service commissions. Consequently, where commissions have been active in these areas, public employee unions have rarely bargained about criteria for movement of personnel.

Manning requirements or regulations governing the number of employees performing a certain task are sometimes bargained in the private sector but rarely in the public sector, because such decisions are usually considered managerial prerogatives. Executive Order 11491 specifically lists manning requirements as a managerial prerogative. An arbitration decision in New York City gave the police department the authority to determine the number of policemen assigned to patrol cars. On the other hand, in some cases teacher organizations have bargained about use of teacher aides or the number of staff members assigned to team teaching or to other innovative programs.

As in private employment, public employees often negotiate other working conditions—temperature of the work place and safety and health practices, for example. One item of particular concern to policemen has been whether they shall be required to appear in court during their off-duty hours without extra compensation.

The early collective bargaining agreements negotiated in private employment almost always expired at the end of one year. As the parties became more familiar with the process and with each other, the duration of collective bargaining agreements tended to increase. Presently most private employment agreements are in effect for at least two years. The same pattern of events is developing in public employment except in states where statutes limit negotiated agreements to one year. In the few cases where the parties have negotiated several collective bargaining agreements, two- and three-year agreements are common. Collective bargaining agreements negotiated for the first time, however, tend to last no more than a year or a budget period, whichever is shorter. Reopening clauses, which provide that either party may reopen negotiations after a specific period, have been negotiated in some long-term teacher agreements. Municipal employees in Detroit negotiated a reopener that can be exercised only if both parties agree to reopen negotiations.

Management rights clauses are present in both private and public employment. Executive Order 11491 delimits the scope of negotiations, specifying certain rights for management—directing, assigning, and disciplining employees; maintaining the efficiency of the government operations; determining methods, means, and personnel by which government operations are to be conducted; and taking whatever actions are necessary to carry out the mission of the agency in emergencies.[6] These rights are included in all collective bargaining agreements covering federal employees.

In a study of municipal employee relations, evidence was found that public sector collective bargaining agreements were less likely to have a management prerogative clause than private sector contracts. Furthermore, management prerogative clauses in the municipal agreements tended to be general statements, while in private sector contracts there was usually an enumerated statement of management prerogatives.[7]

The sovereignty principle probably explains the reason why many public employers rely on strong management rights clauses.

Some public employers believe that this clause protects their sovereign rights in areas not negotiated. This attitude is similar to that of private employers who insist on including managerial prerogative clauses in their collective bargaining agreements to protect their rights of ownership and property.

EMPLOYEE ORGANIZATION MATTERS

As in private employment, collective bargaining agreements in public employment typically include clauses on recognition and dues deduction. Employee organization leaders frequently have attempted, and in some cases succeeded, in negotiating clauses providing for released time and special privileges for employees who negotiate for the organization or process grievances.

Organization security clauses are rare, but are increasing, in public employment. In private employment, on the other hand, union shop clauses requiring employees to join the union after being employed for a specified period are common. Considerable controversy exists regarding union shops in private employment, and nineteen states have passed "right to work" laws, which prohibit the union shop and other forms of union security.

The rationale for opposing union shop clauses in public employment differs from that in private employment. In public employment, the union shop conflicts with civil service systems and tenure. Public employees working under these systems typically may be discharged only for reasons specified in the laws, such as immoral conduct or incompetence. Furthermore, merit systems require public employers to hire any person possessing the necessary qualifications regardless of his union sentiments. Union shop clauses would require discharge of public employees if they refused to join the employee organization. Under existing laws, such union security provisions would probably be illegal.

In spite of these arguments, union security provisions have been negotiated in public employment. One study found over 150 union shop clauses in public employment jurisdictions, and pressure from employee organizations probably will increase this number in future years.[8]

A compromise form of union security that may be more acceptable to legislative bodies and public employers than the union shop is the agency shop. Under this type of clause, an employee need not join the organization, but, as a condition of employment, he must pay a service fee to the organization for representing him. The Wisconsin legislature passed a law permitting agency shops for municipal employees, but it was vetoed by the governor. The Michigan Labor Mediation Board ruled in 1967 that agency shop clauses are a mandatory subject of collective bargaining.

> A requirement that employees pay their share of the cost of negotiating and administrating a collective bargaining agreement neither discourages nor encourages *membership* in the labor organization selected by the majority of employees in the bargaining unit to represent them. It is not discriminatory, as the requirement that each employee pay his pro rata share of the costs applies alike to all employees in the bargaining unit, whether they are or are not members of the union.[9]

This ruling will probably result in a sharp increase in the number of agency shop clauses in Michigan.

A few public employers have negotiated "maintenance of membership" clauses, that necessitate an employee who joins the organization to maintain his membership for a specified period, usually one year. The clause guarantees a steady flow of income to the employee organization.

The absence of union security provisions in public employment may present some disadvantages to management. If the employee organization has no guarantee of membership support, it frequently will become more militant and will attempt to satisfy all demands placed on it by individual members. It is difficult for a union leader to refuse to process a member's grievance when he knows that his refusal may cause the member to resign from the organization. An organization uncertain about its membership also has difficulty mediating among various groups of members in presenting unified proposals to management.

GRIEVANCE PROCEDURES

Grievance procedures, which are essential to collective bargaining agreements in the private sector, are becoming equally widespread in the public sector. Some important differences occur, however, particularly in the dual grievance procedures that have developed in public employment. Before the advent of collective bargaining in public employment, many government agencies had unilaterally established grievance procedures applying to civil service regulations. Negotiated grievance procedures have not eliminated previously existing grievance procedures; instead they provide a second avenue of appeal for the employee.

In some government agencies, different topics must be handled through one of the two grievance procedures. For example, agency regulations on preexisting policies can be appealed only through the grievance procedure established by the agency. On the other hand, interpretations of the collective bargaining agreement can be appealed only through the negotiated procedure. Executive Order 11491 permits agencies and labor organizations to negotiate a single grievance procedure, thus eliminating the dual system to resolve employee grievances.

In cases where an employee may now choose either grievance procedure for his appeal, he may not appeal the same grievance in both procedures. Unions of federal employees have opposed agency grievance procedures and have encouraged their members to use negotiated procedures. The importance of agency procedures will most likely decrease in future years. Grievance procedures in private employment usually permit appeals only on interpretations or applications of the collective bargaining agreement. In public employment, open-end grievance procedures that permit appeals on interpretation of any government agency regulations or on any action of their supervisors are much more common. The absence of grievance arbitration encourages this broad scope for grievance procedures, but, in many cases, open-end procedures have been negotiated along with grievance arbitration clauses.

Very little is known about the use of grievance procedures in public employment as compared to private employment. Most grievances in both sectors are settled at the first or second step, at which stages no written records are kept. Relatively few cases have been submitted to arbitration in public employment, and no data are available on the frequency of use of intermediate steps in grievance procedures.

Few differences exist between public employment and private

employment in terms of the subject matter of grievances. Except for policemen and fire fighters, probably more cases involving the arbitrability of an issue occur in public employment than in private employment because of the relative newness of collective bargaining. On the other hand, discipline cases are relatively rare in public employment, partly because a smaller proportion of employees are discharged for disciplinary reasons. Civil service rulings, or tenure, provide many public employees strong protection against arbitrary dismissal. Discharge of a public employee is an extremely complicated matter, and many agencies find it easier to wait for an employee to leave voluntarily. Many public employees are therefore assured a good deal of job security.

The widespread use of informal methods that adjust employee grievances probably accounts for the relatively infrequent use of formal machinery. Many public employees are accustomed to by-passing the formal machinery and presenting their case to the person or administrator with ultimate authority. A parallel situation occurs when union members take their grievances directly to the union president, instead of to the shop steward. The president then consults the head of the government agency and settles the grievance informally. Discussions are frequently carried on by telephone, thereby expediting grievance processing but by-passing the formal machinery. Once a formal grievance procedure is negotiated, it is difficult for union leaders and public employers to change the informal practices.

GRIEVANCE ARBITRATION

BINDING ARBITRATION

Arbitration, under which a neutral person decides unresolved grievances, is widely accepted and utilized in private employment. Over 90 percent of all grievance procedures in private employment contain an arbitration clause as the terminal point of the procedure. Public employers have been reluctant to accept binding arbitration in grievance procedures. Executive Order 10988 prohibited binding arbitration of grievances for federal employees, and some state attorneys general orders and court decisions prohibit grievance arbitration for state and municipal employees. Other court decisions, however, permit grievance arbitration on an ad hoc basis.[10]

The rationale for prohibiting grievance arbitration in public employment is based on the sovereignty principle. According to this principle, a public employer cannot legally delegate his decision-making authority to a person not responsible to the electorate. Proponents of grievance arbitration claim, however, that public employers permit arbitration of construction contracts and similar matters and that they apply the sovereignty principle to retain their accustomed unilateral decision-making authority in grievances.

Regardless of the legal arguments, grievance arbitration clauses are increasing in public employment. Executive Order 11491 permits binding arbritration of grievances. Public employee unions will most likely continue to press for grievance arbitration, and public employers will continue to accept arbitration clauses.

Monetary awards pose special problems for arbitrators in public employment. In private employment, arbitrators commonly order payment of back pay. Such an award in public employment would require an increase in the budget of the agency or the reallocation of funds within the budget. These decisions imply a degree of legislative authority and pose a serious question whether such authority should be delegated to a person not responsible to the electorate. This reasoning has already been used in ruling on the nonarbitrability of certain grievances.

ADVISORY ARBITRATION

Advisory arbitration is identical to binding arbitration except that the award of the arbitrator may be rejected by the head of the government agency. In a sense, under advisory arbitration the union and the arbitrator are not the equals of the employer, who always may have the final word on a grievance. Advisory arbitration was recommended by the Task Force on Federal Employee Relations and later incorporated in Executive Order 10988 to provide an appeals machinery for grievances without violating the sovereignty of government officials. Implicit in advisory arbitration is the concept that awards will be rejected only if they violate the law or if they are clearly unworkable. Obviously, advisory arbitration will serve little purpose if awards are consistently rejected.

It is interesting to speculate why the term "advisory arbitration" is used instead of "grievance fact-finding with recommendations." "Advisory arbitration" is a misnomer, because "arbitration" implies an award the parties must accept. The term probably was developed to encourage public employers to accept awards and to placate employee organizations.

Although advisory arbitration clauses are included in many collective bargaining agreements in the federal service, relatively few grievance cases have been submitted to advisory arbitration. Likewise, only a small number of cases involving state, county, and municipal employees have been submitted to advisory arbitration. Although some teacher collective bargaining agreements provide for advisory arbitration, a greater number use binding arbitration. An interesting arbitration clause occurs in the collective bargaining agreement of Milwaukee municipal employees; it provides for both binding arbitration and advisory arbitration, depending on the topic of the grievance.

Leaders of public employee unions view advisory arbitration as tantamount to binding arbitration. Public employers share this view, although they have rejected a few decisions on grounds of illegality. From January 1962 to August 1968, four out of sixty-two advisory arbitration decisions were rejected by federal agency heads.

The relationship between advisory arbitration and binding arbitration is somewhat paradoxical. Regardless of management's attitude toward advisory arbitration, this procedure tends to evolve into binding arbitration or de facto binding arbitration. For example, the more willing management is to accept advisory arbitration awards, the more advisory arbitration resembles binding arbitration. On the other hand, if management begins to reject advisory arbitration awards, the employee organizations will have less confidence in advisory arbitration and will intensify their attempts to change it to binding arbitration. Even a single rejection of an advisory arbitration award can cause the unions and their members to lose confidence in the appeals system.

ISSUES ON THE SCOPE OF BARGAINING

If collective bargaining is to be viable, the agreement must include topics relevant to employees. Placing unwarranted restrictions on the scope of collective bargaining limits the institution of collective bargaining as a method of determining employment conditions. Obviously the *number* of issues negotiated is not the important criterion, as some issues are much more important than others—for example, wages generally are of prime importance to employees. Collective bargaining limited to wages would serve an important function in many cases. On the other hand, if the scope of bargaining becomes too narrow or if important issues, such as wages, are eliminated from bargaining, employees will move away from collective bargaining to other means of participation in decision making. These alternatives usually consist of lobbying and political pressures. Once the employee organization devotes considerable effort to lobbying and political pressures, employees, unions, and management reduce their interest in collective bargaining. Even if some topics remain bargainable, the parties will not invest much time and effort to bargaining on these items. The more the parties ignore collective bargaining, the less training and experience they will have in the process, and the more likely the system will fall into disuse.

Limiting the scope of collective bargaining also lessens the ability of the employee organization to claim credit for direct gains. Because it is more difficult for an employee organization to claim credit for a lobbying victory than for a bargaining victory, the organization will try to expand the scope of collective bargaining. Its ability to demonstrate success will affect its ability to retain and recruit new members.

Ironically, when too many topics are negotiated, other issues arise in some sectors of public employment. This factor is sometimes a problem in private employment, and a large body of National Labor Relations Board cases and court decisions has been issued on whether certain topics are negotiable. Guidelines have been developed in private employment, labeling topics either mandatory, permissive, or prohibited subjects of collective bargaining. Parties *must* bargain on mandatory subjects if either party desires to bargain on these topics; they *may* bargain on permissive topics; and they may *not* bargain on prohibited subjects. A similar set of criteria has not evolved in public employment.

Some problems arise in public employment because a large number of public employees are professionals. Salaried professional employees increasingly want to exercise professional autonomy, and they frequently view collective bargaining as the appropriate mechanism to achieve this end. For example, teacher organizations sometimes wish to bargain on curriculum and other matters of educational policy. Similarly, social workers desire some voice in setting procedures for handling welfare cases. Such policy decisions should presumably be decided by the representatives of the citizenry. Public employers may wish to develop alternative means of giving professional employees a voice in these decisions, which, in some cases, have already been issues in collective bargaining.

Some working conditions of public employees, such as assignment and transfer, also affect the quality of the service provided. Citizens will probably become increasingly concerned about the effect of collective bargaining on the quality of government services, because all citizens must pay for these services and all receive indirect benefits from them. The consumer in private employment has alternative purchasing opportunities; he can shift to other products if he is dissatisfied with the service. Public agencies, however, usually have a monopoly, and the only way citizens can influence the quality of the service is to persuade government officials to take certain actions. Consequently, the larger the scope of bargaining in public employment and the more bargaining relates to the quality of the service, the more likely it is that citizens will become involved in these issues.

VIII the process of collective bargaining in public employment

Bargaining Environment

Collective bargaining in public employment takes place in a political environment, which is quite different from the economic environment of private employment. Private employers attempt to maximize profits or to reach an acceptable level of profits. As long as they do this satisfactorily, they will continue in their positions. In making decisions, they can always rely ultimately on economic criteria.

The public agency has different motivations and criteria for decision making. Ultimately the public employer must rely on his constituents—the public. Although the agency's customers may be a small segment of the total citizenry, in the end the voters, through political institutions, determine its future. Decisions on budgets of public agencies are essentially political decisions—not economic decisions, as in the private sector. The public employer is elected or appointed by someone who is elected. Internal corporation politics may be important in private employment, but they differ greatly from the external politics faced by the public agency. These differences between

252

public employment and private employment affect the process and presumably the results of collective bargaining in public employment. This chapter examines the process of collective bargaining in this unique environment.

Political pressures are generally more successful at local levels of government than they are at higher levels. Local government officials are closer to their constituents than are state and federal administrators. Local businessmen pass them on the street and housewives call them by telephone. In general, the more direct control the electorate has over an individual's job, the more "political" or politically motivated his behavior will be. Public officials who rely on their jobs as a sole source of income or as the major source of potential future advancement will tend to be more responsive to their constituency. Similarly, when political institutions permit or encourage opposition, the public official will be more responsive to his constituency.

The greater the scope of collective bargaining and the more controversial the issues discussed, the greater the chance that political pressures will become part of the collective bargaining process itself. Citizens will attempt to consult the public agency's negotiator directly or the elected official responsible for the negotiator's actions. When subjected to such political pressures, elected officials behave in a variety of ways. Sometimes they enter the negotiating sessions; at other times they get in touch with their negotiators informally. Other officials wait for an impasse and then enter the dispute by serving as mediator or catalyst. The latter course has great political advantages, because the public official receives credit for "solving" the dispute. The actions of public officials in collective bargaining appear to depend more on the particular person and his perceptions rather than on the existing collective bargaining relationship.

Public Participation: Multilateral Bargaining

Collective bargaining in private employment is usually a bilateral process between the employer and the organization representing the employees. In public employment, bargaining is much more complex. Because of the political environment, individual citizens, organized interest groups, and elected officials may participate in the bargaining process and may affect the actions of the negotiators. Collective bargaining in the public sector is sometimes therefore characterized as a multilateral process instead of a bilateral one.[1]

The introduction of collective bargaining in public employment gives public employees a greater say in decisions affecting them. This increase in decision-making power often occurs at the expense of interest groups and individual citizens.

The participation of citizens or their representatives in bargaining in the public sector usually results from the pricing characteristic of the market for a public service. Most public services are supplied at no direct cost to the consumer; other services are usually provided at a price below the cost of the service. In either case, the consumers directly benefiting from the service are subsidized from tax revenues provided by both users and nonusers of the service. Consequently, all taxpayers have an interest in labor-management negotiations whose outcome may raise their tax burden. In some cases taxpayers organize into groups that represent their views to decision makers and, if dissatisfied, can threaten to impose a political cost. In other cases, individual taxpayers communicate with negotiators or elected officials responsible for negotiations.

Participation may also occur on nonmonetary questions, especially if essentiality of the service, public policy, or public convenience are at stake. For instance, interest groups, educational policy groups, and citizens are particularly concerned with such issues of public policy as integration of school faculties and class size—topics that have been the subject of negotiations.

The market for public services exhibits a high degree of monopoly, because most public services are faced with little competition. The political process in the public sector is a substitute for the market mechanism in the private sector— political pressures instead of consumer withholding of services influence the nature of cost and services provided.

TIMING OF PUBLIC PARTICIPATION

The public may participate at several different stages of the bargaining process. Before bargaining begins, local government agencies often conduct hearings on their proposed budget—

hearings at which testimony is heard from individual citizens and interest groups. The views of these groups may not necessarily be those of the community, but they undoubtedly carry some weight with government officials, because they are frequently the only citizen opinions presented. After the budget hearings, these views are used by the employer and the union representatives to support their respective positions in collective bargaining. Of course it is not possible to measure quantitatively the impact of the budget testimony on the resulting collective bargaining agreement.

Citizens and interest groups often participate indirectly before or during bargaining by consulting with elected officials, agency heads, or installation heads to persuade them to consider their viewpoints in negotiations. The elected officials transmit the public's views to agency negotiators or administrators responsible for negotiations. This form of participation appears to be more prevalent at the local level, although it takes place in state and federal agencies as well. The actual effect of these pressures on the agencies' positions in negotiations and in the result of negotiations varies, depending on the validity of the arguments and on the elected official's perception of the political importance of the citizen or the interest group. In some cases, government officials have mistakenly thought that groups communicating with them had broad support from the community.

Most public activity, pressure, and participation in negotiations occur prior to or during a work stoppage. At such time citizens, interest groups, and elected officials transfer their focus from the contents of the agreement to avoidance of a work stoppage. The amount of public pressure depends on the anticipated or the actual effect of the stoppage on the public. A transit strike that inconveniences many citizens will cause enormous public reaction; a strike of clerical employees that does not affect the public will generally go unnoticed.

The public participates further in the negotiation process when legislative bodies review budgets of public agencies that incorporate wage settlements negotiated in collective bargaining. This form of "public ratification" occurs at all levels of government. The legislative body often has authority to change specific items in the proposed budget; in some cases, it can change only the aggregate amount and can permit the agency to reallocate its funds. Legislative bodies often take testimony at hearings similar to those of the autonomous government agencies described at the beginning of this section.

Negotiating sessions are usually held in private, but some citizens and interest groups have demanded the right to attend sessions as observers. Open negotiating sessions are thus another means of public participation in collective bargaining. Some public employers and public employee organizations react to the demands by the public by having an open meeting for presentation of initial proposals and counterproposals and by holding private sessions later. Other public employers do not allow the public to attend negotiating sessions but have permitted newspaper reporters to attend. In a few cases, negotiators have met on the stage of an auditorium and have permitted anyone to attend as an observer. In California and a number of other states, state laws prohibit school boards from having closed meetings except in certain specified instances. In these states, negotiating sessions must be held at public meetings.

Open negotiating sessions prolong collective bargaining and make it more difficult to reach agreement. Participants often make statements in order to impress observers; employer and employee representatives are less likely to let their hair down. Similar problems occur sometimes in private employment when the parties reveal negotiating positions to newspaper reporters and conduct negotiations via the press.

VARIATIONS IN PUBLIC SECTOR MULTILATERAL BARGAINING

Multilateral bargaining varies among public employment jurisdictions and among different services within a jurisdiction. The extent of multilateral bargaining depends on the existence of an interest group structure, the scope of bargaining, the perceived impact of a work stoppage, and, in some measure, the bargaining tactics of the parties.

The interest group structure consists of groups or individuals who represent sections of the community to the suppliers of the service. Well-defined interest group structures tend to develop when the public places considerable importance on the quality of the service. In general, organized interest groups at the federal and the state levels are likely to be more permanent and have better financial backing than those at the local level. Many local interest groups are voluntary organizations, whose effectiveness depends partly on the personality and the enthusiasm of their leaders. In small communities, the lack of a permanent well-defined interest group is likely to restrict the amount of communication between the negotiating parties and segments of the community. Hence, one can expect the potential extent of multilateral bargaining in small communities to be much less than that in large cities. It is possible, of course, for an individual holding a key position in the power structure of the community to perform the same function as the interest group structure.

As discussed in the last chapter, the scope of bargaining varies within the public sector. Obviously, interest groups will be more active in negotiations if the topics being negotiated relate to their major goals. Because of the present limited scope of bargaining for federal employees, theoretical considerations suggest that multilateral bargaining is currently minimal at that level.

Particularly just prior to a strike deadline and once a strike has begun, the amount of multilateral bargaining depends largely on perceived impact of a work stoppage—the larger the perceived impact, the more the multilateral bargaining. Not all services within the public sector directly affect the public, however, and in some instances an acceptable alternative is available.

The tactics of the negotiating parties reflect, in part, their desire to increase their relative bargaining power by gaining support of important interest groups. Since few alternative sources of supply exist for most public services, it is expected that each side in negotiations in the public sector will be more aware of the need for public support than is the case in the private sector.

This theoretical discussion of the variations in multilateral bargaining is illustrated in Figure 2 which shows expected interest group activity during negotiations for the private sector and for selected public services in urban areas. Bargaining is divided into three stages: the Initial Probing Stage (I), the Hard Bargaining Stage (II), and the Strike Stage (III). Interest group activity in the initial probing stage is concerned mostly with the quality of the service. In Stage II, interest group motives begin to shift to concern over possible interruption of the service. Once a strike takes place, interest group activity focuses almost entirely on ending the work stoppage. These three stages, of course, represent a general pattern of multilateral bargaining in the public sector. Exceptions from this pattern may occur in some cases. For example, during the strike stage of the prolonged New York City teacher's dispute in 1968, interest group activity was divided between those whose main concern was ending the stoppage and others who still focused primarily on the quality of education.

The shape of the "Expected Interest Group Activity" (EIGA) line depends on the four variables discussed earlier in this section: the interest group structure, the scope of bargaining, the perceived impact of a work stoppage, and the tactics of the parties. In the initial probing stage, the EIGA line depends primarily on the interest group structure and the scope of bargaining. In public education and social welfare services, interest groups are well organized, and bargaining frequently includes such topics as class size, case load, and procedures for professional employees to participate in policy decisions. As a result, third party activity is relatively higher in the initial probing stage in these services than in the other services depicted in Figure 2.

Third party activity is likely to increase slightly for all services in the hard bargaining stage, because the negotiations are given widespread publicity in the news media. Once the strike deadline is reached, interest group activity increases rapidly if the groups believe that the strike will have a large impact. Interest group activity continues to increase after the strike occurs, but at some point the activity levels off or possibly decreases as the public adjusts to the work stoppage or establishes substitute services. The rate at which activity levels off varies according to the difficulty involved in providing acceptable substitute services. For instance, substituting national guard troops for striking police would probably reduce public pressure for ending a police work stoppage. In the event of a strike, management may deliberately "keep the plant open" or provide a partial service in order to relieve interest group pressure to end the strike and to increase its relative bargaining power. During a recent strike of social workers, monthly checks were mailed to welfare recipients so

Figure 2—EXPECTED INTEREST-GROUP ACTIVITY IN URBAN AREAS

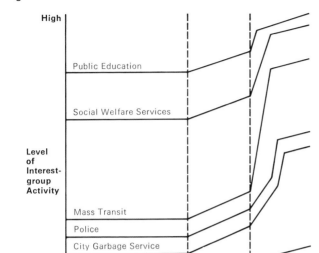

*For explanatory purposes, it is assumed that the private sector is a homogenous group of producers. In practice, the perceived impact of an interruption of services varies among products. Consequently, it would be more accurate to represent the private sector with several different curves.

that pressure from "customers" to end the strike was reduced substantially. This type of management action, which rarely occurs in the private sector, results partly from multilateral bargaining in the public sector. In addition, the illegality of public sector strikes gives management added incentive to attempt to provide services during a strike. A similar effect occurs when the consumers try to provide a substitute service. For example, parents sometimes have threatened or attempted to keep schools open during teacher strikes.

The shape of the EIGA line in the hard bargaining and strike stages most likely will be different in nonurban areas. The perceived impact of a garbage strike in an urban area is depicted as relatively high in Figure 2, but the perceived impact of a similar strike in a rural area would undoubtedly be much less because consumers would be often able to dispose of their garbage.

COMPARISON OF MULTILATERAL BARGAINING: PRIVATE SECTOR AND PUBLIC SECTOR

The bilateral nature of private sector bargaining generally restricts third party action, particularly during the initial probing stage of negotiations when the supply of the product or the service to the consumer is not interrupted. The likelihood of third party activity is somewhat greater during the hard bargaining stage when the strike is imminent and after the strike has occurred. The consumer then becomes aware of the likelihood of economic loss or inconvenience through the interruption of supply, and he will attempt to find substitute sources of supply. This potential loss of customers pressures the negotiators to reach a settlement.

The characteristics of multilateral bargaining in the private sector, however, are quite different from those in the public sector. First, as already mentioned, the timing is different because in the private sector multilateral pressures occur only in the final stages of negotiations. Second, the amount of third party influence is different, because in the public sector, consumer preferences and demands are transmitted by interest groups rather than market mechanisms. Third party activity in the private sector is less prevalent because the market allows the consumer some choice in selecting the product or the service.

Consumer choice in the private sector is in some instances more apparent than real. Little incentive exists for the consumer to switch to another supplier in noncompetitive product markets where oligopolistic pricing is common. In cases where the consumer may switch to avoid interruption of service, the supplier will build up inventories before the strike to avoid losing the customer. If the product or service is perishable, as in the case of transportation or newspapers, employers will cooperate to avoid permanent loss of customers to any one employer. One example of such cooperation is the "Mutual Aid Pact" of the airline industry.

Finally, an important difference in multilateral bargaining between the public and the private sectors is that, apart from the rare cases of government intervention in bargaining, the multilateral influence in the private sector is characterized by autonomous individual action. This approach is significantly different from the highly organized cooperative activity in many areas of public employment.

Interunion Relations

Some public employee unions have received much organizing assistance from established unions in the private sector. From 1961 to 1968, the Industrial Union Department (IUD) of AFL-CIO gave financial assistance and lent organizing personnel to several public employee unions. Under the leadership of Walter Reuther, IUD recognized the tremendous membership potential in the public sector and the possibility that it might be a stepping stone to the organization of white-collar employees. AFSCME, AFT, and AFGE joined the IUD during this period. With Reuther out of IUD, there is some question whether the IUD will continue to support actively public employee unions. Regardless of future developments in IUD, public employee unions will require less support from other unions because of recent increases in their membership.

A few local and international unions of private employees have also assisted public employee affiliates. For example, during the collective bargaining election in 1961, the United Federation of Teachers in New York City received sizable contributions from the International Association of Machinists, the Amalgamated Clothing Workers of America, the United Steelworkers of America, and other unions.

Generally public employee unions have not coordinated their organizing and bargaining efforts in dealing with the same employer. Although picket lines have been respected, in many cases the unions appear to compete with each other for larger wage packages. On the other hand, private sector unions appear to rely more on coalition or coordinated bargaining. Once collective bargaining relationships become more firmly established, more coordination may occur among unions in the public sector.

Greater cooperation among public employee unions has occurred in lobbying activities, but individual public employee unions frequently lobby separately for their own favorable legislation. Union-coordinating councils for lobbying are rare. Even the postal unions, which have nation-wide joint collective bargaining, do not unify their lobbying activities. Police and fire fighters have not joined forces either, although they may have common interests for lobbying. Private employee unions have provided minimum support for public unions only when mutual interests are present. In some cases, state AFL-CIOs have opposed tax increases that would be used primarily for salary increases for groups of public employees.

Ratification

Ratification of agreements negotiated by union representatives is basically the same in both public and private employment. The negotiators for the employee organization attempt to satisfy as many groups of constituents as possible in order to help assure ratification by the membership. This often results in across-the-board wage increases, so all members get "something" and no group then envies another group because of disparate increases. Membership rejections of negotiated agreements have occurred at about the same rate among public sector unions as among private employee unions.

The ratification often required of the employer, however, is unique to public employment. In private employment, negotiating authority is delegated to negotiators within limits set by top management. In smaller companies, top managers or owners negotiate themselves and, of course, have authority to make final agreements. Such authority is rarely delegated to public employers; instead, usually they are required to obtain budgetary approval from another government agency or from the electorate. Negotiating authority, of course, depends upon the level and form of government. Many school boards can set their own tax rates, whereas state and municipal agencies must almost always obtain budgetary approval of settlements.

Employer negotiators sometimes do not have authority in nonmonetary matters. In federal employment, each agency has the right to review local agreements and to make changes in the agreed-upon conditions of employment. This authority has been exercised infrequently because of its potential disastrous effects on local bargaining.

The absence of negotiating authority tends to complicate and prolong collective bargaining. Negotiators usually act more cautiously, and time lags occur while final approval is obtained. In some cases, additional negotiating sessions are required after budget cuts are made.

Lobbying

Lobbying is direct representation by an interest group to the legislative branches of federal, state, or local government. A lobbying group "makes certain claims upon other groups in the society for the establishment, maintenance or enhancement of forms of behavior. . . ."[2]

The term "lobbying" has sinister connotations; a popular conception is that lobbyists wine and dine legislators, offer bribes, and contribute to or withhold support in elections. Although such methods are used, lobbyists can more effectively influence politicians by marshaling widespread public support.

Actually, lobbyists perform an important service in a democracy. They provide legislators with important technical information and convey to legislators the implications of legislation for voters. At the state level particularly, legislators have neither the time nor the staff to assess such implications adequately.

LOBBYING IN PUBLIC EMPLOYMENT

Lobbying activity by public employee organizations is unique, because the lobbyists are employees of the political jurisdiction or of a jurisdiction subordinate to that of the legislators. Certain advantages flow from this unique relationship. The lobbyist for the public employee is generally more sensitive to the location of power because members of his group work in close proximity with the legislators. Public employees may lobby informally with legislators directly. The constant proximity of the public employee to the employer may give disproportionate weight to the views of the public employee.

Three separate groups lobby to influence the terms and the conditions of public employment: employers, employees, and the general public. The goals of these groups do not necessarily conflict, because their goals are frequently independent of one another. For example, in the same situation a public employee organization might lobby for a better pension plan; a taxpayers group might oppose such a plan; and a good-government group might call for higher initial salaries. In this situation the employing organization has the option of siding with one of the parties, of taking an independent course of action, or of generating no pressure whatsoever.

LOBBYING EXPENDITURES

Public employee organizations have spent considerable sums on lobbying activity. In 1966 three public employee organizations were ranked among the first twenty-five spenders in lobbying at the federal level: in first place was the United Federation of Post Office Clerks ($287,000); in fifteenth place was the National Education Association ($73,100); and in twenty-first place was the National Association of Letter Carriers ($58,500).[3] Other large spenders among public employee organizations include the National Federation of Federal Employees, the National Rural Letter Carriers,[4] and District Lodge 44 of the International Association of Machinists (AFL-CIO).

These lobbying expenditures were used for different purposes. The International Association of Machinists supported federal pay increases and opposed the closing of government installations.[5] The National Association of Letter Carriers pursued federal pay increases and retirement benefits. The National Education Association spent funds to obtain federal grants for education.

No comprehensive listing of expenditures for lobbying on the state or local level is available. Where states require filing of such expenditures, state public employee organizations are prominent among reporting lobbying groups.

Expenditures are not the only effective means used in lobbying. Personal relationships can influence decision-makers. For example, fire fighters of one southern city requested the head of the state federation of labor, a former fire fighter, to plead their case to the state legislature. As a result of his lobbying efforts, and at minimal cost to the fire fighters' organization, municipal fire fighters gained increases in various state benefits.

LEVELS OF LOBBYING ACTIVITY

Public employee organizations lobby at various levels of government. Lobbying activities are directed at sources of authority where decisions over terms and conditions of employment take place. A municipal union may attempt to simultaneously persuade aldermen on the city council to act favorably on certain matters within their purview and exert pressures on the state legislature to approve other matters that the legislature controls. In some cases, a city employee organization will engage in much greater lobbying activity at the state level than at the city level.

Despite the lobbying efforts of public employee groups at higher levels of government, a local group will probably have less success lobbying at the state level than it will have at the local level. As a general principle in lobbying, the probability of success is likely to decrease as the level of authority increases— because higher levels of authority are subject to a larger number of lobbying groups and more diversified pressures than are lower levels.

Public employee organizations composed of workers who perform essential services, such as organizations of fire fighters and policemen, are reputed to be astute lobbyists. Some observers suggest that the essential nature of the public safety services helps make their lobbying activities particularly effective. Part of the effectiveness of police and fire-fighting organizations has also resulted from the ability of these groups to wield a cohesive power block, which originates in the paramilitary nature of their occupations. Moreover, public safety personnel are more likely than any other group of public employees to be excluded from collective bargaining. When such personnel do bargain, the scope of the bargaining is often more restricted than that for employees performing nonessential services. Public safety organizations therefore have a greater propensity to turn to lobbying in order to secure benefits than do those organizations of employees performing nonessential services. In other words, public safety organizations may be more skilled at lobbying because of their greater experience with, and their greater reliance on, lobbying.

TYPOLOGY OF PUBLIC EMPLOYEE LOBBYING

Lobbying is used by public employee organizations to achieve a number of different goals, which may add or detract from viable collective bargaining in the public sector. This section presents a typology of different forms of lobbying by public employee organizations. At any particular time an employee organization may engage in one or in a number of the different lobbying techniques discussed.

LOBBYING FOR COLLECTIVE BARGAINING LEGISLATION

Public employee organizations may use lobbying to obtain or to strengthen collective bargaining legislation for public employees. In particular, public employee organizations that have difficulty securing consent recognition may lobby to secure recognition through legislation. If lobbying is undertaken to obtain collective bargaining legislation, the rules of collective bargaining are established or fortified, thereby encouraging and stabilizing bargaining. If the resulting legislation is permissive, the employer legally may bargain. If the legislation is mandatory, the employer *must* bargain.

There are exceptions to the above generalization that legislation strengthens collective bargaining. Legislation allowing for proportional representation could, for instance, detract from collective bargaining.

LOBBYING FOR NONNEGOTIABLE TOPICS

Public employees may also lobby for benefits that have been excluded from negotiations either by law or by tradition. For example, after moonlighting by police was declared nonnegotiable in New York City, police lobbied with the state legislature and secured legislative permission to moonlight. Lobbying for non-bargainable issues shifts the attention of the parties from bargaining to political involvement. The total effect of such lobbying on bargaining depends upon the importance and the number of issues excluded from bargaining.

LOBBYING AS A SUBSTITUTE FOR BARGAINING

Lobbying may also substitute for bargaining. Rather than bargain, the organization may lobby for a wage increase with members of the finance committee, because it believes it can secure a larger wage increase. Lobbying for items that can be collectively bargained weakens the bargaining process. Every increment of such lobbying activity diminishes the importance of bargaining. The ultimate point is reached when the organization rejects bargaining completely and resorts to lobbying for all issues.

LOBBYING FOR LIMITS ON WORKING CONDITIONS

Lobbying may establish limits on a working condition subject to bargaining and thereby affect the range of bargaining on that condition. For example, state laws often specify minimum hours teachers must teach each day for the district to qualify for state aid. The maximum number of hours that a fire fighter may work per week is also frequently legislated. These minimums and maximums affect the parties' maneuverability in collective bargaining. Whether this kind of lobbying adds to or detracts from collective bargaining depends on whether the results of the lobbying widen or narrow the range for bargaining in the specific working condition. In some cases, lobbying may have little effect on negotiations—for instance, if state legislated maximum working hours are reduced to a level above the existing negotiated schedule of hours.

"END RUN" LOBBYING

The employee organization may engage in "end run" lobbying while collective bargaining negotiations are in process. If the organization is dissatisfied with the progress of negotiations, it may attempt to place pressures on the negotiator through the elected officials. This type of political pressure undercuts the negotiator's position and undermines collective bargaining. Agreement is formally reached through the bargaining process, but in reality the outcome is achieved through lobbying.

"CAROM" LOBBYING

The employee organization may engage in "carom" lobbying if negotiations do not yield the desired result. Carom lobbying occurs after the union and the negotiator have reached agreement. The union may then attempt to improve the package by getting in touch with the chief executive or the legislative body. Carom lobbying subverts collective bargaining and affects future bargaining. It also destroys the trust of one party in the other. For example, management may have given a quid pro quo in order to induce the union to make a concession. But if the union has attempted to obtain further benefits from the legislative body, management will be reluctant to make concessions in future bargaining.

EMPLOYER LOBBYING

Employer lobbying may add to or detract from collective bargaining. Management may feel that collective bargaining legislation will improve labor relations. The employer may also assist the employee organization in making a bid for increased appropriations to enhance the jurisdiction's ability to pay. On the other hand, employers may oppose legislation to establish collective bargaining or to increase the scope of bargaining.

LOBBYING OR COLLECTIVE BARGAINING?

An employee organization has certain goals that reflect the desires and needs of its leaders, its members, and the organization as an institution. Organization policies depend on the power positions of the leadership and the rank and file and on the survival and the growth requirements of the organization.

Public employee organizations often use lobbying both as an alternative and a supplement to collective bargaining. The key to the selection of tactics is the perception of the employee organization decision makers. To some extent perception will be colored by past experiences; new events and the nature of the issue may also be factors in determining the tactic to be used.

The organization will use collective bargaining when the perceived benefits per dollar of expenditure are greater than the perceived benefits per dollar of expenditure in lobbying. This decision may be represented by the formula

$$\frac{dCBb}{dCBc} > \frac{dLb}{dLc}$$

where: $dCBb$ = change in collective bargaining benefits
$dCBc$ = change in collective bargaining costs
dLb = change in lobbying benefits
dLc = change in lobbying costs.

As the relationship of the four factors changes, so, too, will the behavior of the employee organization. For instance, an organization that has had success with lobbying may believe that $dLb > dCBb$ and $dCBb > 0$ (the benefits of lobbying outweigh those of collective bargaining, and collective bargaining involves costs). In this case, the organization will continue to lobby. Where one method results in no benefits, the organization will inevitably employ the other.

The costs and benefits used in the decision whether to lobby or to bargain are largely anticipatory. The benefits may not be realized because there is no guarantee that the employee organization will win what it expects to win with either method. A certain portion of the costs may be fixed—for example, lobbyists on a retainer or professional staff preparing for collective bargaining. Other costs, however, are variable and less determinable. For example, the union may make political contributions to curry favor with certain legislators.

Pressure Tactics

This section analyzes pressure tactics other than lobbying. A pressure tactic may be defined as an action or a threat of an action to impose a cost on a party in order to influence his decision. In private sector bargaining, economic cost is probably most important. The primary costs in the public sector are political, psychological, and social. Economic cost, however, can be of major importance in public pay-as-you-go or pay-as-you-receive operations; examples of such operations are the post office, toll roads, transit companies, and bridge authorities.

Pressure tactics in the public sector may be classified according to their influence on production. Some pressure tactics do not affect production. For example, pressures may be used directly on legislators to approve a pension plan, possibly with an offer of campaign support as a reward to the legislators. Such direct attempts to influence the employing authority through political threats or payoffs do not affect production.

Labor organizations may also use techniques to exert public pressure on appointed employers or on appointing authorities. Such tactics may involve impugning the professional integrity of an employer such as the head of a hospital or a superintendent of schools. In addition, publicity may be used to predispose the public in favor of labor. Informational picketing has been widely used by municipal public safety employees. None of the above techniques has a significant impact on production.

Other tactics may be used which partially affect production. Workers may engage in a slowdown or may work specifically according to the rules, which has the same effect as a slowdown. In 1968, toll collectors on a Philadelphia bridge followed work rules to the letter by carefully counting change and noting the license number of every car passing their booths. This detailed adherence to the work rule resulted in massive traffic jams and in wide publicity and apparently served to get increased wages for the collectors.

Teachers and fire fighters have refused to do nonessential or nonrequired work—for example, extracurricular activities or maintenance of equipment. Large-scale sick calls have been used by public employees to withhold their services and yet to remain free from the charge of strike. Policemen in various cities have used the "blue flu" to withhold their labor. Nurses and school bus drivers in large numbers have reported sick as an alternative to striking. Teachers organizations have used another means to affect production by invoking sanctions on certain jurisdictions, thereby warning other teachers to remain away, and thus decreasing the potential number of entrants to the sanctioned labor market.

Finally, pressure tactics may result in a complete halting of production. Strikes, mass resignation, professional meetings, or all employees calling in sick have the intent of halting production completely. Whether the employee organization is successful in its attempt depends to a great extent on what measures management takes to counter the pressure tactic.

LEGALITY

In private employment, the major pressure tactic is the strike. In the United States, until 1969, the strike was never legal in public employment. With few exceptions, the courts and legislative bodies have opposed the use of the strike by public employees. The courts have ruled that state legislatures may pass laws legalizing public employee strikes; in the absence of such legislation, however, public employee strikes have almost always been declared illegal. The legality of mass resignations and mass sick calls has been tested on only a few occasions. In 1967, the New York State Public Employment Relations Board ruled that the "mass resignation" by New York City teachers was a strike, and the board fined the United Federation of Teachers for violating the Taylor Act. Earlier that year, a New Jersey district court judge enjoined the Camden Education Association from a mass sick call, which he interpreted as a strike.

One question crucial to the courts in determining whether a mass resignation or a mass sick call is a strike is: Did the employee organization lead the action, or was the action taken spontaneously by individuals acting autonomously? No one in the United States can be forced to work, but employee organization leaders can be penalized for leading a work stoppage and individuals for engaging in a work stoppage.

Pressure tactics partially affecting production have been used to a greater extent than tactics completely halting production. There has been little litigation involving such tactics as slowdowns, work to rule, and sanctions, because some of these methods are difficult to prove, and others, such as the tactics employed by the Philadelphia toll collectors, are legal. Furthermore, penalties can be imposed only for actual work stoppages.

Penalties may be levied against individuals and employee organizations for engaging in pressure tactics. The civil service rules of many jurisdictions call for automatic discharge of any employee involved in a work stoppage. Most state laws permitting collective bargaining impose penalties for work stoppages; penalties include fines, loss of job tenure, postponement of salary increases, and in some cases discharge. Discharges are usually automatic, but the employee may usually be rehired at the discretion of management.

Penalties may also be leveled against an employee organization. In Maryland and New York, the union may lose its right to dues checkoff and may be fined for leading strikes. In federal employment, employee organizations are required to state that they do not assert the right to strike against the government in order to be recognized. If they engage in strike activity, they may lose their representation rights.

It is difficult to penalize employees individually or in groups for engaging in work stoppages. Such penalties have rarely been meted out to individual employees, and enforcement is completely ignored in some jurisdictions. The penalties are often thought to be too severe, and the enforcers fear political retaliation by those who are penalized. Government administrators are often reluctant to initiate penalties, because they do not want organization leaders to be sent to jail. Jail sentences often make martyrs of organization leaders and frequently strengthen the employee organization. Moreover, if one party is in jail, it becomes difficult to settle a dispute. The subject of penalties thus poses a paradox: Although penalties for strike activity are the norm, unions oppose such penalties and employers rarely make use of them.

INCIDENCE OF WORK STOPPAGES

In 1968, there were 254 work stoppages in public employment. In 1967 and 1968, the number of work stoppages as well as days lost because of work stoppages increased sharply over those of the previous years. The 1967 and 1968 New York City teachers strikes accounted for a large share of the man days lost during those years (Table VIII–1).

A work stoppage has been defined by the Bureau of Labor Statistics as "a temporary stoppage of work by a group of employees to express a grievance or enforce a demand." This definition includes a number of pressure tactics, such as mass sick leave, protests, and similar activities of public employees, whether or not the term "strike" has been used.

Historically, local employees have accounted for most work

Table VIII-1
Work Stoppages in Government, 1958–68*

Year	NUMBER OF STOPPAGES	TOTAL WORKERS INVOLVED	MAN-DAYS IDLE DURING YEAR	State Government			Local Government		
				NUMBER OF STOPPAGES	WORKERS INVOLVED	MAN-DAYS IDLE DURING YEAR	NUMBER OF STOPPAGES	WORKERS INVOLVED	MAN-DAYS IDLE DURING YEAR
1958	15	1,720	7,510	1	30	60	14	1,690	7,450
1959	25	2,050	10,500	4	410	1,650	21	1,640	8,850
1960	36	28,600	58,400	3	970	1,170	33	27,600	57,200
1961	28	6,610	15,300	—	—	—	28	6,610	15,300
1962	28†	31,100	79,100	2	1,660	2,260	21	25,300	43,100
1963	29	4,840	15,400	2	280	2,160	27	4,560	13,300
1964	41	22,700	70,800	4	280	3,170	37	22,500	67,700
1965	42	11,900	146,000	—	—	1,280‡	42	11,900	145,000
1966	142	105,000	455,000	9	3,090	6,010	133	102,000	449,000
1967	181	132,000	1,250,000	12	4,670	16,300	169	127,000	1,230,000
1968	254§	201,800	2,545,200	16	9,300	42,800	235	190,900	2,492,800

* Includes stoppages lasting a full day or shift or longer and involving 6 workers or more.

† Includes five stoppages of Federal employees, affecting 4,190 workers, resulting in 33,800 man-days of idleness.

‡ Idleness in 1965 resulting from a stoppage that began in 1964.

§ Includes three stoppages of Federal employees, affecting 1,680 workers, resulting in 9,600 man-days of idleness.

Data on stoppages and workers refer to stoppages beginning in the year; man-days idle refer to all stoppages in effect during the year. Because of rounding, sums of individual items may not equal totals.

SOURCE: U.S. Bureau of Labor Statistics.

stoppages; stoppages at the federal level have been rare. In 1968, only 3 stoppages of work by federal employees were reported. Only sixteen stoppages occurred on the state level, and 235 at the local level.

Teachers and librarians were responsible for the largest number of work stoppages, one hundred twelve. Sanitation workers accounted for sixty-three stoppages. Administration and protection service employees took part in twenty-eight stoppages. Hospital and health service employees accounted for twenty-one stoppages.

The major matters responsible for work stoppages were salary and fringe benefits. There were 196 such stoppages for these reasons. Recognition disputes were second, with sixty stoppages; administrative matters were responsible for thirty-three stoppages. Although the 1968 statistics indicated a major strike year in public employment, only about ten days were lost to work stoppages for every 10,000 days worked. In private industry the ratio was about twenty days lost for 10,000 days worked.

ROLE OF THE STRIKE

In private employment the strike or the threat of the strike is the major means of resolving impasses in negotiations. A strike is costly, placing economic pressures on both parties and inducing them to come to an agreement. The employer loses potential profits and still has to pay fixed costs; the employees receive no wages during a strike. Conceivably the parties may not reach an agreement. In such a case the employer may be forced out of business and/or the strikers may lose their jobs. Such a situation is the exception rather than the rule, however, because both parties usually have an interest in the survival and the prosperity of the business.

Strikes in private employment have different effects on the parties depending upon such variables as capital-labor ratio, size of inventories, competitiveness of the industry, business conditions, perishability of the product or the service, seasonality, size of the strike fund, actions of rival unions, behavior of factions within the union, and union leadership's perception of the temperament of the rank and file. These factors also affect the length of the strike and the efforts of the parties to reach a settlement. Generally strikes are not called during collective bargaining, be-

cause the threat of the strike is sufficient to encourage the parties
to reach an agreement.

Many persons see the strike as a necessary tool for resolving
impasses and forcing the parties to come to agreement. Some
critics argue that the strike saps the strength of both parties and
has intolerable effects on the public. It is because the strike imposes such costs, however, that the parties are forced to come to
agreement. In private employment, the role of the strike in collective bargaining has permitted labor relations to be left primarily
in the hands of the parties.

In the private sector, the product market limits the size of the
wage settlement in collective bargaining. Wage increases that
exceed productivity increases *must* cause a rise in product prices,
if profit margins are to remain constant. Depending on the elastic-
ity of demand for the product, price increases may result in decreases in sales and, consequently, a loss of jobs for some workers.
The product market thus theoretically protects the public interest
by preventing excessive increases in prices and wages. On the
other hand, if the union is willing to sacrifice employment opportunities, excessive increases in cost of a product may occur. Few
employee unions are willing to pay such a price for wage increases.

In the public sector, most services are not subject to pressure
from the product market because the government is the only
source of supply. In most instances a user of the service does not
individually pay for the service. Instead, all citizens pay for the
services through taxes. Government agencies cannot lock out
their employees, and, as pointed out in Chapter I, it is difficult to
cut back services in light of the increased public demand for those
services.

In public employment, little economic pressure can be exerted
against the government. The primary pressures are political,
though the amounts and kinds of pressures vary among jurisdictions. In some cases, political pressure may be combined with
indirect economic pressure. For example, a strike by city harbor
pilots results in severe economic hardships on shippers and re-
ceivers, who, in turn, generate political pressure on city authorities.

The extent of political pressure generated by a strike of public
employees depends, in part, on the essentiality of the service as

perceived by the public. The more essential the service in the public view, the more effective will be the pressure put on the government. The amount of pressure also depends on the politician's relative power vis-à-vis the size of the union, the amount in its treasury, its political cohesiveness, its alliance with labor groups, and other factors. The determinants of the power positions in public employment differ from those in private employment primarily because the emphasis is on political rather than economic pressure.

The strike in both public and private employment is more than a collective bargaining tool. A strike may have therapeutic and participative benefits for the individual union member. He may feel he is part of a group doing something to better his position. He may view the strike as a blow against arbitrary authority—perhaps the boss or the government. The union as an institution may need a strike to increase the interest, militancy, and loyalty of its members.

Although numerous alternatives to the strike have been proposed, no widely accepted substitute has thus far been developed. Union leaders see the strike as their most effective weapon. This viewpoint leads to their demands that the strike be made legal in public employment. Furthermore, they argue that effective collective bargaining cannot be carried on without the right to strike.

Impasse Procedures

Because the strike is generally illegal in the public sector, a variety of different procedures have been developed to resolve impasses in negotiations. This section analyzes the various proposals for resolving impasses in public employment.

DECISION BY EMPLOYER

Impasses in negotiations in federal employment were submitted to agency heads for final approval. Fact-finding by neutral individuals or mediation by FMCS may be used as interim steps, but the final authority rested with agency heads. Although employee organizations had not been willing to accept this procedure at lower levels of government, they had no alternative at the federal level until Executive Order 11491.

Unions on the federal level object to the employer unilaterally resolving impasses. The practice limits the employee organization's bargaining power to the rationality of its arguments and its political power within the agency.

RELATIVE POLITICAL POWER IN LEGISLATURE

George W. Taylor, a prominent mediator and arbitrator, and the other .members[6] of Governor Nelson A. Rockefeller's Committee on Public Employee Relations in New York rejected the strike as a means of resolving impasses in public employment. The strike in public employment "introduces an alien force in the legislative process"[7] and interferes with the proper functioning of representative government.

The Taylor Committee recommended mediation, fact-finding, and voluntary arbitration as a means of resolving impasses in public employment negotiations. If either party were to reject the award of a neutral tribunal, the final step would be submission of the dispute to the appropriate state or local legislative body, which would hold a "show cause hearing" ". . . prior to final legislative action on the budget or other enactment."[8] The legislative body, which usually bases its decisions on the relative political power of constituent groups becomes the final step in the impasse procedure.

> It is ultimately the legislature and the political process which has to balance the interests of public employees with the rest of the community, to relate the compensation of public employees to the tax rate, and to appraise the extent and quality of public services and the efficiency of their performance to the aspirations of public employees. The methods of persuasion and political activity, rather than the strike, comport with our institutions and traditions as means to resolve such conflicts of interest.[9]

The Taylor Committee emphasized that joint determination of working conditions by unions and management as practiced in the private sector "cannot be transferred literally to the public employment sector."[10]

The committee favored a statutory prohibition against strikes in public employment. If a strike occurred, the agency administering the statute would determine if the employee organization had called the strike and "whether these were such acts of extreme provocation on the part of the public employer as to detract from the fault of the employee organization in permitting the strike to take place." Presumably the penalties of fines and loss of dues checkoff would be waived if the employing agency was found to have provoked the strike.

The committee proposal of deciding impasses ultimately by relative political power tends to give greater bargaining power to numerically larger unions because a larger bloc of voters will have greater political power with the legislative body. Equating political influence with size of a union is the basis of most government decisions in a democratic country, so that criticism of the proposal on these grounds is really criticism of representative government. The committee proposal is also similar to the Taft-Hartley Act eighty-day injunction procedure in private employment, whereby, after fact-finding, the President may submit an unresolved dispute to Congress.

The success of the Taylor Committee proposal depends on the vast majority of disputes being settled independently by the parties. The experience to date suggests, however, that, until the parties develop greater sophistication in bargaining, many disputes will be submitted to the legislative body.

Relying on relative political power in the legislative body as the final determinant in impasses will affect bargaining strategy of the parties. As discussed under lobbying, the party possessing greater political power will be reluctant to bargain and will prefer that the legislative body determine working conditions. A union with strong political power will have little incentive to bargain if it believes it can get better working conditions from the legislative body. A union with relatively less political power than the employing agency will probably settle for a lower wage package in bargaining rather than attempt to submit the dispute to the legislative body.

MEDIATION AND FACT-FINDING

In almost all states, statutes regulating collective bargaining in public employment prohibit the strike, but none, except in New York State, provide that impasses be referred to the legislative body. The impasse procedures in the other statutes end with mediation and fact-finding. The study commissions appointed to recommend or review public employee legislation in Illinois and Michigan also favored mediation and fact-finding as the terminal point of the impasse procedure.

It is important to recognize the differences among mediators, fact-finders and arbitrators. The mediator provides a channel of communications for the parties. Sometimes he carries messages between the parties; at other times he helps to clarify arguments. He makes recommendations only when he is confident that they will be accepted by both parties. The fact-finder establishes the relevant facts in the dispute and usually issues recommendations for settlement. The arbitrator issues an award that, if binding, must be accepted by the parties. The recommendations or award of all three often provides a "face saver" for one or both of the parties. "Face savers" are particularly important in public employee bargaining, because the employer often does not have control of the purse strings, and because the negotiators can use the recommendation or award to justify the settlement to their constituencies.

Mediation and fact-finding are voluntary processes. Neither party is compelled to accept the assistance of the mediator in resolving the dispute or the recommendations of the fact-finder in ending the impasse. The success of these methods depends on the acceptability and ingenuity of the third parties. FMCS mediators have substituted their own time limitations for a strike deadline to break impasses in federal-level bargaining. In several cases, the threat of the mediator's withdrawing his services has accelerated negotiations to a successful conclusion. A landmark study of fact-finding in public employment has suggested:

> the fact finder in the public sector must understand that his role or function will vary according to the circumstances in which he finds himself. Fact finding is not necessarily adjustment or adjudication. It may often be a mixture of both with a large infusion of political and strategic consideration.[11]

The fact-finder's recommendations may be used to bring pressure on the other side in negotiation (usually the public employer), the legislative or budget-approving body, or the public. With some exceptions, fact-finding awards have been accepted by both parties. Two fact-finding awards were rejected by boards of education in New York State in 1968, and 5 out of 50 fact-finding reports were rejected by municipalities in Wisconsin from 1967 to 1968. Fact-finding does not always provide a terminal point for collective bargaining. In many cases disputed issues submitted to fact-finding have been resolved prior to the issuance of the fact-finder's recommendations. Even a fact-finding award may not end the impasse. Early experience under the New York State statute and other state laws indicated that a fact-finding award sometimes forms the basis of subsequent negotiations between the parties and even a later fact-finding award.

The proponents of mediation and fact-finding claim that these procedures minimize strikes in public employment. Of course mediation and fact-finding will not prevent all strikes. Nor will they necessarily guarantee collective bargaining in good faith. Particularly in the early rounds of collective bargaining, the parties may seize upon the availability of third parties before serious bargaining—or indeed sometimes before any bargaining —has taken place. Such premature involvement of third parties is in part due to the limited number of issues at stake, usually a few economic issues. A more important explanation, however, is the parties' inexperience with the bargaining process. Mediators and fact-finders cite examples of public employers believing they have bargained in good faith if they have given the employee represent- ative what the employer considers a "fair" offer. When the em- ployee representative rejects the offer, the parties have concluded their bargaining and turn to the third party for a solution. The pro- ponents of mediation and fact-finding argue that once the parties gain collective bargaining experience, resorting to these impasse procedures will be less automatic and proportionately lower. In addition, the availability of these deadlock procedures will sub- stantially lessen the chances of strikes in the public sector.

Fact-finding has been used exclusively in states with impasse procedures established by law. To prevent overuse of fact-find- ing, it has been suggested that the neutral be prohibited from is- suing an award that to some extent favors each party.[12] Instead, the neutral would have to accept completely either one party's position or the other's. This suggestion is intended to encourage bargaining and to discourage submitting extreme positions to a neutral; because the parties would be risking complete acceptance of the other side's demands by agreeing to fact-finding. Although this suggestion has never been implemented, it encourages innovation in developing penalties for parties who adhere to extreme positions in bargaining. Probably a more workable suggestion would be to permit the neutral to issue a two-part award. The first part would publicly state whether either party or both parties had bargained in good faith, making sincere attempts to reach agreement. The second part would issue a recommendation for settlement according to the neutral's own criteria.

BINDING ARBITRATION

Binding arbitration is another procedure for resolving impasses in negotiations. Under binding arbitration, a neutral person or committee listens to the point of view of each party and then issues a decision for settlement which the parties must accept. Binding arbitration can be either compulsory or voluntary. If the procedure is established by statute, it is compulsory; if it is agreed to in advance by the parties, it is voluntary.

Pennsylvania and Rhode Island provide for compulsory binding arbitration as the ultimate impasse procedure for disputes involving policemen and fire fighters. Wyoming has similar procedures for fire fighters only. Rhode Island also has a statute on binding compulsory arbitration for impasses involving teachers, but the binding aspect of the arbitrator's award is limited to "all matters not involving the expenditure of money."

Over sixty cases went to arbitration in Pennsylvania in 1968, the first year the compulsory arbitration statute was in effect. The principal issue at dispute in these cases was invariably economic terms of employment.

Compulsory arbitration has been opposed on the grounds that it violates the principles of representative government. If a binding decision is made by an arbitrator, the public employer is no longer responsible to the electorate. If an arbitrator issues a monetary award that must be implemented and financed by the representatives of the citizenry, some legal problems are clearly present. The constitutionality of the Rhode Island, Pennsylvania, and Wyoming statutes that provide for compulsory arbitration has been challenged. The courts in all three of these states have upheld the constitutionality of the statutes.

The neutral party issuing an award under compulsory binding arbitration may be less sensitive to political pressures than the neutral in fact-finding or voluntary arbitration. In theory, the use of any kind of neutral is supposed to remove the impasse from political pressures, and the neutral may select his own criteria to make recommendations or awards. In practice, the neutral may take political pressures into account, particularly if the parties need not accept his decision. He wants the parties to accept his recommendation, and he does not want to get a reputation for issuing unworkable awards. The neutral under compulsory arbitration need not worry about the parties accepting his award.

A major disadvantage of compulsory arbitration, as in fact-finding, is that the parties are often reluctant to bargain if they know that a neutral person will later make an award for settlement of the dispute. The party with weaker bargaining power has nothing to lose by taking an extreme position at the start of negotiations and adhering to this position until the matter is submitted to the arbitrator. He always has a chance of convincing the neutral. Prior to this point, concessions he makes weaken his presentation to the arbitrator.

MODIFIED RIGHT TO STRIKE

The modified right to strike may take several forms; in each case the right is conditional. In 1969 two states adopted laws enacting a modified right to strike for specific groups of public employees. The Vermont statute for teachers leaves the question of determining the legality of a teachers' strike to the courts. The courts may issue an injunction against a strike if the strike endangers "a sound program of school education which . . . is in the best interest to prevent." Until experience accumulates under this act, it is impossible to know how narrowly or broadly the courts will interpret the criteria for granting injunctions. The revised Montana law for nurses in public and private institutions conditions the right to strike on (1) 30 days' notice of the strike, and (2) absence of any other strike in a health care facility within a radius of 150 miles.

The "Governor's Commission to Revise the Public Employment Law of Pennsylvania" recommended a procedure similar to the one in the Vermont statute. Public employee strikes are not prohibited unless enjoined by the courts when "the welfare, health and safety of the general public" are being adversely affected. Penalties are provided for violations of court injunctions.

Another procedure, first suggested by Donald H. Wolett and later expanded by Robert E. Doherty and Walter E. Oberer, combines advisory arbitration with a limited right to strike.[13] The right to strike is available only if a board of education rejects an award of a fact-finder or an arbitrator. Under such circumstances, the teachers are given the legal right to strike. Presumably this procedure would limit the number of legal strikes and provide some assurance to teacher organizations that bargaining will be meaningful. Its major disadvantage is that neither party has an incentive to bargain and to adopt moderate positions. Furthermore, union leaders point out that the procedure is onesided in that only public employers are permitted to reject awards of neutrals.

UNLIMITED RIGHT TO STRIKE

Theodore Kheel, the well-known mediator and arbitrator, is the most prominent supporter of the legal right of public employees to strike.[14] Kheel makes exception of public employees whose absence endangers the health and safety of the public—for example, policemen and fire fighters. To these groups of public employees Kheel recommends that compulsory arbitration be granted. A similar proposal to Kheel's would give *all* public employees the right to strike, but have the courts or a special governmental agency enjoin strikes that endanger public health and safety.

The advocates of the right to strike reason that the strike is a necessary ingredient to collective bargaining; the employees must have some power to reject management's proposals. Only such force will induce meaningful bargaining and subsequent agreement. Without the right to strike to back up their demands, public employees are merely able to make suggestions and recommendations, which the employer is free to reject without fear of reprisal. The strike or the threat of a strike thus resolves impasses in public employee negotiations in the same way it operates in private employment.

The authors do not believe that the absolute right to say "no" (the right to strike) is always necessary in order to have joint determination. The key ingredient to joint determination is the ability of each party to impose a cost on the other. In public employment, the employee organization can impose some costs on the employer without actually calling a strike. For example, slowdown, work to rule, picketing, disseminating publicity unfavorable to the administrators of the employing agency, or impugning the integrity of these administrators have all been used to induce public employers to bargain.[15] Another opportunity for the employee organization to say no to the employer is inherent in arbitration or fact-finding. A favorable decision by the neutral party increases the employee organization's ability to pressure the employer—especially if there is a cost of disagreement imposed on the employer who rejects the recommendations of the neutral.

The strike in the public sector is a strong political demonstration. Political pressures encourage agreement, but the effects of these pressures vary depending on the essentiality of the service and the constituency affected by the strike. A strike of social welfare workers results in very little political pressure on the employer, because those affected by such a strike have comparatively little political power. Little incentive was provided for settlement of the strike of social workers in New York City in 1966, especially since the city continued to mail welfare checks to recipients during the strike. Similarly, few citizens would object to a prolonged strike of internal revenue investigators.

If no other impasse procedure is used and public employees are permitted to strike, the parties would eventually be forced to bargain and to reach agreement. Some strikes, however, would last much longer than a strike by comparable employees in the private sector, because no continuous and increasing economic pressure is placed on the employer in the public sector. The essentiality of the service would determine the length the strike would be and perhaps the size of the wage package. Groups of public employees that can most inconvenience the public by withdrawing their services would have the greatest bargaining power. In the private sector, the key determinant for settlement is usually the economic cost to both parties; in the public sector it is the political cost to the public officials and the impact of lost wages upon the employees.

Fact-finding and arbitration interfere with collective bargaining as it is carred on in the private sector. These procedures may likewise interfere with the opportunity of public employees to participate effectively in the determination of their wages and working conditions. On the other hand, strikes by public employees interfere with two goals of public policy. First, strikes may shut down public services considered essential. Second, the right of an employee organization to strike may place so much stress on a democratic government that it becomes authoritarian instead of democratic. Public employee strikes constitute "coercive pressure" possessed by no other interest group. If public employers can force elected officials to accede to their demands, can these officials be responsible to the entire electorate?

Some institutional modification must be found to balance the conflicting goals of public policy. Very little experimenting has been done in resolving public employee impasses; much more is needed in the future.

IX the future of collective bargaining in public employment

The preceding discussions indicate that collective bargaining is well established in many jurisdictions in public employment. What will become of the institution of collective bargaining? Will it continue to spread rapidly to other public employee jurisdictions? Or has it reached its saturation point? Will collective bargaining become an integral part of employee-employer relations in the public sector? If so, is the institution mature, or will it continue to change substantially in future years? These questions form the focus of this final chapter.

Predictions are often hazardous in a field as new as collective bargaining in public employment. It is only since 1962, when Executive Order 10988 was issued, that public employee bargaining has become widespread. In this sense, the following "predictions" resemble "speculations." Nevertheless, some discussion of the future direction of public employee labor relations is warranted at this point.

Growth of Collective Bargaining

Collective bargaining in public employment is not a fad. It has already become a permanent part of employee-employer relationships in many governmental jurisdictions, and will spread to other jurisdictions. Furthermore, the practice will probably spread more rapidly in public employment than in the still unorganized areas of private employment. When unions attempt to organize in the private sector, they usually deal with individual employees who lack any form of structure or group cohesion. In the public sector, however, unions frequently encounter employees already organized into lobbying and social welfare organizations. Either these employees, accustomed to belonging to organizations, are prone to join a union to represent them in collective bargaining, or the competition from unions forces the existing organizations to adopt collective bargaining as a major goal.

The question of legality has been a primary limitation to the growth of collective bargaining in public employment. In the absence of permissive legislation many public employers believe it is illegal for them to recognize and bargain with an employee organization. This limitation, however, is rapidly disappearing. The federal government has issued two Executive Orders and 18 states have passed laws providing for recognition and bargaining with public employees organizations. On the basis of experience, some future changes will undoubtedly occur in existing bargaining laws. Moreover, many other states will pass statutes granting public employees the right to bargain collectively.

A possibility also exists that Congress will pass federal legislation regulating collective bargaining for state and local employees. This type of legislation could be either an amendment to existing federal labor statutes or an entirely new statute. Several events in the late 1960's may have opened the door to passage of such legislation. The U.S. Supreme Court approved the extension of federal minimum wage legislation to state and local government employees, thereby presumably permitting further federal regulation of employment relations for such employees. In addition, the National Education Association introduced a federal statute regulating employment relations for all public school teachers. Although the proposed bill has little chance of passage, its introduction is significant. Similarly, the AFL-CIO has been drafting federal legislation to grant collective bargaining rights to all state and local employees.

Public employee unions and private employee unions having members employed in the public sector will most likely continue to increase in membership. Private employee unions will multiply their efforts to organize public employees in the future; given the current momentum, however, public employee unions will probably continue to be more successful. Much of the future growth in public employee unions will occur at the state, county, and municipal levels—most of it occurring among municipal employees, but some also among state employees, in view of the relatively small number currently organized. Federal white-collar employees, the only major unorganized group in the federal government, will also contribute to the increase in membership in public employer unions.

The extent of future organizing gains in public employment will vary according to occupation. Because of the increase in demand for health services and in the number of persons employed in these occupations, many unions will concentrate on the health service occupations. Private employee unions will enjoy their greatest success among employees in blue-collar occupations such as those commonly found in highway maintenance, sanitation, building service, and parks. Only limited increases will occur in public education because of the current high degree of organization by professional associations; but collective bargaining will continue to spread rapidly among teachers and other public school employees.

As a result of the spread of collective bargaining, some structural changes will occur among public employee unions and associations. More private employee unions will form separate departments to focus on the organization of public employees. Some mergers probably also will take place. The Post Office Mail Handlers Union has already agreed to become a special division of the Laborers International Union. The merger of AFT and NEA is a distinct possibility, although it may occur outside AFL-CIO. Merger of some state employee associations and AFSMCE is also possible.

Coalition bargaining, in which various unions bargain simultaneously with an employer, has become increasingly popular in the private sector, but has been rare in the public sector—the only exception being unions of postal employees at the national level. The immediate prospect for wider acceptance of coalition bargaining in the public sector is not promising, because of established jurisdictions and of division of crafts among unions.

As collective bargaining spreads in the public sector, personnel departments will place greater emphasis on employee relations. As a result of this emphasis, additional personnel staff will be required, and additional training seminars and courses on labor relations will be developed for staff members.

Joint bargaining, or the joining together of separate agencies at a single level of government for bargaining, which has occurred mainly in large cities, will probably increase in public employment in future years. Where collective bargaining is currently conducted by separate agencies within a single political unit, union whipsawing may also encourage joint bargaining.

Association bargaining, common in the private sector, has not yet occurred among public employers. In the public sector, association bargaining would require employers of different governmental units to unite for collective bargaining. Obviously, such joint action could not occur at the federal level, since only one employer exists. And it is unlikely that different states, counties, or municipalities will unite for collective bargaining, because of the uniqueness of their problems and of their financial structure. Public education probably offers the only prospect for joint bargaining. For example, a group of school districts could bargain jointly with an organization representing employees in all the districts. The conditions necessary for such bargaining exist among school districts with equal financial structure and with similar employee and school problems.

Scope of Bargaining

The scope of bargaining in the public sector will continue to widen in future years. As the parties get accustomed to each other and as collective bargaining relationships mature, more topics will be negotiated.

Pressure for organizational security clauses will intensify. If the benefits a member receives from his organization are not dependent on his contributions, he will probably end his support of the organization. The organization wants support from all the people that it represents. The strongest form of organizational security would be requiring an employee to join an employee organization before he can get a job. Physicians often must be members of county medical associations in order to obtain hospital privileges in that county. In over one-half the states, attorneys must belong to state bar associations before they can practice law in that state.

This requirement has been modified in different ways to guarantee support for employee organizations. In private industry, unions have relied on the union shop as a guarantee of support from their members. Because the union shop is usually considered illegal in public employment, public employee unions will increase their efforts to obtain the agency shop. At the same time these unions may attempt to legalize the union shop by changing laws that ban it.

The number of grievance arbitration clauses will continue to grow in the public sector. Many federal employees, municipal employees, and public school teachers have already negotiated grievance arbitration clauses. The importance of dual grievance procedures will decrease as more emphasis is placed on the grievance procedure negotiated by the employee organization. Finally, advisory arbitration of grievances probably will evolve into binding arbitration.

Where impasse procedures have not been included in negotiation statutes, the parties in the public sector have frequently negotiated their own procedures. Private sector unions and employers rarely negotiate their own impasse procedures, even though many labor relations authorities have encouraged them to do so. Impasse procedures will probably be negotiated more among federal employees and teachers, who have already negotiated some procedures, than among other public employees.

Decisions affecting professional employees pose new problems for unions and public employers. Professional employees like to participate in many of these decisions, but crisis bargaining is clearly not the most desirable procedure to follow in decision making. Some formal procedures will probably be developed to allow professional employees a voice in these important decisions. An increase in informal contacts between professionals and administrators might possibly make such formal procedures unnecessary. If these approaches do not work, however, employee organizations will press to include the matters in collective bargaining.

Wages, instead of fringe benefits, will continue to be the major topic of negotiations except in federal employment, where they are not negotiable, as most government employers already provide for pension, vacation, sick leave, leaves of absence, and so on.

Process of Bargaining

Both public employers and public employee unions will become increasingly sophisticated in collective bargaining as they gain more experience in the process. In the near future, the number of public employee strikes will probably increase, because many strikes are a function of political pressures and of the immaturity of the relationship between the parties. In the long run, however, the number of public employee strikes will level off and will probably decrease. In spite of the illegality of strikes in public employment, some unions will continue to apply this sometimes effective weapon.

Public employee organizations will continue their efforts to remove the legal ban on strikes by these employees. Probably only organizations of policemen and fire fighters will accept the illegality of strikes if a substitute such as compulsory arbitration is available.

Some labor experts predict that by the mid-1970's public employee strikes will be legal for all nonessential services. Others predict that strikes by public employees will never be made legal, because the majority of people in the United States are opposed to such strikes. Legislators generally react to the wishes of their constituents, and most citizens do not want to be inconvenienced by strikes of public employees. With few exceptions, the authors do not anticipate that strikes by public employees will be declared legal in the near future.

Binding arbitration on monetary and nonmonetary issues will become more frequent in public employment. More states will soon pass laws requiring compulsory arbitration for such essential services as those provided by police and fire fighters. Some public employers and unions representing employees in other occupations will voluntarily accept binding arbitration in contract negotiations. Eventually some public employee laws requiring arbitration as an impasse procedure will be extended from essential services to nonessential services.

Despite the increasing scope and sophistication of collective bargaining in public employment, political pressures will remain important. Attempts by the parties to insulate themselves from these pressures will be of little avail. The nature of collective bargaining in the public sector and the political environment will not permit collective bargaining to replace completely other systems of employee participation. Matters such as the total number of persons employed by a government agency may not be bargainable issues, but they will continue to be subjects of lobbying. Other matters, such as pensions, which are negotiated in private employment, will probably continue to be subjects of lobbying instead of becoming part of bargaining in the public sector. As a result, the scope of collective bargaining most likely will not be as comprehensive in public employment as it is in private employment.

Collective bargaining will continue to expand among unorganized public employees. Where collective bargaining has already been instituted, the pace will intensify. Collective bargaining in the public sector is an important new front in the public scene, and its impacts will be felt in areas far beyond the employees covered.

notes

Chapter I Government and Public Employment

1. M. Slade Kendrick, *Public Finance* (Boston: Houghton Mifflin, 1951), pp. 46–59.
2. James A. Maxwell, *Financing State and Local Governments* (Washington, D.C.: The Brookings Institution, 1967), p. 23.
3. Charles R. Adrian, *State and Local Governments* (New York: McGraw-Hill, 1967), p. 451.
4. Claudius O. Johnson, *American State and Local Government* (New York: Crowell, 1956), pp. 195–203.
5. U.S. Civil Service Commission, Annual Report, *Occupations of Federal White Collar Workers*, 1963.
6. *Ibid.*
7. U.S. Department of Labor, *The Economic Situation of Negroes* in the United States, Bulletin 5–3, 1963.
8. U.S. Civil Service Commission, *Study of Minority Group Employment in the Federal Government*, 1967, p. 3.
9. *Ibid.*, p. 7.
10. Samuel Krislov, *The Negro in Federal Employment* (Minneapolis: University of Minnesota Press, 1965), p. 94.
11. Pennsylvania Human Relations Commission, *Survey of Non-White Employees in State Government* (Harrisburg: Pennsylvania Human Relations Commission, March 28, 1963).
12. U.S. Department of Labor, *Manpower Report of the President* (Washington, D.C.: April 1967), p. 269.
13. An excellent description of the impact of the sovereign doctrine on public employment organization is given by Kurt L. Hanslowe in *The Emerging Law of Labor Relations in Public Employment* (Ithaca, N.Y.: New York State School of Industrial and Labor

Relations, 1967), Part II; see also Terrence Kiely, "Right of Public Employees to Strike," *De Paul Review*, Vol. 16 (Autumn–Winter 1966), 151–165.

14. The Bureau of National Affairs, *Government Employee Relations Report*, No. 243 (Washington, D.C.: May 6, 1968), pp. D–1–D–6.

Chapter II Collective Bargaining for Federal Employees

1. *Manpower Report of the President, 1968* (Washington, D.C.: 1968), Tables G–2 and G–4.

2. U.S. Department of Labor, Bureau of Labor Statistics, *Handbook of Labor Statistics, 1967,* Bulletin No. 1555 (Washington, D.C.: undated), Table 33.

3. U.S. Department of Labor, *Manpower Report of the President, April, 1967* (Washington, D.C.: 1967), Table E–9.

4. Herbert Kaufman, "The Growth of the Federal Personnel System," in the American Assembly, Wallace S. Sayre (ed.), *The Federal Government Service* (Englewood Cliffs, N.J.: Prentice-Hall, 1965), p. 2.

5. National Manpower Council, *Government and Manpower* (New York: Columbia University Press, 1964), p. 16.

6. *Ibid.*, p. 142.

7. U.S. Civil Service Commission, *Federal Workforce Outlook, Fiscal Years 1966–1969* (Washington, D.C.), p. 3.

8. U.S. Civil Service Commission, *84th Annual Report, 1967* (Washington, D.C.), Table A–2.

9. National Manpower Council, *op. cit.*, pp. 157–159.

10. U.S. Civil Service Commission, *Annual Report, op. cit.*, Tables A–4 and A–5.

11. Kaufman, *op. cit.*, pp. 41–43 and 52.

12. National Manpower Council, *op. cit.*, p. 173.

13. U.S. Civil Service Commission, *Annual Report, op. cit.*, p. 25.

14. Frederick C. Mosher, "Features and Problems of the Federal Civil Service," in the American Assambly, Wallace S. Sayre (ed.), *The Federal Government Service* (Englewood Cliffs, N.J.: Prentice-Hall, 1965), p. 173.

15. Kaufman, *op. cit.*, p. 67.

16. Sterling D. Spero, *Government as Employer* (New York: Remsen Press, 1948), p. 81.

17. *Ibid.*, p. 85.

18. *Ibid.*, p. 95.

19. *Ibid.*, pp. 105–113.

20. *Ibid.*, p. 175.

21. *Ibid.*, p. 190.

22. U.S. Civil Service Commission, "Analysis of Data on Union Recognition in the Federal Service," Bulletin 711–6 (May 15, 1969).

23. Mosher, *op. cit.*, p. 192.

24. U.S. Department of Labor, Bureau of Labor Statistics, *Directory of National and International Unions*, 1965, Bulletin No. 1493 (Washington, D.C., April 1966), pp. 51–55.

25. U.S. Department of Labor, Bureau of Labor Statistics, *Directory of National and International Labor Unions in the United States, 1967*, Bulletin No. 1596 (Washington, D.C.), pp. 56–62.

26. National Association of Letter Carriers, *Postal Record* (Washington, D.C.: October 1967), p. 22.

27. Spero, *op. cit.*, p. 199.

28. R. Hart Wilson, *Collective Bargaining in the Federal Service* (New York: Harper & Row, 1961), p. 34.

29. Spero, *op. cit.*, p. 149.

30. Hart, *op. cit.*, p. 75.

31. Congressional Quarterly Service, *Legislators and the Lobbyists* (Washington, D.C.).

32. Hart, *op. cit.*, pp. 87–92.

33. Spero, *op. cit.*, p. 167.

34. Louis J. Van Mol, "The TVA Experience," in *Collective Bargaining in the Public Service*, Kenneth O. Warner (ed.), (Chicago: Public Personnel Association, 1967), pp. 85–94; Hart, *op. cit.*, pp. 96–106.

35. Memorandum from the President to Heads of Departments and Agencies on the Subject of Employee-Management Relations in the Federal Service, June 22, 1961.

36. Executive Order 10988, Section 13.

37. Department of Defense Directive, "Employee-Management Cooperation," August 18, 1964, No. 1426.1.

38. U.S. Civil Service Commission, FPM Letter No. 711–6, dated December 14, 1966.

39. U.S. Department of Labor, *Rules for the Nomination of Arbitrators*, August 20, 1964.

40. American Bar Association, *Report of the Committee on Government Employer-Employee Relations*, 1968.

41. H. J. Lahne and E. H. Ghearing, "Federal Employee Bargaining Unit Determinations," *Monthly Labor Review*, July 1964, pp. 763–766.

42. In the matter of arbitration involving a unit determination at Norfolk Naval Shipyard, Portsmouth, Virginia in repetition of Local No. 1 of the Planners-Estimators and Progressmen's Association, September 20, 1967, Joseph M. Stone, Arbitrator.

43. AFGE v. NMU, Dredges Goethals and Comber, U.S. Army Engineer District, Philadelphia, Case No. 64–37, June 15, 1964, 43 LA 111.

44. The Bureau of National Affairs, *Government Employee Relations Report*, No. 210 (Washington, D.C.: September 10, 1967), p. A–1.

45. AFGE v. IAM, Aircraft Services Base, Oklahoma City, Oklahoma, May 2, 1966, 48 LA 63.

46. Executive Order 10988, Section 6(b).

47. Executive Order 10988, Section 7.

48. W. V. Gill, "Labor-Management Relations in the Federal Service," an address to Town Hall of California, February 21, 1967 (mimeographed).

49. "An Analysis of 55 GSA-Union Agreements Negotiated Under Executive Order 10988, May 1967," internal document.

50. U.S. Civil Service Commission, Bureau of Inspections, *op. cit.*, p. 13.

51. U.S. Civil Service Commission, Office of Labor-Management Relations, *Union Recognition in the Federal Government*, November 1968, Table A.

52. U.S. Civil Service Commission, Bureau of Inspections, *Summary Report on Employee-Management Cooperation*, March 1967, p. 5.

53. The Bureau of National Affairs, *Government Employee Relations Report*, No. 263 (Washington, D.C.: September 23, 1968), p. A–1.

54. The Bureau of National Affairs, *Government Employee Relations Report*, No. 229 (Washington, D.C.: January 29, 1968), p. A–3.

55. The Bureau of National Affairs, *Government Employee Relations Report*, No. 284 (Washington, D.C.: February 17, 1969), p. A–3.

56. The Bureau of National Affairs, *Government Employee Relations Report*, No. 220 (Washington, D.C.: November 27, 1967), p. A–1.

57. The Bureau of National Affairs, *Government Employee Relations Report*, No. 235 (Washington, D.C.: March 11, 1968), Grievance Arbitration 47

58. See, for instance, Otto Pragan's comments in the panel discussion, "Is Private Sector Industrial Relations the Objective in the Federal Service?" in *Collective Bargaining in the Public Service*, Gerald G. Somers (ed.) (Madison, Wisconsin: Industrial Relations Research Association, 1966), pp. 37–48.

59. A. H. Raskin, "Strikes by Public Employees," *The Atlantic*, January 1968, p. 48.

60. The Bureau of National Affairs, *Government Employee Relations Report* No. 234 (Washington, D.C.), March 4, 1968, p. A–8; No. 243, May 6, 1968, p. A–1; No. 251, July 1, 1968, p. A–5.

61. The Bureau of National Affairs, *Government Employee Relations Report* (Washington, D.C.), No. 258, August 19, 1968, p. A–I; No. 259, August 26, 1968, p. A–9; No. 263, September 23, 1968, p. A–8.

62. U.S. Civil Service Commission, Federal Personnel Manual System Letter No. 711–3, February 7, 1966.

63. *Ibid.*

64. Richard J. Murphy, "Labor-Management Relations—Where Do We Stand?" p. 6. U.S. Civil Service Commission, *Civil Service Journal*, July–September 1967.

65. Federal Mediation and Conciliation Service, *Twenty-First Annual Report, 1968* (Washington, D.C.), p. 44.

66. See, for instance, bills proposed in the 91st Congress, First Session (1969): S. 309, H.R. 4, and H.R. 4803; also the testimony before the House Post Office and Civil Service Committee in *Government Employee Relations Report*, No. 253, July 15, 1968, pp. A–4 and A–5.

67. Message of President Johnson in appointing the Review Committee on Federal Employee-Management Relations, September 8, 1967.

Chapter III Collective Bargaining for State, County, and Municipal Employees

1. Charles R. Adrian, *State and Local Governments* (New York: McGraw-Hill, 1967), pp. 199–202.

2. Russell W. Maddox and Robert T. Fuquay, *State and Local Government* (Princeton, N. J.: Van Nostrand, 1966), p. 87.

3. U.S. Bureau of the Census, *County Boards and Commissions* (Washington, D.C., 1947).

4. Maddox and Fuquay, *op. cit.*, p. 504.

5. Adrian, *op. cit.*, pp. 224–225.

6. James A. Maxwell, Financing State and Local Governments (Washington, D.C.: The Brookings Institution, 1965), pp. 128–129.

7. *Ibid.*

8. *The Municipal Year Book, 1967* (Chicago: The International City Managers Association, 1967), p. 161.

9. Maddox and Fuquay, *op. cit.*, p. 511.

10. Chester A. Newland, *Public Employee Unionization in Texas* (Austin: Institute of Public Affairs, University of Texas, 1962), p. 43.

11. For a thorough discussion of AFSCME's early history see Leo Kramer, *Labor's Paradox* (New York: Wiley, 1962), pp. 1–23.

12. Richard L. Harris "Independent Municipal Employee Associations in California," reprinted in Kenneth O. Warner (ed.), *Management Relations with Organized Public Employees* (Chicago, Public Personnel Association, 1963), p. 198.

13. Joseph Krislov "The Independent Public Employee Association," reprinted in Warner *ibid.*, pp. 173–176.

14. *Municipal Yearbook*, 1967, p. 163.

15. *Ibid.*

16. Harris, *op. cit.*, pp. 194–195.

17. *Ibid.*

18. Department of Industrial Relations, State of California, *Independent State and Local Public Employee Associations in California, 1963*, March, 1965.

19. Winston W. Crouch, *Employer-Employee Relationships in Council-Manager Cities* (Washington, D.C.: International City Managers' Association, 1968), Tables 9 and 12.

20. American Bar Association, Committee on Government Employee Relations, 1966, as cited in Andrew W. J. Thomson, "Unit Determination in Public Employment," *Public Employee Relations Reports* No. 1, (Ithaca, N.Y.: N.Y. State School of Industrial and Labor Relations, undated), p. 10.

21. The Bureau of National Affairs, *Government Employee Relations Report* (Washington, D.C.: May 15, 1967), p. B–1.

22. *Ibid.*, July 31, 1967, p. B–1.

23. Crouch, *op. cit.*, p. 73.

24. Wisconsin Employment Relations Board, *op. cit.*, p. 5.

25. State of New York, Governor's Committee on Public Employee Relations, *Final Report,* March 31, 1966, p. 31.

26. Newland, *op. cit.*, p. 45.

27. Crouch, *op. cit.*, pp. 142–143.

28. The Bureau of National Affairs, *Government Employee Relations Report*, No. 234 (Washington, D.C.: March 4, 1968), pp. D–1–D–3.

29. Winston W. Crouch, *The American City and its Organized Employees* (Washington, D.C.: International City Managers Association, 1969), p. 32–33.

30. American Federation of State, County, and Municipal Employees, AFL-CIO, *Public Employee* (Washington, D.C.: December 1967).

31. *Ibid.*, June 26, 1967.

32. *Agreement Between City of Milwaukee and* AFSCME *District Council 48,* January 1, 1966, pp. 12–16.

33. *Agreement Between City of Detroit and* AFSCME *District Council 77,* 1967, p. 6.

34. Wisconsin Employment Relations Board, "Anatomy of Assembly Bill 866, a Bill to Repeal and Recreate Subchapter IV of Chapter III of the Wisconsin Statutes Relating to Municipal Employment Relations" (Madison: 1967) (mimeographed), pp. 18–26.

35. Wisconsin Employment Relations Board, *Digest of the Wisconsin Employment Relations Board and the Courts Involving the Wisconsin Employment Peace Act and Section 111.70, Wisconsin Statutes (Municipal Employer-Employee Labor Relations Law)*, Vol. 1, June 1, 1966, p. 240.
36. The Bureau of National Affairs, *Government Employee Relations Report*, No. 185 (Washington, D.C.: March 27, 1967).
37. The Bureau of National Affairs, *Government Employee Relations Report*, No. 148, July 11, 1966.

Chapter IV Collective Bargaining for Teachers

1. U.S. Bureau of the Census, *Government Finances in 1966–67*, Series GF67 No. 3 (Washington, D.C., 1968), p. 7.
2. NEA, Research Division, *Estimates of School Statistics, 1968–69*, Research Report 1968–R16 (Washington, D.C.), p. 19.
3. *Ibid.*, p. 6.
4. *Ibid.*, p. 18.
5. Department of Commerce, Bureau of the Census, *Public Employment in 1967* (Washington, D.C.), pp. 7–9.
6. NEA, Research Division, *op. cit.*, p. 13.
7. *Ibid.*, p. 6.
8. U.S. Department of Health, Education, and Welfare, Office of Education, 1956–1958. *Biennial Survey of Education, 1961* Chapter II.
9. NEA, Research Division, *Estimate of School Statistics, 1963–64* (Washington, D.C.), p. 13; Department of Health, Education, and Welfare, Office of Education, *Projections of Educational Statistics to 1977–78*, OE 1003–68 (Washington, D.C.), p. 47.
10. *NEA, Research Division, NEA Research Bulletin*, Vol. 43, No. 3, (Washington, D.C.), p. 68.
11. U.S. Census of Population, 1960: *Subject Reports, Occupational Characteristics*, Final Report PC (2)–7A, Table 25. Reprinted in William J. Baumol and William G. Bowen, *Performing Arts—The Economic Dilemma* (New York: The Twentieth Century Fund, 1966), p. 104.
12. *Teachers Association of Newport vs. Newport School Committee*, No. 1130–Di87–67, reprinted in NEA, Research Division, *Negotiation Research Digest*, Vol. 1, No. 5 (Washington, D.C.).
13. Hereinafter referred to as IUD.
14. Walter Reuther, "Reports to the Industrial Union Department of the AFL-CIO," *Proceedings of Fifth Constitutional Convention*, Washington, D.C., November 7–8, 1963.

15. American Federation of Teachers, *Convention Proceedings* (abridged), Forty-eighth Annual Convention (Chicago, 1964), pp. 8, 96.

16. American Federation of Teachers, AFL-CIO, *American Teacher*, XI, No. 2 (Washington, D.C.: November 1964), 1, 2.

17. Myron Lieberman and Michael H. Moskow, *Collective Negotiations for Teachers* (Chicago: Rand McNally, 1966), p. 58.

18. Lieberman and Moskow, *op. cit.*, p. 59.

19. National Education Association, *NEA Handbook* (Washigton, D.C.: National Education Association, 1965), p. 13.

20. Dayton David McKean, *Pressures on the Legislature of New Jersey* (New York: Columbia University Press, 1938).

21. Virgil Blanke, "Educational Policy Formulation at the State Level by Chief State School Officers" (unpublished Ph.D. dissertation, University of Chicago, Department of Education, 1961).

22. Ronald F. Campbell, *et al., The Organization and Control of American Schools* (Columbus, Ohio: Charles E. Merrill, 1965), p. 268.

23. Myron Lieberman, *The Future of Public Education* (Chicago: University of Chicago Press, 1960), p. 192.

24. Constitution of the American Federation of Teachers (October, 1964), p. 3.

25. *The Wall Street Journal,* April 5, 1962, p. 1.

26. American Federation of Teachers, *AFT in Action* (Chicago: American Federation of Teachers, January 1962), p. 8.

27. National Education Association, *Address and Proceedings,* 1962 (Washington, D.C.: The Association, 1962), p. 181.

28. *Ibid.,* pp. 24, 28.

29. *Ibid.,* pp. 245–246. (Emphasis by authors.)

30. National Education Association, *Financial Report* (Washington, D.C.: The Association, 1965), p. 11.

31. Proceedings of the 1963 American Federation of Teachers National Convention. Resolution No. 79.

32. Philip Kochman, "The Developing Role of Teachers Union" (unpublished Ph.D. dissertation, Teachers College, Columbia University, 1939).

33. *Negotiation Research Digest,* Vol. I, No. 2, October 1967, p. B–1.

34. National Education Association, Research Division, *State Minimum Salary Laws and Goal Schedules for Teachers, 1964–65* (Washington, D.C.: National Education Association, 1965), p. 5.

35. National Education Association, Research Division, *Research Bulletin,* 38, No. 3 (Washington, D.C.: October 1960), p. 84.

36. Michael H. Moskow, *Teachers and Unions* (Philadelphia: University of Pennsylvania Press, 1966), p. 218.

37. NEA, Research Division, *Negotiation Research Digest,* Vol. 1, No. 1 (Washington, D.C.: September, 1967), p. B–1.

38. NEA, Research Division, *Negotiation Research Digest,* Vol. 1, No. 5 (Washington, D. C.: January 1968).

39. NEA, Research Division, *Negotiation Research Digest,* Vol. 1, No. 7 (Washington, D.C.: March 1968), p. B–4.

40. Research Division, "*Local Association—Organization, Practices, and Programs, 1958–59*" (Washington, D.C.: National Education Association, 1960), p. 28–29.

41. Moskow, "Teacher Organizations: An Analysis of the Issues," *Teachers College Record,* 66 (February 1965), p. 457.

42. National Education Association, *NEA Handbook* (Washington, D.C.: National Education Association, 1965), p. 65.

43. *Negotiation Research Digest,* Vol. 1, No. 4 (December 1967), p. C–11.

44. Myron Lieberman and Michael H. Moskow, *Collective Negotiations for Teachers* (Chicago: Rand McNally, 1966).

45. National Education Association, *Guidelines for Professional Sanctions* (Washington, D.C.: The Association, 1963), p. 9.

46. *Ibid.,* p. 16.

47. *Newsweek,* Vol. 64, No. 22, November 30, 1964, p. 67.

48. American Federation of Teachers, *President's Report* (Washington, D.C.: August 1964), p. 50.

49. AFT, *President's Report, op. cit.,* p. 47.

50. *The New York Times,* December 20, 1964, p. 28.

51. AFT, *President's Report, op. cit.,* p. 48; *The New York Times,* December 23, 1964, p. 24.

52. AFT, *President's Report, ibid.,* p. 48.

53. *The New York Times,* December 20, 1964, p. 28.

54. Martin S. Estey, "The Strategic Alliance as a Factor in Union Growth," *Industrial and Labor Relations Review,* 9, No. 1 (October 1955), p. 42.

Chapter V Collective Bargaining for Police and Fire Fighters

1. Winston W. Crouch, "Employee Organizations in Council-Manager Cities," *Municipal Yearbook 1967* (Chicago: International City Managers' Association), pp. 140–141.

2. U.S. Department of Commerce, Bureau of the Census, *City in 1966,* Series GE No. 3, (Washington, D.C., March 1967), Table 2.

3. Cf., Sterling D. Spero, *Government as Employer* (New York: Remsen Press, 1948), pp. 252–284.

4. International Association of Fire Chiefs, "First Annual IAFC Fire Department Statistical Report," February-March, 1967.

5. *Municipal Yearbook, 1967,* p. 441.

6. *Municipal Yearbook, 1966,* p. 370, *Washington Post,* December 26, 1967, p. B–1.

7. *Municipal Yearbook, 1967,* p. 448.

8. Data supplied by International Association of Fire Fighters.

9. See, for instance, The President's Commission on Law Enforcement and Administration of Justice, *Task Force Report: The Police* (Washington, D.C., 1967), pp. 15–16.

10. Boyd A. Hartley, "Elements of Fire Department Management and Operation: A Statistical Analysis," *Municipal Yearbook, 1967,* pp. 337–390.

11. *The New York Times,* September 1967.

12. David B. H. Martin, Town of Windsor and Windsor Police Department Employees Association, Inc., Case 6667–FF22, State of Connecticut, Board of Mediation and Arbitration, July 27, 1967.

13. *Wall Street Journal,* July 25, 1967, pp. 1, 13.

14. See, for instance, Emma Schweppe, *The Firemen's and Patrolmen's Unions in the City of New York* (New York: King's Crown Press, 1948).

15. Richard Reeves, "Is the Mayor the Number One Cop on the Beat?" *The New York Times,* December 17, 1967, p. 6E.

16. For a report of civilian review boards, see The President's Commission on Law Enforcement and Administration of Justice, *op. cit.,* pp. 200–202.

17. *Municipal Yearbook 1967,* p. 377.

18. Crouch, *op. cit.,* p. 141.

19. *Ibid.,* p. 139.

20. Schweppe, *op. cit.,* p. 28.

21. International Association of Chiefs of Police, *Police Unions,* rev. ed. (Washington, D.C.: 1958), p. 67.

22. *Municipal Yearbook 1966,* pp. 440–442.

23. Statement of Commissioner Donald D. Pomerlean Concerning a Proposal to Recognize a Union within the Baltimore City Police Department, State House, Annapolis, Maryland, March 16, 1967, I.A.C.P. Abstract 67–1, pp. 1–2.

24. *Municipal Yearbook 1966,* pp. 377, and 442.

25. Schweppe, *op. cit.,* p. 32.

26. The Bureau of National Affairs, *Government Employee Relations Report,* No. 217 (Washington, D.C.: November 6, 1967), p. B–12.

27. Patrick V. Murphy, *Police Employee Organizations* (M.P.A. thesis, College of the City of New York, June 1960), p. 29.

28. Connecticut State Board of Labor Relations, *Town of West Hartford (Police Department)* Decision No. 649 and 649A.

29. Connecticut State Board of Labor Relations, Twenty-First Annual Report, pp. 6–7.

30. Michigan Public Employment Relations Act, Section 13.

31. State of Washington Department of Labor and Industries, Case No. 0–281, May 14, 1968.

32. The Bureau of National Affairs, *Government Employee Relations Report,* No. 242 (Washington, D.C.: April 29, 1968), p. D–1.

33. The Bureau of National Affairs, *Government Employee Relations Report,* No. 258 (Washington, D.C.: August 19, 1968), pp. B–4–B–6.

34. Massachusetts Labor Relations Commission, City of Springfield (Police Department) and Public Employees Local 571, Service Employees' International Union, Case No. MUP 40, July 1, 1968.

35. International City Managers' Association, *Municipal Yearbook, 1967* (Chicago).

36. American Federation of State, County and Municipal Employees, *Public Employee,* (Washington, D.C.: March 1968).

37. *Municipal Yearbook, 1967.*

38. Bureau of National Affairs, *Government Employee Relations Report,* No. 218, November 13, 1967, p. B–7.

39. Bureau of National Affairs, *Government Employee Relations Report,* No. 251, July 1, 1968, p. B–10.

40. *Municipal Yearbook, 1966.*

41. Patrick V. Murphy, *op. cit.,* Table XVIII.

42. Ziskind, David, *One Thousand Strikes of Government Employees* (New York: Columbia University Press, 1940), pp. 33–71.

43. Bureau of National Affairs, *Government Employee Relations Report,* No. 232, February 19, 1968, p. B–5.

44. Bureau of National Affairs, *Government Employee Relations Report,* No. 259, August 26, 1968, p. A–9.

45. *Harney v. Russo et al.,* 435 Pa. 183 (1969).

46. See, for instance, Schweppe, *op. cit.,* p. 227.

Chapter VI Participants in Collective Bargaining

1. John T. Dunlop, *Industrial Relations Systems* (New York: Holt, Rinehart and Winston, 1958), p. 7.

2. U.S. Department of Labor, Bureau of Labor Statistics, *Directory of National and International Unions in the United States,* 1959 and 1969.

3. *Wall Street Journal,* May 7, 1968, p. 1.

4. U.S. Department of Labor, Bureau of Labor Statistics, *op. cit.*

5. Maryland vs. Wirtz, 389 U.S. 1031 (1967).

Chapter VII Recognition and the Scope of Negotiations

1. State of New York, Governor's Committee on Public Employee Relations, *Final Report,* March 31, 1966, pp. 29–30.

2. This distinction is made by Neil Chamberlain, "Determinants of Collective Bargaining Structures," John Dunlop, "The Industrial Relations System in Construction," and Arnold R. Weber, "Introduction" appearing in Arnold R. Weber (ed.), *The Structure of Collective Bargaining* (New York: Free Press, 1961).

3. Paul F. Gerhart, "The Scope of Bargaining in the Public Sector." Paper presented at the Spring 1969 Meeting of the Industrial Relations Research Association.

4. National Labor Relations Act, Section 1, 9–2.

5. *Labor Law Course: 1964* (Chicago: Commerce Clearing House, Inc., 1963), p. 1605.

6. Executive Order 11491, *Labor-Management Relations in the Federal Service,* Section 12 (Washington, D.C.: 1969).

7. Gerhart, *op. cit.*

8. Alan Rubin, "Union Security Agreements in Public Employment," (study in progress).

9. NEA Research Division, *Negotiation Research Digest,* Vol. 1, No. 7 (Washington, D.C.: March 1968).

10. Norwalk Teachers Association v. Board of Education, 138 Conn. 269, 83A 2d 482, 31 ALR (2d) 1133 (1951).

Chapter VIII The Process of Collective Bargaining in Public Employment

1. This secion draws heavily on a paper entitled "Multilateral Bargaining in the Public Sector," by Kenneth McLennan and Michael H. Moskow, appearing in the *Twenty-First Annual Proceedings* of the Industrial Relations Association, 1969, pp. 31–40.

2. Harmon Zeigler, *Interest Groups in American Society* (Englewood Cliffs, N.J.: Prentice-Hall, 1964), p. 13.

3. *Congressional Quarterly,* Congressional Quarterly Service, Washington, D.C., August 22, 1966.

4. *Op. cit.,* July 7, 1967.

5. *Ibid.,* p. 1848.

6. George W. Taylor, *et al.*, *Governor's Committee on Public Employee Relations, Final Report*. The other members of the Committee, all well-known authorities in labor relations, were E. Wight Bakke, David L. Cole, John T. Dunlop, and Frederick H. Harbison.
7. *Ibid.*, p. 15.
8. *Ibid.*, p. 8.
9. *Ibid.*, p. 39.
10. *Ibid.*, p. 11.
11. Jean T. McKelvey, "Fact Finding in Public Employment Disputes: Promise or Illusion?" in Industrial Relations Research Association, *Twenty-First Annual Proceedings* (1968), p. 45.
12. B. V. H. Schneider, "Collective Bargaining and the Federal Civil Service," *Industrial Relations*, 3 (May 1964), p. 100.
13. Robert E. Doherty and Walter E. Oberer, *Teachers, School Boards, and Collective Bargaining: A Changing of the Guard* (Ithaca, N.Y.: New York State School of Industrial and Labor Relations, Cornell University, 1967), p. 105.
14. Theodore W. Kheel, "Report to Speaker Anthony T. Travia on the Taylor Case," February 21, 1968. Many others have favored this approach, among them Myron Lieberman, "Teacher Strikes: An Analysis of the Issues," *Harvard Educational Review*, Vol. 81 (Winter 1956), pp. 39–70; and Jack Stieber, "A New Approach to Strikes in Public Employment," *MSU Business Topics* (October 1967), pp. 67–71.
15. For an analysis of alternative means of bargaining power used by teacher organizations see Michael H. Moskow, *Teachers and Unions* (Philadelphia: Industrial Research Unit, University of Pennsylvania, 1966), pp. 194–210.

bibliography

Books

ADRIAN, CHARLES R. *State and Local Governments*. New York: McGraw-Hill, 1967.

American Civil Liberties Union. *Policy Statement on Civil Rights in Government Employment*. New York: American Civil Liberties Union, 1959.

ANDERSON, HOWARD J. *Public Employee Organization and Bargaining*. Washington, D.C.: Bureau of National Affairs, 1968.

Arkansas Legislative Council. *The Right of Public Employees to Organize, Bargain Collectively, Picket and Strike Against Their Employer*. Little Rock: Arkansas Legislative Council, Research Dept., 1963.

BARBASH, JACK. *The Practice of Unionism*. New York: Harper & Row, 1956.

BEAGLEY, THOMAS L. "Problems from the Viewpoint of Employees and Union," in *Collective Bargaining for Public Employees: 18th Annual Central Labor Union Conference*. Urbana: University of Illinois, Institute of Labor and Industrial Relations, 1966.

BELASCO, JAMES A. *Public Employee Dispute Settlement: The Wisconsin Experience; Collective Bargaining in City X*. Ithaca: New York School of Industrial and Labor Relations, (Reprint No. 188), 1966.

California State Library. *Public Employee Labor Relations;* a bibliography prepared by Carleton W. Kenyon. Sacramento: State of California, 1966.

CASE, HARRY L. *Personnel Policy in a Public Agency: The TVA Experience*. New York: Harper & Row, 1955.

CHAMBERLAIN, NEIL W. and J. W. KUHN. *Collective Bargaining*. 2 ed. New York: McGraw-Hill, 1965.

CRISPO, JOHN H. G. (ed.). *Collective Bargaining and the Professional Employee.* Toronto: Centre for Industrial Relations, University of Toronto, 1966.

CROUCH, WINSTON W. "Employee Organization in Council Manager Cities," in *1967 Municipal Yearbook,* Chicago: International City Managers' Association, 1967.

DOHERTY, ROBERT E. (ed.). *Employer-Employee Relations in the Public Schools.* Ithaca: New York State School of Industrial and Labor Relations, Cornell University, 1967.

———, and WALTER E. OBERER. *Teachers, School Boards, and Collective Bargaining: A Changing of the Guard.* Ithaca: New York State School of Industrial and Labor Relations, Cornell University, 1967.

DUNLOP, JOHN T. *Industrial Relations Systems.* New York: Holt, Rinehart and Winston, 1958.

———, and NEIL W. CHAMBERLAIN, (eds.). *Frontiers of Collective Bargaining.* New York: Harper & Row, 1967.

EPSTEIN, BENJAMIN. *The Principal's Role in Collective Negotiations Between Teachers and School Boards.* Washington, D.C.: National Association of Secondary School Principals, 1965.

FRANKEL, SAUL J. and PRATT, R. C. *Municipal Labor Relations in Canada.* Montreal, Canada: Canadian Federation of Mayors and Municipalities, 1954.

GODINE, MORTON R. *The Labor Problem in the Public Service.* Cambridge, Mass.: Harvard University Press, 1951.

HAGBURG, EUGENE C. (ed.). *Problems Confront Union Organization in Public Employment.* Columbus: Ohio State University, Labor Education and Research Service, 1966.

HANSLOWE, KURT L. *The Emerging Law of Labor Relations in Public Employment.* Ithaca: New York State School of Industrial and Labor Relations, Cornell University, 1967.

HART, WILSON R. *Collective Bargaining in the Federal Civil Service.* New York: Harper & Row, 1961.

HEISEL, W. D., and J. D. HALLIHAN. *Questions and Answers on Public Employee Negotiation.* Chicago: Public Personnel Association, 1967.

HERRICK, H. T. *Unions for Government Employees.* New York: New York University, 1962.

HOLLAND, ANN U. *Unions are Here to Stay; A Guide for Employee— Management Relations in the Federal Service,* Washington, D.C.: Society for Personnel Administration, 1962.

HOWLETT, ROBERT G. "Resolution of Impasses in Employee Relations in Public Education," paper delivered at Cornell University Conference, July 16, 1966, conference proceedings published in *Employer-Employee Relations in Public Schools,* Robert E. Doherty (ed.). Ithaca: New York State School of Industrial and Labor Relations, Cornell University, 1967.

Industrial Relations Research Association. *Collective Bargaining in the Public Service*. Proceedings of the 1966 Annual Spring Meeting, at Milwaukee, Wisconsin, May 6–7, 1966.

KLAUS, IDA. "Collective Bargaining by Government Employees" in *Conference on Labor*. Proceedings. New York University, 1959, pp. 21–38.

————. *Collective Bargaining Will Help Staff Morale*. New York: Society for the Experimental Study of Education, Yearbook, 1963.

KRAMER, LEO. *Labor's Paradox*. New York: Wiley, 1962.

LEVIN, EDWARD (ed.). *New York State Public Employment Labor Relations*. Ithaca: New York State School of Industrial and Labor Relations, Cornell University, 1968.

LIEBERMAN, MYRON, and MICHAEL H. MOSKOW. *Collective Negotiations for Teachers*. Chicago: Rand McNally, 1966.

LONG, WILLIAM A. *The Development and Techniques of Collective Bargaining in the Municipal Service*. Washington, D.C.: International Association of Fire Fighters, 1966.

MAXWELL, JAMES A. *Financing State and Local Governments*. Washington, D.C.: The Brookings Institution, 1967.

MILLER, GLEN W. *Collective Bargaining by Public Employees*. Columbus: Ohio State University, Labor and Education Research Services, College of Commerce and Administration, 1966.

MOSKOW, MICHAEL H. *Teachers and Unions*. Philadelphia: University of Pennsylvania Press, 1966.

National Education Association. *Guidelines for Professional Negotiations*. Washington, D.C.: National Education Association, 1963.

————. *NEA Handbook*. Washington, D.C.: National Education Association (published annually).

————. *Professional Negotiation with School Boards: A Legal Analysis and Review*. Washington, D.C.: National Education Association, 1965.

NEWLAND, CHESTER A. *Public Employee Unionization in Texas*. Austin: The University of Texas, 1962.

NIGRO, FELIX A. *Modern Public Administration*. New York: Harper & Row, 1965.

OCHELTREE, KENNETH (ed.). *Government Labor Relations in Transition*. Chicago: Public Personnel Association, 1966.

OLSON, MANCUR. *The Logic of Collective Action: Public Goals and the Theory of Groups*. Cambridge, Mass.: Harvard University Press, 1965.

POLISAR, ERIC. *Strikes and Solutions*. Chicago: Public Personnel Association, 1968.

REHMUS, CHARLES M., and EVAN WILNER. *The Economic Results of Teacher Bargaining: Michigan's First Two Years.* Ann Arbor, Michigan: Institute of Labor and Industrial Relations, The University of Michigan-Wayne State University, 1968.

ROBERTS, HAROLD S. (ed.). *A Manual For Employee Management Cooperation in the Federal Service.* Honolulu: Industrial Relations Center, University of Hawaii, 1967.

SALIK, RICHARD L. (ed.). *The Right to Meet and Confer-Laws and Policies.* Chicago, Ill.: Public Personnel Association, 1968.

SCHMIDT, CHARLES T., JR., HYMAN PARKET, and BOB REPAS. *A Guide to Collective Negotiations in Education.* East Lansing: Michigan State University, Social Science Research Bureau, 1967.

SHILS, EDWARD B., and C. TAYLOR WHITTIER. *Teachers, Administrators and Collective Bargaining.* New York: Crowell, 1968.

SMYTHE, CYRUS F. (ed.). *Conference on Employee Management Personnel of Selected U.S. Government Agencies.* (Proceedings.) Minneapolis: Industrial Relations Center, University of Minnesota, 1963.

SOLOMON, BENJAMIN. *Teachers and Nurses: The Issue of Group Power for Professional Employees.* Chicago: University of Chicago, Industrial Relations Center, 1966.

SPERO, STERLING, D. *Government as Employer.* New York: Remsen Press, 1948.

STAHL, GLENN O. *Public Personnel Administration.* 5th ed. New York: Harper & Row, 1962.

STINNETT, T. M., JACK KLEINMANN, and MARTHA WARE. *Professional Negotiation in Public Education.* New York: Macmillan, 1966.

STURMTHAL, ADOLF (ed.). *White-Collar Trade Unions: Contemporary Developments in Industrialized Societies.* Urbana: University of Illinois Press, 1966.

STUTZ, ROBERT L. *Collective Dealing by Units of Local Government in Connecticut.* Storrs, Conn.: University of Connecticut, Labor Management Institute, 1960.

TOMKINS, DOROTHY C. (ed.). *Strikes by Public Employees, Professional Personnel and Social Workers: A Bibliography.* Berkeley: University of California, Institute of Governmental Studies, 1966.

VOSLOO, WILLIAM B. *Collective Bargaining in the United States Federal Civil Service.* Chicago: Public Personnel Association, 1966.

WALLERSTEIN, LOUIS S. "Labor Relations in Public Employment—the Federal Experience" in *Conference on Labor.* New York: New York University, 1966.

WARNER, KENNETH O. (ed.). *Collective Bargaining in the Public Service: Theory and Practice.* Chicago: Public Personnel Association, 1967.

————, (ed.). *Developments in Public Employee Relations: Legislative, Judicial, Administrative*. Chicago: Public Personnel Association, 1965.

————, (ed.). *Management Relations with Organized Public Employees*. Chicago: Public Personnel Association, 1963.

————, and MARY L. HENNESSY. *Public Management at the Bargaining Table*. Chicago: Public Personnel Association, 1967.

WEBER, ARNOLD, (ed.). *The Structure of Collective Bargaining*. New York: Free Press, 1961.

WILDMAN, WESLEY A. *Implications of Teacher Bargaining for School Administration*. Chicago: University of Chicago, Industrial Relations Center, 1964.

ZEIDLER, FRANK P., FELIX A. NIGRO, J. D. LOVE, and W. D. HEISEL. *Rethinking the Philosophy of Employee Relations in the Public Service*. Chicago, Ill.: Public Personnel Association, 1968.

ZIEGLER, HARMON. *Interest Groups in American Society*. Englewood Cliffs, N.J.: Prentice-Hall, 1964. ,

ZISKIND, DAVID. *One Thousand Strikes of Government Employees*. New York: Columbia University Press, 1940.

Reports

American Bar Association. "Report on Government Employee Relations," *Government Employee Relations Report*. Bureau of National Affairs, No. 204 (August 7, 1967), D–1.

California State Employees Association. *37th General Council Annual Report*. Los Angeles: State Employees Association, 1967.

Conference on Employee-Management Relations in the Public Service. *Report and Findings of the Conference on Employee-Management Relations in the Public Service*. Ithaca: New York State School of Industrial and Labor Relations, Cornell University, 1964.

GRIFFENHAGEN-KROEGER. *Employer-Employee Relations for the County of Sacramento, California*. A Report to the Board of Supervisors Through the Management Committee. Sacramento: Griffenhagen-Kroeger Inc., August, 1967.

KHEEL, THEODORE W. Report to Speaker Anthony T. Travia on the Taylor Law: New York, February 21, 1968.

National Governors Conference. *Report of Task Force on State and Local Government Labor Relations*. Chicago: Public Personnel Association, 1967.

National School Boards Association. *Report on State Survey on Board-Administration-Teacher Relations*. Chicago: National School Boards Association, April 24, 1964.

Wisconsin Association of School Boards. *School Board-School Employee Negotiations.* A Report of the Conference on School Board-School Employee Negotiations, Winneconne, Wisconsin: Wisconsin Association of School Boards.

Commission Reports

Illinois. Governor's Advisory Commission on Labor-Management Policy for Public Employees. *Report and Recommendations.* Springfield: State of Illinois, 1967.

Michigan. Advisory Committee on Public Employee Relations. *Report to Governor George Romney.* Lansing: State Capital, Feb. 15, 1957.

New Jersey. Public and School Employees' Grievance Procedures Study Commission. *Final Report to the Governor and the Legislature.* Trenton: State House, January 9, 1968.

New York State. Governor's Committee on Public Employee Relations. *Final Report.* Albany: Executive Chamber, March 13, 1966.

———. *Interim Report,* June 17, 1968.

———. *Report of January* 23, 1969.

Pennsylvania. Governor's Commission to Revise the Public Employee Law of Pennsylvania. *Report and Recommendations.* Harrisburg: Department of Labor and Industry, June 1968.

Public Documents

City of New York. *Executive Order No. 49.* An Order on the Conduct of Labor Relations Between the City of New York and Its Employees. March 31, 1958.

———. *The Report of the Tri-Partite Panel on Collective Bargaining Procedures in Public Employment.* (Reprinted and available from District Council 37, 68 Trinity Place, New York City.) March 31, 1966.

Commonwealth of Pennsylvania. *Human Relations Commission, Survey of Non White Employees in State Government.* March 28, 1963.

State of California. *Collective Bargaining and Right to Strike for Public Employees.* State Personnel Board Memorandum. June 16, 1966.

State of Connecticut. *Report of the Interior Commission to Study Collective Bargaining by Municipalities* (1965).

State of Illinois. *Report and Recommendations.* A Report prepared by the Governor's Advisory Commission on Labor-Management Policy for Public Employees. Springfield, 1967.

State of Michigan. *Report to Governor George Romney.* A Report by the Advisory Committee on Public Employee Relations. Lansing, February 15, 1967.

State of New York. *Public Employee Relations Final Report*. A Report Prepared by the Governor's Committee on Public Employee Relations. Albany, 1966.

―――. Department of Labor Division of Research and Statistics. *Employer Associations Engaged in Collective Bargaining in New York State: A Directory of Associations and a Report on Their Characteristics* (Publication No. B–150). New York, 1965.

State of Wisconsin. *Digest of Decision of the Wisconsin Employment Relations Board and the Courts Involving the Wisconsin Employment Peace Act and Section 111.70, Wisconsin Statutes (Municipal Employer-Employee Labor Relations Law)*. Vol. I, June 1, 1966.

―――. *Wisconsin Employment Relations Board Administrative Code*. November 1, 1964.

STEFFENSON, JAMES P. *Teachers Negotiate with Their School Boards*. USOE Bulletin No. 40. Washington, D.C.: U.S. Government Printing Office, 1964.

U.S. Civil Service Commission, *Conducting Hearings on Employee Appeals*. Washington, D.C.: U.S. Government Printing Office, 1964.

―――. *Employee Management Cooperation in the Federal Service*. Personnel Methods Series No. 15. Washington, D.C.: U.S. Government Printing Office, 1962.

―――. *Exclusive Recognition and Negotiated Agreements in Federal Agencies Under Executive Order 10988*. Washington, D.C.: U.S. Government Printing Office, 1966.

―――. *Résumé of Collective Bargaining for Civil Servants in Canada*. 1966.

―――. *Statistical Report of Exclusive Recognitions and Negotiated Agreements in the Federal Government Under Executive Order 10988*. Washington, D.C.: U.S. Government Printing Office, 1966.

U.S. Department of Labor. *Work Stoppages: Government Employees, 1942–1961*. Bureau of Labor Statistics (1963). (Report No. 247.)

―――. *Work Stoppages Involving Government Employees, 1966*. A Bureau of Labor Statistics Summary Release.

―――. *Procedural Guide for Advisory Arbitration Proceedings Under Section 11 of Executive Order 10988*. 1963.

―――. *Standards of Conduct for Employee Organizations and Code of Fair Labor Practices*. 1963.

U.S. Navy Department, *How to Conduct a Hearing*. Washington: U.S. Government Printing Office, 1963.

―――, Office of Industrial Relations, *Employee Management Cooperation*. 1963.

U.S. President. President's Task Force on Employee-Management Relations in the Federal Service. *A Policy for Employee Management*

Cooperation in the Federal Service. Washington, D.C.: U.S. Government Printing Office, 1961.

———. Executive Order 10988, January 17, 1962.

———. Executive Order 11491, October 29, 1969.

Articles and Periodicals

ANDERSON, ARCHIE E., and EDDY, WILLIAM B. "Collective Bargaining for Federal Employees," *University of Missouri Business and Government Review*, Vol. 6 (May-June 1965), pp. 30–38.

ANDERSON, ARVID. "Labor Relations in the Public Service: Analysis of the Present Status of Public Employee Unions," *Labor Law Journal*, Vol. 12 (November 1961), pp. 1069–1094.

———. "Labor Relations in the Public Service," *Wisconsin Law Review*, July 1961.

———. "Public Employees and Collective Bargaining; Comparative and Local Experience," *Proceedings of the 21st Annual Conference on Labor*, New York University, New York, 1969.

ARONSON, ROBERT L. "Employee-Management Cooperation in the Federal Service (Document)," *Industrial and Labor Relation Review*, Vol. 15 (July 1962), pp. 548–553.

ASNARD, ROBERT R., and DONALD P. WALKER. "NEA's Digest of Negotiation Research," *NEA Journal*, Vol. 56, pp. 34–35.

BALL, LESTER B. "Collective Bargaining: A Primer for Superintendents," *Saturday Review*, Vol. 50 (January 21, 1967), pp. 70–71.

BARBRICK, JAMES J. "White Collar Unionization," *Personnel Administrator*, March–April 1964, pp. 1–7, 31.

BARR, DAVID S. "Executive Order 10988: An Experiment in Employee-Management Cooperation in the Federal Service," *Georgetown Law Journal*, Vol. 52 (Winter 1964), pp. 420–454.

BECKER, HARRY A. "Collective Bargaining May Force School Boards to Organize," *American School Board Journal*, Vol. 153 (October 1966), pp. 57–58.

———. "The Role of School Administrators in Professional Negotiations," *American School Board Journal*, Vol. 150 (May 1965), pp. 9–10.

BELASCO, JAMES A. "Resolving Disputes over Contract Terms in the State Public Service: An Analysis." *Labor Law Journal*, Vol. 16 (September 1965), pp. 533–544.

———. "The American Association of University Professors as a Private Dispute Settlement Agency," *Industrial and Labor Relations Review*, Vol. 18 (July 1965), pp. 535–553.

BELENKER, JERRY. "Binding Arbitration for Government Employees," *Labor Law Journal*, Vol. 16 (April 1965), pp. 234–236.

BERGER, HARRIET F. "Grievance Process in the Philadelphia Public Service," *Industrial and Labor Relations Review*, Vol. 13 (July 1960), pp. 568–580.

BERRODIN, EUGENE F. "Recent Changes in Public Employee Relations," *Michigan Municipal Review*, Vol. 39, No. 2 (February 1966), pp. 42–43.

BLAINE, HARRY R., HAGBURG, EUGENE C., and ZELLER, FREDERICK. "Discipline and Discharge in the United States Postal Service," *Industrial and Labor Relations Review*, Vol. 19, (October 1965), pp. 92–98.

BLUM, SHELLEY. "Issues in Teachers' Union Negotiations." *Labor Today*, Vol. 6 (August–September, 1967), pp. 18–28.

BROOKS, THOMAS R. "Collective Bargaining in Education," *Dissent*, Vol. 13 (May–June 1966), pp. 306–311.

BROWN, GEORGE W. "Teacher Power Techniques: Serious New Problems," *American School Board Journal*, Vol. 152 (February 1966), pp. 11–13.

CARVER, CHARLES B. "Bargaining in the Federal Sector," *Labor Law Journal*, September 1968, pp. 569–589.

CHRISTRUP, HELEN J. "Why do Government Employees Join Unions?" *Personnel Administration*, Vol. 29, pp. 49–54.

CLARK, R. THEODORE, JR. "Public Employee Labor Legislation: A Study of the Unsuccessful Attempt to Enact a Public Employee Bargaining Statute in Illinois," *Labor Law Journal*, Vol. 20 (March 1969), pp. 164–73.

CLARY, JACK R. "Pitfalls of Collective Bargaining in Public Employment," *Labor Law Journal*, Vol. 18 (July 1967), pp. 406–411.

COHANY, HARRY P., and H. JAMES NEARY. "Collective Bargaining Agreements in the Federal Service," *Monthly Labor Review*, Vol. 88 (August 1965), pp. 944–950.

COHEN, FREDERICK, "Legal Aspects of Unionization Among Public Employees," *Temple Law Quarterly*, Vol. 30 (Winter 1957), pp. 187–198.

"Collective Bargaining and Strikes? Or Profession Negotiations and Sanctions?" *Phi Delta Kappan*, Vol. 44 (October 1962), pp. 1–2.

Congressional Quarterly, Washington, D.C., (August 22, 1966, and July 7, 1967).

COOK, ALICE H. "Union Structure in Municipal Collective Bargaining," *Monthly Labor Review*, Vol. 79 (June 1966), pp. 606–608.

COONEY, TIMOTHY J. "Civil Service Unionism—How to Avert Another Strike," *The Nation*, Vol. 202, No. 4 (January 24, 1966), pp. 88–89.

CORNELL, HERBERT W. "Collective Bargaining by Public Employee Groups," *University of Pennsylvania Law Review*, Vol. 107 (November 1958), pp. 43–64.

CUNNINGHAM, W. B. "Public Employment, Collective Bargaining and the Conventional Wisdom," *Industrial Relations Quarterly Review*, Vol. 21, No. 3 (July 1966), pp. 406–433.

DAILEY, WILLIAM A. "Changing Patterns of Union Relations in the Federal Service," *Personnel Journal*, Vol. 44 (May 1965), pp. 258–262.

DERBER, MILTON. "Labor Management Policy for Public Employees in Illinois: The Experience of the Governor's Commission, 1966–1967," *Industrial and Labor Relations Review*, Vol. 21, No. 4 (July 1968), pp. 541–558.

DEWALD, FRANKLIN K. "Bargaining—Unit Relationships in Public Service," *Personnel Administration*, Vol. 33, No. 1 (January–February 1967), pp. 40–42.

DEWEY, ALLEN C. "Labor Law—Collective Bargaining—Right or Power of Municipalities to Engage in Collective Bargaining," *Michigan Law Review*, Vol. 56 (February 1958), pp. 645–648.

DOHERTY, ROBERT E. "Determination of Bargaining Units and Election Procedures in Public School Teacher Representation Election," *Industrial and Labor Relations Review*, Vol. 19 (July 1966), pp. 573–595.

———. "Labor Relations Negotiators on Bargaining Factories vs. the Schools," *ISR Journal*, I Number 1 (Winter 1969), pp. 5–14.

———. "Law and Collective Bargaining for Teachers," *Teachers College Record*, Vol. 68 (October 1966), pp. 1–12.

DONOIAN, HARRY A. "Organizational Problems of Government Employee Unions," *Labor Law Journal*, Vol. 18 (March 1967), pp. 137–144.

DONOVAN, B. E., A. ANDERSON, C. COYER, and A. W. WALPERT. "Collective Bargaining vs. Professional Negotiations," *School Management*, Vol. 9 (November 1965), pp. 68–75.

DORROS, SIDNEY. "The Case for Independent Professional Teachers' Association," *Monthly Labor Review*, Vol. 87, No. 5 (May 1964), p. 543.

DUNN, J. D., and ED D. ROACH. "The Collective Bargaining Unit in the Federal Service," *Public Personnel Review*, Vol. 28, No. 1 (January 1967), pp. 19–25.

ELAM, STANLEY M. "NEA-AFT Merger—and Related Matters," *Phi Delta Kappan*, Vol. 47 (February 1966), pp. 285–286.

———. "Rift Without Differences," *The Nation*, October 18, 1965, pp. 247–249.

———. "Union or Guild," *The Nation*, June 29, 1964, pp. 651–653.

FOEGEN, J. H. "A Qualified Right to Strike—In the Public Interest," *Labor Law Journal*, Vol. 18 (February 1967), pp. 90–102.

FOSTER, HOWARD G. "Dispute Settlement in Teacher Negotiations," *ILR Research*, Vol. 12 (February 1967), pp. 3–12.

FREDERICKSON, H. GEORGE. "Public Employee Militancy: Attitudes, Politics, and Bargaining." Proceedings of the American Political Science Association, Washington, D.C. 1968.

FUSILIER, H. L. and LAWRENCE L. STEINMETZ. "Public Employee Strikes: An Operational Solution," *Quarterly Review of Economics and Business*, Vol. 7, No. 3, (Autumn 1967), pp. 29–36.

GALLOP, A. L. "Professional Teachers Must Solve Negotiation Problems," *Minnesota Journal of Education*, Vol. 47 (October 1966), pp. 21–22.

GARBARINO, JOSEPH W. "Professional Negotiations in Education," *Industrial Relations*, Vol. 12, No. 2 (February 1968).

GARBER, LEE O. "How to Free Superintendents from Negotiation Hazards," *Nation's Schools*, Vol. 77 (March 1966), p. 139.

GERHART, PAUL F. "The Scope of Bargaining in the Public Sector," Paper prepared for the Spring 1969 meeting of the Industrial Relations Research Association.

GLASS, RONALD W. "Work Stoppages and Teachers: History and Prospect," *Monthly Labor Review*, Vol. 90 (August 1967), pp. 43–46.

GOLDBERG, JOSEPH P. "Labor-Management Relations Laws and Public Service," *Monthly Labor Review*, XCI, No. 6 (July 1968), pp. 48–55.

GRAY, HERMAN A. "Topics: The City Unions Need One Bargaining Table," *The New York Times*, December 16, 1967.

GROSSMAN, HARRY. "Adverse Actions and Appeals Therefrom—A New System for Federal Civil Servants," *Labor Law Journal*, Vol. 14 (March 1963), pp. 265–270.

HAMILTON, DAVID. "Will the College Teacher Organize?" *IUD Digest*, Vol. 7 (Spring 1967), pp. 121–128.

HARPER, DEAN. "Labor Relations in the Postal Service," *Industrial and Labor Relations Review*, Vol. 17 (April 1964), pp. 443–453.

HART, WILSON R. "The Impasse in Labor Relations in the Federal Civil Service," *Industrial and Labor Relations Review*, Vol. 19 (January 1966), pp. 175–189.

———. "The U.S. Civil Service Learns to Live with Executive Order 10988, An Interior Appraisal," *Industrial and Labor Relations Review*, Vol. 17 (January 1964), pp. 203–220.

HAZARD, WILLIAM R. "Collective Bargaining in Education: The Anatomy of a Problem," *Labor Law Journal*, Vol. 18 (July 1967), pp. 412–419.

HEIMBACH, WILLIAM W. "Cooperation and Arbitration in the Federal Service," *Monthly Labor Review*, Vol. 89 (June 1966), p. 614.

HEISEL, W. D., and J. P. SANTA-EMMA. "Unions in City Government: the Cincinnati Story," *Public Personnel Review*, Vol. 22 (January 1961), pp. 35–38.

HEPBRON, JAMES M. "Police Unionization Means Disorganization," *American City*, Vol. 73 (November 1958), pp. 131–132.

HERMAN, EDWARD E. "Bargaining by Civil Servants in Canada," *Monthly Labor Review*, Vol. 89 (June 1966), pp. 603–606.

HOFFMAN, HERBERT. "Right of Public Employees to Strike," *De Paul Law Review*, Vol. 10, No. 2 (Autumn–Winter 1966), pp. 815–839.

HOLLADY, RAY E. "Police Unions—Programs of Negation," *Police*, Vol. 6 (November–December 1961), pp. 63–69.

IRONS, WARREN B. "Employee-Management Cooperation: the Federal Program in Perspective," *Public Personnel Review*, Vol. 25 (July 1964), pp. 146–150.

KASSALOW, EVERETT M. "Public Employee Bargaining in Europe: What Lessons for the United States," *Proceedings of the Twenty-First Annual Meeting*, Industrial Relations Research Association, Madison: IRRA, 1969, pp. 48–58.

KAUFMAN, JACOB, J. "Compulsory Arbitration: Other Perspectives," *Industrial and Labor Relations Review*, Vol. 18 (July 1965), pp. 588–590.

KERESMAN, PETER. "Constructive Employee Relations in Police Departments," *Labor Law Journal*, Vol. 8 (August 1957), pp. 556–558.

KHEEL, THEODORE W. "How to Prevent Strikes by Public Employees," *Proceedings of the 21st Annual Conference on Labor*, New York University, New York, 1969.

KIELY, TERRENCE. "Right of Public Employees to Strike," *De Paul Review*, Vol. 16 (Autumn–Winter 1966), pp. 151–165.

KILLINGSWORTH, CHARLES C. "Grievance Adjudication in Public Employment," *American Arbitration Journal*, XIII, No. 1, pp. 3–15.

KLAUS, IDA. "Labor Relations in the Public Service: Exploration and Experiment," *Syracuse Law Review*, Vol. 10 (Spring 1959), 183–202.

KLEIN, LAWRENCE. "The NEA Convention and the Organizing of Teachers," *Monthly Labor Review*, Vol. 87 (August 1964), pp. 882–885.

KLEINGARTNER, ARCHIE. "Nurses, Collective Bargaining and Labor Legislation," *Labor Law Journal*, Vol. 18 (April 1967), pp. 236–245.

KNOWLTON, THOMAS A. "Is Collective Bargaining the Answer? Comments on a Municipal Labor Crisis (New York City)," *Arbitration Journal*, Vol. 21, No. 2 (1966), pp. 93–97.

KRAUSE, ROBERT D. "The Short, Troubled History of Wisconsin's New Labor Law," *Public Administration Review*, Vol. 25, No. 4 (December 1965), pp. 302–307.

KRINSKY, EDWARD B. "Public Employment Fact-Finding in Fourteen States," *Labor Law Journal*, Vol, 17, No. 9 (September 1966), pp. 532–540.

KRISLOV, JOSEPH. "The Independent Public Employee Association: Characteristics and Functions," *Industrial and Labor Relations Review*, Vol. 15 (July 1962), pp. 41–57.

———. "Prospects for the Use of Advisory Grievance Arbitration in Federal Service," *Industrial and Labor Relations Review*, Vol. 18, No. 3 (April 1965), pp. 420–432.

———. "The Union Shop, Employment Security and Municipal Workers," *Industrial and Labor Relations Review*, Vol. 12, No. 2 (January 1959), pp. 256–258.

———. "Work Stoppages of Government Employees, 1942–1959," *Quarterly Review of Business and Economics*, Vol. 1 (February 1961), pp. 87–92.

LAHNE, HERBERT J. "Bargaining Units in the Federal Service," *Monthly Labor Review*, December 1968, pp. 37–39.

LIEBERMAN, MYRON. "Battle for New York City's Teachers," *Phi Delta Kappan*, Vol. 43 (October 1961), pp. 2–8.

———. "Teacher Strikes: An Analysis of the Issues," *Harvard Educational Review*, Vol. 81 (Winter 1956), pp. 39–70.

———. "Teachers Strikes: Acceptable Strategy," *Phi Delta Kappan*, Vol. 46 (January 1965), pp. 237–240.

LOVE, THOMAS M. "Municipal Employment Relations in Wisconsin: Administration," *Wisconsin Law Review*, Summer 1965, pp. 652–670.

MACY, JOHN W. "The Federal Employee—Management Cooperation Program," *Industrial and Labor Relations Review*, Vol. 19 (July 1966), pp. 549–561.

McCAFFERTY, BART. "Unionized Municipal Employees: Financial Aspects," *Municipal Finance*, Vol. 33 (November 1960), pp. 98–103.

McGINN, ARTHUR J., JR. "The Role of Employee Organizations in Government," *Industrial and Labor Relations Research*, Vol. 9, No. 9, pp. 3–7.

McKELVEY, JEAN. "Cook County Commissioners' Fact Finding Board Report on Collective Bargaining and County Public Aid Employees," *Industrial and Labor Relations Review*, Vol. 20, No. 3 (April 1967), pp. 457–477.

———. "Fact Finding in Public Employment Disputes: Promise or Illusion," *Twenty-First Annual Proceedings,* Industrial Relations Research Association, Madison: IRRA, 1969, pp. 41–47.

———. "The Role of State Agencies in Public Employee Labor Relations," *Industrial and Labor Relations Review*, Vol. 20, No. 2 (January 1967), pp. 179–197.

McLennan, Kenneth and Michael H. Moskow. "Multilateral Bargaining in the Public Sector," *Twenty-First Annual Proceedings,* Industrial Relations Research Association, Madison: IRRA, 1969, pp. 31–40.

Moberly, Robert B. "The Strike and Its Alternatives in Public Employment," *Wisconsin Law Review,* Vol 17 (Spring 1966), pp. 549–582.

Morse, Muriel M. "Shall We Bargain Away the Merit System?" *Public Personnel Review,* Vol. 24 (October 1963), pp. 239–243.

Moskow, Michael H. "Collective Bargaining for Public School Teachers," *Labor Law Journal,* Vol. 15, No. 12 (December 1964), pp. 787–794.

———. "Recent Legislation Affecting Collective Negotiations for Teachers," *Phi Delta Kappan,* Vol. 47, No. 3 (November 1965), pp. 136–141.

———. "Representation Among Teachers," *Monthly Labor Review,* Vol. 66 (July 1966), pp. 728–732.

———. "Teacher Organizations: An Analysis of the Issues," *Teachers College Record,* Vol. 66 (February 1965), pp. 453–463.

Muir, J. Douglas. "The Strike as a Professional Sanction: The Changing Attitude of the National Education Association," *Labor Law Journal,* October 1968, pp. 615–27.

Mulcahy, Charles. "A Municipality's Rights and Responsibilities Under The Wisconsin Municipal Labor Law," *Marquette Law Review,* Vol. 49, No. 3 (February 1966), pp. 512–532.

Mysliwiec, Frank A. "Municipal Employees' Unions: The Climb Up Labor's Ladder," *Duquesne University Law Review,* Vol. 4, No. 1 (Fall 1965), pp. 137–145.

Newland, Chester A. "Trends in Public Employee Unionization," *The Journal of Politics,* XXVI, No. 3 (August 1964), pp. 586–611.

Nigro, Felix A. (ed.). "A Symposium: Collective Negotiations In the Public Service," *Public Administration Review,* Vol. 27 (March–April 1968), pp. 11–147.

Nolte, M. C. "Is the Board an Employer Under a State's Labor Relations Law?" *American School Board Journal,* Vol. 151 (September 1965), pp. 9–10.

Parker, Hyman. "The Role of the Michigan Labor Mediation Board in Public Employee Labor Disputes," *Labor Law Journal,* September 1959, pp. 632–642.

Parks, Michael. "Cities on Strike," *American,* Vol. 115 (October 15, 1966), pp. 455–457.

———. "The Government Worker Goes Union," *American Federationist,* Vol. 71 (March 1964), pp. 8–12.

PHELPS, ORME W. "Compulsory Arbitration: Some Perspectives," *Industrial and Labor Relations Review*, Vol. 18 (October 1964), pp. 81–91.

PRAGAN, OTTO. "Grievance Procedures in the Federal Service," *Monthly Labor Review*, Vol. 89, No. 6 (June 1966), p. 609.

"Public Employee Relations: Proposals for Change in Present State Legislation," *Vanderbilt Law Review*, Vol. 20, No. 3 (April 1967), pp. 700–722.

RAINS, HARRY H. "Collective Bargaining in Public Employment," *Labor Law Journal*, Vol. 8, pp. 548–550.

RASKIN, A. H. "Strikes by Public Employees," *The Atlantic*, Vol. 201, No. 1 (January 1968), pp. 46–51.

REHMUS, CHARLES M. "Developments in Federal Union-Management Relations," *Monthly Labor Review*, Vol. 89 (June 1966), p. 613.

RICH, J. M. "Civil Disobedience and Teacher Strikes," *Phi Delta Kappan*, Vol. 45 (December 1963), pp. 151–154.

RICHE, MARTHA F. "American Federation of Government Employees," *Monthly Labor Review*, Vol. 87 (November 1964), pp. 1256–1257.

RICK, MICHAEL B. "Labor Law: Public Employees' Right to Picket," *Marquette Law Review*, Vol. 50 (April 1967), pp. 541–549.

ROACH, ED D., and J. D. DUNN. "The Collective Bargaining Unit in the Federal Service," *Public Personnel Review*, Vol. 28 (January 1967), pp. 19–25.

ROCK, ELI. "Practical Labor in the Public Service," *Public Personnel Review*, Vol. 18 (April 1957), pp. 71–80.

———. "Research on Municipal Collective Bargaining," *Monthly Labor Review*, Vol. 89, No. 6 (June 1966), pp. 615–616.

———. "Role of the Neutral in Grievance Arbitration in Public Employment," Address to the 20th Annual Meeting of the National Academy of Arbitrators, reprinted in *Government Employees Relations Report*, No. 191, (May 8, 1967), pp. D–1–D–11.

ROSS, IRWIN. "The Newly Militant Government Workers," *Fortune*, Vol. 78, No. 2 (August 1968), pp. 104–107, 131.

ROWLANDS, DAVID D. and JERRY WURF. "Unions Enter City Hall," *Public Management*, Vol. 48 (September 1966), pp. 244–252.

RUBIN, RICHARD S. *A Summary of State Collective Bargaining Law in Public Employment*, Public Employee Relations Report No. 3, New York State School of Industrial and Labor Relations, Cornell University, Ithaca, 1968.

SASO, CARMEN D. "Massachusetts Local Government Goes to the Bargaining Table," *Public Personnel Review*, Vol. 28 (July 1967), pp. 146–152.

SCHMIDT, CHARLES T., JR. "Representation of Classroom Teachers. Two Case Studies in the Selection of Bargaining Representatives for Michigan Teacher Groups," *Monthly Labor Review,* Vol. 91, No. 7 (July 1968), pp. 27–36.

SCHNEIDER, B. V. H. "Collective Bargaining and the Federal Civil Service," *Industrial Relations,* Vol. 3 (May 1964), pp. 97–120.

SEIDMAN, JOEL. "The Trend Among Professional Groups Today," *American Journal of Nursing,* Vol. 65, No. 1 (January 1965), pp. 72–78.

SELDEN, DAVID. "Why the AFT Maintains its AFL-CIO Affiliation," *Phi Delta Kappan,* Vol. 47 (February 1966), pp. 298–300.

SHARPE, CARLETON F., and ELISHA C. FREEDMAN. "Collective Bargaining in a Nonpartisan, Council-Manager City," *Public Administration Review,* Vol. 22 (Winter 1962), pp. 13–18.

SHENTON, DAVID G. "Compulsory Arbitration in the Public Service," *Labor Law Journal,* Vol. 17 (March 1966), pp. 138–147.

SILVER, RICHARD A. "Collective Bargaining with Public Employees," *Personnel Administration,* Vol. 22 (January–February 1959), pp. 27–34.

SIMON, HARRY. "The Right to Strike in the Public Service," *Canadian Labour,* Vol. 9 (November 1964), pp. 19–21.

SMITH, RUSSELL A., and DORIA B. MCLAUGHLIN. "Public Employment: A Neglected Area of Research and Training in Labor Relations," *Industrial and Labor Relations Review,* Vol. 16 (October 1962), pp. 30–44.

———, and ROBERT K. BURNS. "Unionization of White Collar Employees: Extent, Potential and Implications," *The Journal of Business of the University of Chicago,* Vol. 36, No. 2 (April 1963).

SMYTHE, CYRUS F. "Collective Bargaining Under Executive Order 10988—Trends and Prospects," *Public Personnel Review,* Vol. 26 (October 1965), pp. 199–202.

SPERO, STERLING D. "Collective Bargaining in Public Employment: Form and Scope," *Public Administration Review,* Vol. 22 (Winter 1962), pp. 1–5.

STAMBLER, HOWARD V. "State and Local Government Manpower in 1975," *Monthly Labor Review,* Vol. 90 (April 1967), pp. 13–17.

STERN, JAMES L. "The Wisconsin Public Employee Fact-Finding Procedure," *Industrial and Labor Relations Review,* Vol. 20 (October 1966), pp. 3–29.

STEVENS, CARL M. "Is Compulsory Arbitration Compatible with Bargaining?" *Industrial Relations,* Vol. 5 (February 1966), pp. 38–52.

STIEBER, JACK. "A New Approach to Strikes in Public Employment," *MSU Business Topics,* October 1967, pp. 67–71.

STIEBER, JACK. "Collective Bargaining in the Public Sector," *Challenges to Collective Bargaining*, American Assembly, Lloyd Ulman (ed.), Prentice-Hall, 1967, pp. 65–88.

STRAUSS, GEORGE. "Professionalism and Occupational Associations," *Personnel Administration*, Vol. 9 (March–April 1964), pp. 17–23.

STUART, JOHN R. "Personnel Developments in Canadian Cities," *Public Personnel Review*, Vol. 29, No. 2 (April 1968), pp. 70–74.

STUTZ, ROBERT L. "Collective Bargaining by City Employees," *Labor Law Journal*, Vol. 15 (November 1964), pp. 696–701.

SULLIVAN, DANIEL P. "How Can the Problem of the Public Employees Strike Be Resolved?" *Oklahoma Law Review*, Vol. 19 (November 1966), pp. 365–385.

TAYLOR, BENJAMIN J. "Public Employee Union Organization in Arizona," *Arizona Business Bulletin*, Vol. 13 (November 1966), pp. 3–10.

TAYLOR, GEORGE W. "Public Employment: Strikes or Procedures," *Industrial and Labor Relations Review*, Vol. 20 (July 1967), pp. 617–636.

TERRY, NEWELL B. "Collective Bargaining in the U.S. Department of the Interior," *Public Administration Review*, Vol. 22 (Winter 1962), pp. 19–23.

THOMPSON, ARTHUR A. "Collective Bargaining in the Public Service—the TVA Experience and its Implications for Other Government Agencies," *Labor Law Journal*, Vol. 17 (February 1966), pp. 89–98.

———. and IRWIN WEINSTOCK. "White Collar Employees and the Unions at TVA," *Personnel Journal*, Vol. 41, No. 1 (January 1967), pp. 14–21.

THOMSON, ANDREW J. *Strikes and Strike Penalties in Public Employment*, Public Employee Relations Report No. 2, New York State School of Industrial and Labor Relations, Cornell University, Ithaca, 1967.

———. *Unit Determination in Public Employment*, Public Employee Relations Report No. 1, New York State School of Industrial and Labor Relations, Cornell University, Ithaca, 1967.

"Union Activity in Public Employment," *Columbia Law Review*, Vol. 55 (March 1955), pp. 343–366.

WAKEFIELD, JOSEPH C. "Expanding Functions of State and Local Governments," *Monthly Labor Review*, Vol. 40 (July 1967), pp. 9–14.

WEBER, ARNOLD R. "Paradise Lost; Or Whatever Happened to the Chicago Social Worker?" *Industrial and Labor Relations Review*, Vol. 22 (April 1969), pp. 323–38.

WEIFORD, DOUGLAS, and WAYNE BURGGRAAFF. "The Future for Public Employee Unions," *Public Management*, Vol. 45 (May 1963), pp. 102–107.

WEISENFELD, ALLAN. "Collective Bargaining by Public Employees," *Monthly Labor Review*, Vol. 89 (June 1966), pp. 610–612.

———. "Public Employees—First or Second Class Citizens," *Labor Law Journal*, Vol. 16, No. 11 (November 1965), pp. 685–704.

———. "The Philosophy of Bargaining for Municipal Employees," *Arbitration Journal*, Vol. 21, No. 1 (January 1967), pp. 40–47.

WHITE, DONALD J. "Rights and Responsibilities in Municipal Collective Bargaining," *Arbitration Journal*, Vol. 22, No. 1 (1967), pp. 31–39.

WILDMAN, WESLEY A. "Collective Action by Public School Teachers," *Industrial and Labor Relations Review*, Vol. 18 (October 1964), pp. 3–19.

———. "Conflict Issues in Negotiations," *Monthly Labor Review*, Vol. 89 (June 1966), pp. 617–620.

WIRTZ, W. WILLARD. "Local Government and its Employees: Four Guidelines for a Durable Truce," *American County Government*, Vol. 31 (December 1966), pp. 13–15.

WOLLETT, DONALD H. "The Public Employee at the Bargaining Table: Promise or Illusion?" *Labor Law Journal*, Vol. 15 (January 1964), pp. 8–15.

WORTMAN, MAX S., JR. "Federal Civil Service Bargaining," *Monthly Labor Review*, Vol. 87 (June 1964), pp. 659–660.

———. "Collective Bargaining Strategies and Tactics in the Federal Civil Service," *Labor Law Journal*, Vol. 15 (July 1964), pp. 482–492.

WURF, JERRY. "Personnel Opinions," *Public Personnel Review*, Vol. 89, No. 1 (January 1966), pp. 52–53.

———. "Unions Enter City Hall," *Public Management*, Vol. 27, No. 9 (September 1966), pp. 224–252.

YOUNG, DALLAS M. and JAMES D. BROWN, JR. "Two Views on the Right to Strike," *Personnel*, July–August 1967, pp. 34–43.

ZACK, ARNOLD M. "Are Strikes of Public Employees Necessary?" *American Bar Association Journal*, Vol. 53 (September 1967), pp. 808–810.

ZAGORIA, SAM. "A New Frontier in Collective Bargaining: Public Workers and Citizen Bosses," *Labor Law Journal*, Vol. 19 (July 1968), pp. 387–390.

ZANDER, ARNOLD S. "A Union View of Collective Bargaining in the Public Service," *Public Administration Review*, Vol. 22 (Winter 1962), pp. 5–13.

ZANER, THEODORE. "Did the Right to Bargain Collectively Precipitate Closure of the Brooklyn Navy Yard?" *Personnel Administration*, Vol. 30 (July–August 1967), pp. 42–45.

ZLOCHIVER, ISAAC. "Collective Bargaining in the Public Service," *Connecticut Government*, Vol. 17 (October 1963), pp. 1–4.

ZWAKMAN, JOHN C. "Municipal Employment Relations in Wisconsin: The Extension of Private Labor Relations Devices into Municipal Employment," *Wisconsin Law Review*, Summer 1965, pp. 691–701.

index of names

327

index of subjects

ABOUT THE AUTHORS

MICHAEL H. MOSKOW is an Associate Professor of Economics and Director of the Bureau of Economic and Business Research at Temple University. During a leave of absence in 1969–1970 he served as a Senior Staff Economist with the Council of Economic Advisers in Washington. A recipient of the M.A. and Ph.D. degrees from the University of Pennsylvania, Professor Moskow is an experienced mediator and arbitrator in public employee disputes and has held a Rockefeller Brothers Fund grant to study labor relations in the performing arts. The several books and articles he has written include *Teachers and Unions* (1966), *Collective Negotiations for Teachers* (1966), and *Employment Relations in Higher Education* (1969).

J. JOSEPH LOEWENBERG is an Associate Professor of Management at Temple University. He received his A.B., M.B.A., and D.B.A. degrees from Harvard University and has worked with the U.S. Department of Labor in the Bureau of Labor Statistics and the Manpower Administration. His writings on collective bargaining and manpower topics include *The Operation of Severance Pay Plans and their Implication for Labor Mobility,* and articles in *Regulating Union Government, Emerging Sectors of Collective Bargaining* and *Monthly Labor Review.*

EDWARD CLIFFORD KOZIARA, Associate Professor, Drexel Institute of Technology, received his Ph.D. from the University of Wisconsin. Ford Foundation grants enabled him to study minority employment in the hotel and maritime industry and employer attitudes toward federal retraining programs. He recently completed a U.S. Department of Labor study of labor force nonparticipation in a Philadelphia poverty area. Professor Koziara has had articles published in the *Industrial and Labor Relations Review* and other labor journals. He has also coauthored two monographs in the *Racial Policies of American Industry* series published by the University of Pennsylvania Press.